VIRTUE IN POLITICAL LIFE
Yves Simon's Political Philosophy for Our Times

Patrick Lafon

Langaa Research & Publishing CIG
Mankon, Bamenda

Publisher:
Langaa RPCIG
Langaa Research & Publishing Common Initiative Group
P.O. Box 902 Mankon
Bamenda
North West Region
Cameroon
Langaagrp@gmail.com
www.langaa-rpcig.net

Distributed in and outside N. America by African Books Collective
orders@africanbookscollective.com
www.africanbookscollective.com

ISBN-10: 9956-762-83-0

ISBN-13: 978-9956-762-83-5

© Patrick Lafon 2017

All rights reserved.
No part of this book may be reproduced or transmitted in any form or by any means, mechanical or electronic, including photocopying and recording, or be stored in any information storage or retrieval system, without written permission from the publisher

To the memory of my father,
Joseph Noni Lafon (1920-2004),
who did politics the right way.

Table of Contents

Acknowledgments... ix
Preface.. xi

Chapter 1: The Definition of Virtue............................... 1
*I: Modern Substitutes for Virtue and
their Inadequacy*... 1
The Recourse to Natural Goodness................................ 3
Social Engineering.. 13
Psycho-Technology.. 21
II: Towards a Definition of Virtue................................. 31
Problems of Translation Regarding *Hexis*..................... 32
Virtue is not Habit.. 32
Virtue is not Grounded in Opinion................................ 40
Virtue is not Science... 43
III: Understanding Aristotle's Definition of Virtue........... 49
Distinguishing Virtue from a False Intention
and from Vice.. 49
The Intellectual and Moral Virtues in Practice............... 51
The Interdependence of the Virtues:
The Aristotelian and Stoic Positions.............................. 55
The Definition of Moral Virtue..................................... 58
Knowledge of Moral Axioms through Instinct.............. 59

**Chapter 2: Virtue in Public Life:
Simon's Concept of the Common Good**...................... 63
I: Brief Historical Overview... 63
Introduction... 63
The Birth and Evolution of the Concept: Ancient Greek
Philosophy to Medieval Times...................................... 64
The State of the Concept in Modern and
 Contemporary Thought.. 69
*II: The Threefold Classificatory Scheme
of Virginia Held as Outlined in the Public
Interest and Individual Interests and her*

Concept of the Public Interest... 79
Preliminary Considerations..79
The "Preponderance Theories" of Thomas Hobbes,
David Hume, and Jeremy Bentham.................................. 83
The "Public Interest as Common Interest" Theory............... 90
The "Unitary Conception" 94
Virginia Held's Proposed Constituent Elements
of the Common Good... 101
III: Simon's Concept of the Common Good.................... 107
Two Misconceptions of the Common Good. 109
Simon's Concept of the Common Good........................... 118
Drawing the Threads Together... 129

**Chapter 3: Virtue in Public Life:
The Virtue of Theoretical Truth and the
Virtue of the Ruler and the Ruled**.............................. 133
Introduction... 133
I: The Virtue of Theoretical Truth............................... 135
The Truth Value of Witness... 135
The Truth Value of Science... 137
The Truth Value of Creative Freedom............................... 139
Freedom of the Intellect: The Trouble with the
Position of the Liberals... 141
Truth and the Market Place of Ideas................................ 148
The Role of Authority in Teaching Transcendent Truth......... 150
II: The Virtue of the Ruler and the Ruled...................... 153
Rule by the Virtuous.. 153
Rule by the Experts or by an Elite.................................... 165
Freedom from Self: Obedience as Perfective....................... 171

Chapter 4: Virtue In Public Life: Virtue and Law.............. 183
Introduction... 183
*I: Virtue and the Idea of Natural Law and
Philosophical Challenges to the Idea*............................... 185
The Idea of Natural Law... 185
Philosophical Challenges to the Idea of Natural Law............189
II: Virtue and Facets of Positive Law

and Natural Law.. 202
On the Existence of the Just by Nature................................ 202
On Knowledge of Natural Moral Law................................. 206
On Law as Premise and Conclusion: The Role of Virtue......... 213
On God as the Author of Natural Law and
Natural Moral Law... 217

Conclusion.. 223

Bibliography... 229

Acknowledgments

If a good number of human undertakings would be impossible without the help of others, this is even more so in the case of writing a book. This work would have been impossible without the invaluable help of a many people at different levels.

Father Paul Verdzekov, the pioneer Archbishop of Bamenda, who first sent me to do philosophical studies in Rome, remains for all who knew him a beacon that lights up and enlightens. A universally acclaimed intellectual and moral giant, unstinting with his talents, he remains an epitome of the kind of virtue and knowledge with which this book deals. My debt to him is incalculable.

I am very appreciative of the warm welcome to the Catholic University of America (CUA) that I received from Fr. Kurt Pritzl, Dean of the School of Philosophy, when I arrived to do a doctorate in philosophy some decades after earning a licentiate in 1982 at Urbaniana University Rome. While he mentioned what such an enterprise would entail in terms of toil and sweat, he encouraged me at every step. This book is partly the result of his encouragement and support. I continue to pray for the happy repose of his gentle soul.

This work would never have been written without Monsignor Robert Sokolowski who introduced me to the thought of Yves Simon, in a course on Virtue and Human Action in the Spring of 2009 at the Catholic University of America. It examined the thought of Aristotle, Aquinas, Kant, Mill, and Simon on the philosophy of virtue. My debt to Monsignor Sokolowski is immense.

I would also like to thank Monsignor John F. Wippel, perhaps the foremost Aquinas scholar alive, Dr. V. Bradley Lewis, and Dr. Angela Mckay Knobel, all faculty of the Catholic University, with whom I shared philosophical ideas on the above question.

It remains to mention Dr. James A. Oti, and my sisters, Dr. Felicia L. Oti, and Gladys Lafon, whose technical, moral, and material support have been invaluable. The constant discussions I had with Father William Neba, of the ideas in this book, were a source of intellectual ferment.

Preface

Yves R. Simon is one of the greatest contemporary philosophers of moral virtue. After giving up medical studies for philosophy, he enrolled as a student of Jacques Maritain in the Catholic Institute of Paris in 1928. Thanks to this acquaintance and his philosophical formation, he became well versed in the works of Aristotle and Aquinas, developing the conviction that philosophy is not just a mental game aimed at showing theoretical erudition but could and ought to be a tool for resolving life's most difficult dilemmas. Subsequently, Simon began to teach philosophy at the Catholic Institute of Lille in 1930.

His first published book, his doctoral dissertation, entitled *Introduction à l'ontologie du connaître* (1934),[1] was in the field of epistemology. It was followed by *Critique de la connaissance moral*,[2] a work on moral philosophy, published the same year. This work, which Marie-Vincent Leroy, O.P. calls "an excellent introduction to the problems of practical knowledge, the scope and method of moral and political philosophy, and the nature of moral judgment,"[3] lays down some of the principles of many of his later writings.

In 1936, two years after the publication of his first work, what he describes as an "immensely sad event," namely the Italian invasion of Ethiopia, forced him to turn his attention to political matters and how moral philosophy might apply to them. The result was *La campagne d'Ethiopie et la pensée politique française*,[4] in which he sought to

---

[1] Yves R. Simon, *Introduction à l'ontologie du connaître* (Paris : Desclée de Brouwer, 1934). English translation by Vukan Kuic and Richard J. Thompson, *An Introduction to Metaphysics of Knowledge* (New York: Fordham University Press, 1990).

[2] Yves R. Simon, *Critique de la connaissance moral* (Paris: Desclée de Brouwer, 1934). English translation by Ralph McInerny, *A Critique of Moral Knowledge* (New York : Fordham University Press, 2002).

[3] Yves R. Simon, *The Definition of Moral Virtue*, ed. Vukan Kuic, with a Bio-Biography by Marie-Vincent Leroy, O.P., (New York: Fordham University Press, 1986), ix-x.

[4] Yves R. Simon, *La campagne d'Ethiopie et la pensée politique française* (Paris : Desclée de Brouwer, 1936). English translation by Robert Royal, *The Ethiopian Campaign and French Political Thought* (Notre Dame : University of Notre Dame Press, 2009).

expose the hypocrisy of some political actors and intellectuals in France. In 1938 he came to the University of Notre Dame as a visiting teacher. The outbreak of World War II prevented his return to France, and he continued teaching at Notre Dame as a regular member of the faculty. Following the start of the war, and what he considered the culpable hesitation, even tame acceptance of Nazism by some highly placed Catholics, including some in the hierarchy, he wrote *La grande crise de la République Française: Observations sur la vie politique français de 1918 à 1938*[5] in 1941. Simon was to write two other works to urge reconciliation and to propose some principles to help guide action during the post war period. These works were respectively, *La Marche à la délivrance*[6] and *Par delà l'expérience du désespoir*.[7]

There is no question that Simon intended these books to be understood as the works of a political philosopher rather than a political scientist, a fact which earned him the title "the philosopher of the fighting French."[8] He did not hesitate to look history in the eye and apply time-worn principles to it. What characterizes these works, therefore, is the fact that they "transcend the era that saw their birth" or possess a certain timelessness.[9] In a review of *The Community of the Free*, re-issued some forty years after it was written, Robert Speath justifies the fact of its re-issue so many years afterwards by pointing to this timeless quality. He says:

---

[5] Yves R. Simon, *La grande crise de la République Française: Observations sur la vie politique français de 1918 à 1938* (Montreal : Editions de l'Arbre, 1941). English translation by James A Corbett & George J. McMorrow, *The Road to Vichy* (Lanham, MD: University Press of America, 1988).

[6] Yves R. Simon, *La Marche à la délivrance* (New York: Éditions de la Maison Française, 1942). English translation by V. M. Hamm, *The March to Liberation* (Milwaukee: The Tower Press, 1942).

[7] Yves R. Simon, *Par delà l'expérience du désespoir* (Montreal: Lucien Parizeau, 1945). English translation by Willard R. Trask, *The Community of the Free* (Lanham, MD: University Press of America, 1984).

[8] Marie-Vincent Leroy, O. P., "Bio-Bibliography," in Simon, *The Definition of Moral Virtue*, x.

[9] Vukan Kuic, *Yves Simon: Real Democracy* (Lanham, MD: Rowman & Littlefield Publishers Inc., 1999), 2.

Simon's way of treating his subject makes his book readily applicable to social situations that have occurred much later. The concrete conditions that led to his reflections do not dominate the contents of these reflections: rather the concrete gave Simon the occasion to construct arguments of principle and generality that live on. It is not only possible but, in this reviewer's opinion, very beneficial to ponder these essays with the news of the 1980s as a factual accompaniment. *The Community of the Free* has transcended the era that saw its birth.[10]

And these remarks can be seen not only as applying to this book but also to all of the works mentioned above.

After the Second World War, and because of the issues it had thrown up, Simon continued to reflect and write on questions of political philosophy, the only difference consisting in the more generalized nature of the catastrophe. In 1948, he moved from Notre Dame University to the Committee on Social Thought at the University of Chicago and was to stay here till his death in 1961. It was a particularly fruitful time. Not only did he teach twenty seven different courses in preparation for his projected writing of an Encyclopedia of Philosophy,[11] in 1951 he published what has probably become his most famous work, *Philosophy of Democratic Government*. This ground-breaking book has been translated into Japanese, Portuguese, German, Korean, Italian, Polish and French. After his early death in 1961 at the age of fifty-eight, other important works in political philosophy have been put together from his classroom notes, files, and tapes made by his former students. These include, *A General Theory of Authority*, *A Definition of Moral Virtue*, *The Tradition of Natural Law: A Philosopher's Reflections* and *Practical Knowledge* among others. These works and others inform this book.

---

[10] Robert L. Speath, "Simon's Moderate Pessimism," *The Review of Politics* 48 (1986): 122.

[11] Simon intended to publish an "Philosophical Encyclopedia." It would comprise many volumes dealing with logic, philosophy of science, epistemology, ontology, political philosophy including the philosophy of work, and moral philosophy. Because of the illness that led to his death at the young age of fifty eight, Simon scaled back his project renaming it "Philosophical Inquiries."

These works, published posthumously, exhibit the same character of shining the light of the perennial teachings of the past on contemporary issues. Simon is not so much engaged in a restoration of the Aristotelian-Thomistic doctrine as a rereading in the face of different circumstances.[12] Having thoroughly assimilated the thought of Aristotle and Aquinas, Simon expounds it in a manner that is personal, faithful to principle, but without depending on authority. Vukan Kuic makes the point clearly and elegantly:

> What Simon is interested in are not "texts" but actual problems, and he finds the Aristotelian-Thomistic tradition helpful in suggesting solutions. He may thus be considered a follower of that tradition because he succeeded, in a relatively short working life, to clarify, bring up to date, and even improve its teaching on a number of vital philosophical issues.[13]

This book will be concerned specifically with virtue, and how Simon weaves it into various political contexts. I will examine how it affects various actors on the political scene and its role in the different facets of political life. That is: how are we to understand the important and crucial definition of virtue in a time when a number of alternatives are being proposed as more relevant and meaningful? Are these novel theories better than Aristotle's and Thomas Aquinas's? Are we, henceforth, dispensed from the hard and persevering work of acquiring the virtues? How does virtue relate to the common good in the light of the competing theories on the question, such as those that Virginia Held outlines in her influential book, *The Public Interest and Individual Interests*?[14] Why is virtue an indispensable requirement in those who rule, a quality that should help us assess the performance of sit-tight dictators who populate the African and other continents, and how does Simon rescue the bad name of the virtue of obedience? How do natural law, natural moral law, and positive law incorporate the virtues in the way they work?

---

[12]Simon, *The Definition of Moral Virtue*, 55–56.
[13]Vukan Kuic, *Yves Simon: Real Democracy*, 12.
[14] Virginia Held, *The Public Interest and Individual Interests* (New York: Basic Books Inc. 1970).

In this work, I explore how Simon brings the wisdom of the past to bear on various aspects of modern efforts at nation building in the aftermath of the destructive theories of Machiavelli, René Descartes, Thomas Hobbes, Rousseau,[15] and many others.

---

[15]Simon, *The Definition of Moral Virtue*, 56.

Chapter 1

The Definition of Moral Virtue

I: Modern Substitutes for Virtue and their Inadequacy

Yves R. Simon observes that in the Western tradition, virtue theory has its origins in ancient Greek philosophy. The four cardinal virtues of prudence, justice, courage, and temperance, go back to Plato's *Republic*,[1] and have won the general acceptance of philosophers through the ages.[2]

But if there is such unanimity regarding the four traditional moral virtues, defining virtue is not equally straightforward. Not the least of the problems complicating this task is the fact that perception of what constitutes natural law, and thus what is virtuous, seems to change in some cases from one culture to another, from one society to another, and also from one age to another. In this regard Simon writes as follows:

> There would be no eternal return of natural law without an everlasting opposition to natural law. Again, this opposition thrives on the contrast between the notions of actions that are right or wrong by nature, and the lack of uniformity which we observe in actual judgments. If the right or wrong of murdering unborn babies is decided by nature, why should we not be completely agreed on such an

---

[1] Plato, *Republic* 427e; 435b.

[2] Simon, *The Definition of Moral Virtue*, 95. See also Peter Geach *The Virtues* (Cambridge: Cambridge University Press, 1977); James D. Wallace, *Virtues and Vices* (Ithaca: Cornell University Press, 1978). I am aware that in our times Walter Kaufmann has proposed a new list of the cardinal virtues, namely, ambition/humility, love, courage, and honesty. Cf. *The Faith of a Heretic* (New York: Doubleday & Co. 1961), 317-38. These efforts have not, however, been followed up by any other moral philosopher that I know of.

important subject? Even in a well-defined social group divergences are not inconceivable.³

There are other examples of moral diversity such as the question of slavery, which was once thought to be a perfectly acceptable practice but was rapidly seen as vicious between 1760 and 1800 in America, France and Britain.

Conscious of these divergences in perception, and while leaving a complete definition for the end of the chapter, Simon begins his consideration of how virtue is to be understood in *The Definition of Moral Virtue* with a provisional description which all would accept. He says that "what matters is that everyone recognizes the difference between people who are really dependable and those who are not."⁴ A virtuous man is dependable and can be trusted not to steal even if the chances of being caught are nil.

But this is only the beginning since a definition of virtue requires a multitude of clarifications and distinctions starting, for what Simon calls "pedagogic"⁵ reasons, with an articulation of three major modern alternatives. He considers these alternatives as deficient and will, in this work and in other writings, show how they fall short, but he uses them as foils to help him develop the right definition of virtue. The three theories are (1) the recourse to natural or spontaneous goodness, (2) the idea that people can be made good by way of social engineering and (3) the attempt to achieve goodness through psycho-technology. In Part I of this chapter, I will present Simon's discussion of these theories and his explanation of how they fall short.

Given that some modern authors, either through a misunderstanding of Aristotle's thought or a mistranslation of key words in Aristotle's definition of virtue fail to properly grasp this definition, I will look at why Simon insists that virtue is not habit, opinion, or scientific *habitus*. These distinctions which constitute Part

---

³ Yves R. Simon, *The Tradition of Natural Law: A Philosopher's Reflections*, ed. Vukan Kuic (New York: Fordham University Press, 1965), 4-5.

⁴ Simon, *The Definition of Moral Virtue*, 1, 15.

⁵ Ibid.

II of chapter 1, take in chapters three and four of Simon's work. In Part III, which covers the last two chapters of Simon's book, I will conclude by looking at how he explains Aristotle's definition of virtue. This definition is further clarified by an examination of how the virtues work in practice, their interdependence, and how we get to virtue by instinct.

The Recourse to Natural Goodness

The Work of Jean Jacques Rousseau and Ralph Waldo Emerson

If the above introduction proves anything, it is that the idea of virtue is a complex one and trying to understand it has led many astray. Simon warns us not to be misled by Rousseau and his followers, who might continually use the word virtue, but who do not conceive it in traditional terms. Rather they see it exclusively in terms of liberating the native goodness man inherits at birth. They urge people to "be yourself . . . relax and let the goodness in you come out."[6] Simon identifies principally Jean Jacques Rousseau (1712-1778) and Ralph Waldo Emerson (1803-1883) as holding this position.

He traces the origins of the ideas so powerfully expressed by Rousseau regarding natural goodness to the inspiration of Michel de Montaigne (1533-1592), and René Descartes (1596-1650). Montaigne was one of the most influential writers of the French Renaissance. He made the essay popular as a literary genre, something which Rousseau imitated and used effectively in his own work. Montaigne's essays also had a strong influence on Emerson and philosophers such as Descartes, which might explain their connection on the question of the natural goodness of man. In his *Essays*, especially the one entitled "*Of the Education of Children*,"[7] Montaigne credits his success in Latin, which he studied for many years, to the fact that his father aroused his natural interest in the subject rather than use the

---

[6] Simon, *The Definition of Moral Virtue*, 84.

[7] Michel de Montaigne, *Montaigne's Essays and Selected Writings*, trans. and ed. Donald M. Frame (New York: St. Martin's Press, 1963).

unpleasant and harsh teaching methods that were popular and thought to be effective in the sixteenth century. He writes that while nothing was forced on him, he had everything, so that he could take advantage of his freedom to achieve the best in him.[8]

Regarding the influence of Descartes on Rousseau's thought, Simon points to an affinity between Rousseau's idea of the spontaneous goodness of man and Descartes' theory of intellectual perfection, precisely as expressed in Descartes' pregnant phrase "the natural light of reason,"[9] which itself bears a resemblance to the idea of "naturalistic optimism" of his near contemporary Francis Bacon.[10]

But the question Descartes has to answer is why some people fail to apprehend reality correctly if we all possess the natural light of reason. By way of a response, Descartes blames all mistakes we make on our childhood. Whereas the majority of people would name their childhood as a happy time when they did not have to shoulder the responsibilities of adult life, Descartes looks at childhood with regret since he thinks that of all of the reasons responsible for our having wrong ideas, this is the most important contributing factor.[11] Our natural powers, which are good in themselves, are skewed at this stage, because of an imagination that lacks discipline and tends to run wild, but above all because of the bad teaching of our parents and minders who inculcate erroneous ideas in our minds. If the above problem can be resolved, then the powers of human reason would be at their best.

---

[8]. Ibid., 64-65, 75-76. See Simon, *The Definition of Moral Virtue*, 16, 85.

[9] In one of his replies to an objection in the *Meditations*, Descartes writes: "I do not see what I can add to make it any clearer that the idea in question could not be present to my mind unless a supreme being existed.

. . . If (the reader) attends carefully to what I have written he should be able to free himself from the preconceived opinions which may be eclipsing his natural light." *The Philosophical Writings of Descartes*, vol. II., trans. John Cottingham, Robert Stoothoff, Dugald Murdoch (Cambridge: Cambridge University Press, 2005), 97. See also the following pages of the same work: 11, 27-28, 32.

[10] Francis Bacon expressed his aspirations and ideals in the *New Atlantis* released in 1627 and the *New Organon* published in 1620 when Descartes was in his early twenties. In the *New Organon*, he detailed a system of logic superior to the old ways of syllogism.

[11] Simon, *The Definition of Moral Virtue*, 2-3.

Simon is of the view that Rousseau adopted these ideas from these sources and applied them to moral philosophy with the result that whereas virtues are acquired qualities for Aristotle and Thomas Aquinas, for him they result from a freeing of native energies. Simon writes as follows of Rousseau's position:

> The idea of how to achieve moral excellence is not to work for it but rather to tap in the individual a natural spontaneity towards goodness, which Rousseau takes to be antecedent to both rationality and social order. . . . Rather than an acquired quality of the mind or character "virtue" for Rousseau means nothing more than "natural spontaneity."[12]

This rendering by Simon is in harmony with what Rousseau himself wrote in a famous letter to Malesherbes in 1762:

> 'Oh Monsieur, if I had ever been able to write a quarter of what I saw and felt under that tree, with what force would I have exposed all the abuses of our institutions, with what simplicity would I have demonstrated that man is naturally good, and that it is by these institutions that men have become wicked.[13]

I would like to observe, in support of Simon, that this idea of the natural goodness of man is also evident when Rousseau articulates his theory of the state of nature in opposition to that of Thomas Hobbes. Like other philosophers of his day, Rousseau accepts a hypothetical state of nature as a normative guide. But, in his *Discourse on the Origin and Foundations of Inequality Among Men* (or Second Discourse), Rousseau's natural man is very different to that of Hobbes. He criticizes Hobbes for asserting that since man in the state of nature "has no idea of goodness, he must be naturally wicked

---

[12]Ibid., 4.
[13] Quoted in the introduction to Jean Jacques Rousseau, *On the Social Contract*, ed. Roger D. Masters, trans. Judith R. Masters (New York: St. Martin's Press, 1978), 8. See Simon, *The Definition of Moral Virtue*, 17.

because he does not know virtue."[14] Rather, Rousseau sees man as good in the natural state in the sense of having what he calls uncorrupted morals.[15] He is of the view that the state of nature was a primitive condition admittedly without law or morals, but a condition in which, there was *amour de soi*, a positive self love as opposed to *amour propre*, or vanity brought on by society, through competition and an encouragement of the tendency to compare oneself with other people.[16]

The account of Ralph Waldo Emerson makes the same point but has nuances which Rousseau's does not have. Simon tells us that he takes Rousseau's enthusiasm for spontaneous goodness as virtue even further, by adding two features to it that are philosophically significant. He places natural goodness not only before the voluntary but in opposition to it. He thinks that "our moral nature is vitiated by any interference of our will."[17] Secondly, and much more explicitly than Rousseau, Simon points out, he ties spontaneity to a divine agent or a god who is the soul of the world.[18] It is this ultimate source that is responsible for our spontaneous acts becoming virtue, rather than the will or any struggle to acquire virtue through the consistency of our good actions. In support of this interpretation of Emerson, Simon points to Emerson's essay on "*Spiritual Laws*" where he states:

> People represent virtue as a struggle, and take to themselves great airs upon their attainments, and the question is everywhere vexed when a noble nature is commended, whether the man is not better who strives with temptation. But there is no merit in that matter. Either God is there or he is not there. We love characters in proportion as they are

---

[14] Jean Jacques Rousseau, *Discourse on the Origin and Foundations of Inequality among Men or Second Discourse* in *The Discourses and other early political writings*, ed. Victor Gourevitch (Cambridge: Cambridge University Press, 2002) 151.

[15] Ibid., 151, 218.

[16] Ibid.

[17] Ralph Waldo Emerson, *The Selected Writings of Ralph Waldo Emerson*, ed. Brooks Atkinson (New York: Modern Library, 1950), 192. See Simon, *The Definition of Moral Virtue*, 7.

[18] Ralph Waldo Emerson, *The Selected Writings of Ralph Waldo Emerson*, 192. See Simon, *The Definition of Moral Virtue*, 7.

impulsive and spontaneous. The less a man thinks or knows about his virtues, the better we like him.[19]

In this quote, Emerson alludes, both to the divine causality of virtue, and the need to disregard the will.

What does Simon think about this version of what virtue is? Before I begin an elaboration of Simon's case against this version of virtue, this is the place to state what, in his view, is positive about it because even if modern horrors as witnessed especially in the last World Wars have seriously dented belief in natural goodness, it still persists today in some circles. Simon does not dispute that the idea of natural spontaneity has something to be said for it. If the idea was ever put forward at all, and if it has survived for so long, it must have a core truth.[20] The idea of spontaneous goodness is acceptable to a point because underlying it is the presupposition that there is a certain goodness, which needs to be let out, in each person. This core truth has to do with a good pristine disposition. Simon thus gives Emerson and Rousseau "full credit for defending (spontaneous goodness) so passionately, because spontaneity is such an essential ingredient in human fulfillment."[21]

The Role of Childhood Accidents

However, whether it is an adequate substitute for a theory of virtue is the question that Simon wants to put to the test. He does so by pointing to the possibility of childhood accidents, by examining the witness of experience, and by looking at the place of reason in a truly human act. The first argument is mainly drawn from psychology and the second from history. The really philosophical argument is the third. Let us now begin with the first.

Simon points to the fact that it is certainly accepted today that some of the heinous crimes that people commit defy any rational explanation. Some of these crimes, as well as certain ways of behaving point to psychological problems traceable to childhood. He explains

---

[19] Ralph Waldo Emerson, *The Selected Writings of Ralph Waldo Emerson*, 191.
[20] Simon, *The Definition of Moral Virtue*, 15.
[21] Ibid., 85.

that certain accidents during childhood can damage people psychologically, and that this argues against giving free rein to native spontaneity. Rather than originating with Aristotle, Simon thinks that this argument against spontaneous goodness is proposed by modern psychology. He says of the argument:

> Among the lasting achievements of modern psychoanalysis perhaps none is more significant than its having shown that an individual's strongest and most idiosyncratic tendencies are sometimes caused by childhood accidents. An authoritarian father, an authoritarian mother, or two quarreling parents can easily and often do warp their children's sound native inclinations into all sorts of harmful neurotic behaviors.[22]

What Simon clearly refers to above is the fact that we are also the product of the environment in which we grow up. If it is characterized by love and trust and other positive influences, we grow up to be rounded individuals. The reverse can leave people in an unsound state even at that early stage, and this is what Rousseau and Emerson ignore.

Spontaneity and Experience

Simon takes as his example here a favorite theme of Western intellectual history, namely, that of the "noble savage" which some authors attribute to Rousseau but which probably originated with Christian missionaries anxious to protect native populations from colonists.[23] He argues that it was the intellectuals of the second half of the eighteenth century who turned it into a philosophy of history portraying the "noble savage" as living close to nature, in un-spoilt conditions. They thus projected man as good by nature.

Simon is of the opinion that the travelogues and accounts of encounters with people in far-away places were tailored to give the impression of happy natives and are unconvincing if closely examined. He says:

---

[22]Ibid., 84-85.
[23]Ibid., 29.

There is no doubt in my mind that this travel literature, which is supposed to confirm the native goodness in man, is based to a large extent on preconceived opinions. Moreover, I do not think that ethnological enquiry can really tell us anything definitive about this subject, because, for one thing, the very notion of a primitive people is ambiguous. Modern science has firmly established that the species *Homo sapiens* has been in existence for at least several hundred thousand years, perhaps much longer. So how primitive can the natives, say, of New Guinea or Samoa be? Eighteenth-century philosophers may have believed that the tribes of the Canadian wilderness were truly primitive; we tend to be more skeptical. Besides, even among peoples considered more or less primitive, modern anthropologists have found a great variety of mores, manners, and beliefs. Some of these people do seem to be "noble," or at least friendly, but others are definitely hostile and cruel.[24]

The inevitable conclusion is that few today are convinced of spontaneous human goodness by looking at the historical evidence.

I would add in support of what Simon says, that already in the eighteenth century, the idea of the *bon sauvage* was not unanimously held either. One might point to an example from Hobbes. Even if for him the state of nature, when "man was a wolf to man" and "the life of man was solitary, poor, nasty, brutish and short,"[25] is a postulate rather than a description of history, he still conceives of native Americans as primitive in a pejorative sense. He writes:

> For the savage people in many places of America, except the government of small families, the concord whereof dependeth on natural lust, have no government at all; and live at this day in that brutish manner, as I said before.[26]

---

[24]Ibid., 31.
[25] Thomas Hobbes, *Leviathan* (New York: Collier Books, 1962), 100.
[26]Ibid., 101.

Spontaneity and Reason

But it is not only the witness of psychology and the evidence of history which, according to Simon, dent the claims of Rousseau and Emerson regarding the acceptance of spontaneous goodness as virtue. Their theory also ignores the role of reason or, what Simon calls the role of "the dynamic character or the parts of the human psyche,"[27] in a truly human act. Simon argues that the main problem with Rousseau's position is the presumption of "the superiority of primeval feelings over rational deliberation."[28] For Simon, one is entitled to ask if it is really the case that what is best in man is spontaneous, and exists prior to the work of reason and the will? The yearning of the Romantics for action that cuts through the complications of thinking and the time it often takes to work things out might sometimes be understandable, but can such impulsive action be elevated to a general rule?

By way of a response, Simon makes a distinction between human knowledge or understanding and human fulfillment, which corresponds to Aristotle's distinction between theoretical and practical knowledge.[29] For instance, a medical doctor may be well aware of the bad effects of smoking on health and still be a smoker. He has theoretical knowledge but does not use it. Simon says that, "I may know all there is to know about morality in theory and still remain totally undependable in my actual conduct,"[30] and elsewhere quotes John of St. Thomas who writes that, "a man may well be an ethical philosopher and theologian of great distinction and an imprudent sinner."[31] Simon mentions Charles Sanders Peirce,[32] the

---

[27] Ibid.,
[28] Simon, *The Definition of Moral Virtue*, 47.
[29] Ibid., 32.
[30] Ibid.
[31] John of St. Thomas, *The Material Logic of John of St. Thomas: Basic Treatises*, trans. Yves R. Simon, John J. Glanville, G. Donald Hollenhorst (Chicago: University of Chicago Press, 1955), 46. See Yves R. Simon, *Practical Knowledge*, ed. Robert J. Mulvaney (New York: Fordham University Press, 1991), 32. See also Simon, *The Definition of Moral Virtue*, 101,
[32] Charles Sanders Peirce, *Collected Papers of Charles Sanders Peirce*, ed. Charles Hartshorne and Paul Weiss, 6 vols. (Cambridge: Harvard University Press, 1931-

founder of American pragmatism, as having failed to make this important distinction in his philosophy when he says that "logic depends on ethics because ethics is the science of aims."[33] In both *The Definition of Moral Virtue* and *Practical Knowledge* he shows why Peirce is wrong. In the latter he says:

> The aims of logic, say, valid and explanatory reasoning, involve no consideration of human use. There is such a thing as a logical, and such a thing as a non-logical use of reasoning, and logic tells me which is which. But it does not tell me whether I should write papers on logic, or write papers in demonstrative form about something else, or write essays that be persuasive rather than demonstrative, or just cultivate my garden: these are problems of human use with which ethics is concerned.[34]

Logic is about right reasoning and ethics about right actions. Another way of saying this is that logic is about particular use while ethics is about human use.[35] He points out that since knowledge is not virtue which Socrates failed to grasp, nor is Logic subordinated to Ethics as Charles Sanders Peirce argued, we need to work out a "unity of theory and practice where understanding becomes a vital part of human fulfillment."[36] Whenever the aim is good human use "explanation is less important than application."[37]

Simon accepts that it is the case that people's actions are the result of habits formed through parental guidance, or stem from obedience to the mores and laws laid down by society. He adds that when these are good, they lead to fulfillment through upbringing and

---

1935). Vol. 4, *The Simplest Mathematics*, 197-203. See Simon, *The Definition of Moral Virtue*, 21-22

[33] Simon, *Practical Knowledge*, 38.

[34] Ibid., 39.

[35] Simon points out that the only sense in which logic could be said to be subordinated to ethics is if one had to decide how to apply logic to a particular situation, which would be the same of piano playing or carpentry. (See Simon, *The Definition of Moral Virtue*, 21-22). For the distinction between particular use and human use see p. 33.

[36] Simon, *The Definition of Moral Virtue*, 33.

[37] Ibid., 32.

socialization. But it must be said that this is only routine fulfillment, which even if better than no fulfillment, is still not human fulfillment.[38] Discussing this point in *Practical Knowledge*, he says:

> Suppose that the right thing is done without thought, as a result of sheer habit. It is good, indeed, that the right thing should be done at all; this sort of fulfillment may be the best we can expect of feeble-minded persons who have been trained to do, out of habit, what their deficient constitution does not allow them to do according to more human modalities. But clearly, when the right thing is not done in the way proper to man, it is only in a material sense that we can speak of fulfillment. No matter how important it may be that the right thing be done at all, something essential to *human* fulfillment is lacking. Our best chance of getting the true signification of progress in moral philosophy, that is, in the explanation of moral essences, may well consist in rationality, understanding, and explanation as perfections that do matter for proper fulfillment in the life of rational agents.[39]

One might say therefore, that human fulfillment and thus, virtue demands reason rather than just acting from mere habit. It is only when we know and choose, that we are fully human. Simon clinches the point in the following passage which addresses especially Emerson's views but also Rousseau's:

> The truth of the matter is that insofar as it is anterior to the work of reason, human fulfillment lacks the rational modality which belongs to it precisely as human fulfillment. Instinct and custom may make us both behave and be happy; but it is only if we know what we are doing and why that we become fully human.[40]

In support of the principle that reason is constitutive of every human action, Simon indicates that this is the position in the Socratic

---

[38]Ibid., 33.
[39] Simon, *Practical Knowledge*, 37.
[40]Ibid., 33.

dialogues of Plato,[41] and I would point to a passage in *Republic* where Socrates says that it is only when "a mind . . . combines reason and culture (and) when this resides in someone throughout his life that his goodness is kept intact."[42]

Social Engineering

The Birth of the Science of Society

In *The Definition of Moral Virtue* and in several places in *Practical Knowledge,* Simon indicates that one of the characteristics of the period of the Enlightenment was that of rapid progress in science. Simon tells us, that this is the context in which the social sciences were born, with a mandate to imitate the mechanical sciences. Society, it was thought, ought to benefit from the ways of science and the example of physical causality. Specifically the challenge was couched in these terms: the mechanical engineers and the scientists having done their share of work in making the world a better place, the social engineers now had to do their part and thereby complete the salvation through knowledge procured by the science of nature.[43] Simon articulates the challenge as it was conceived at the time:

> Here the image of a science of society patterned after the science of nature could enter the scene. The domain of salvation through knowledge would then comprise, over and above our relation to physical things, the whole universe of social relations. Servitude, exploitation, destitution, and war would fall under the power of science. Hope for the end of exploitation would have as good a foundation as hope for the end of cancer. A good part of the problem of evil would be virtually solved.[44]

---

[41] Simon, *The Definition of Moral Virtue*, 37.
[42] Plato, *Republic*, 549b, trans. Robin Waterfield (Oxford: Oxford University Press, 2008), 284.
[43] Simon, *The Definition of Moral Virtue*, 70.
[44] Simon, *Practical Knowledge*, 119.

The result was the development of the social sciences, which we would point out, is an umbrella term often used to refer to a number of fields. These include anthropology, economics, political science, business administration, and international relations among others.

But, to add a little more background information, we might observe that more specifically, the term 'the science of society' refers to sociology originally founded by Auguste Comte (1798-1857). He is, therefore, usually referred to as the 'Father of Sociology.' The credit for putting social research on concrete foundations, however, belongs to Emile Durkheim (1858-1917) born one year after the death of Comte. He was the one who created the first department of sociology in 1895 in the University of Bordeaux and published the work, *The Rules of Sociological Method*.[45] He further showed how he thought the sociological method to be distinct from the philosophical method in a ground-breaking study of suicide rates among Catholics and Protestants in 1897.[46]

During the two years Simon spent at the Sorbonne, where he enrolled in 1921, he became acquainted with the great French social thinkers of the nineteenth century, who had benefited from the work initiated by Comte and Durkheim. After finishing his studies at the Sorbonne, Simon was employed as a clerk in the French Ministry of Education, and with plenty of time on his hands and the National Library nearby, he decided to do a more thorough reading of the great French social thinkers, delving into the thought of Henri Saint-Simon and his disciples, Considerant, Buchez, but especially the forty odd volumes of P. J. Proudhon, whom he considered the greatest social thinker of the period, and Fourier.[47]

---

[45] Emile Durkheim, *The Rules of Sociological Method and Selected Texts on Sociology and its Method*, ed. Steven Lukes, trans. W. D. Halls (New York: The Free Press, 1982).

[46] Gianfranco Poggi, *Durkheim* (Oxford: Oxford University Press, 2000), chapter 1.

[47] Vukan Kuic, *Yves Simon: Real Democracy*, 5.

Charles Fourier as an Advocate of Social Engineering

While Simon considers Proudhon to be the greatest of the social thinkers of the nineteenth century, it is Charles Fourier (1772-1837) who furnishes an example of the kind of social engineering he finds to be extremely problematic, since unlike the others who had toyed with the idea before or after him, he embraced it with a zeal that was unequalled.[48] The achievements of science during the period of the Enlightenment, had, in Simon's view, a mesmerizing effect on Charles Fourier and the fact that the French refer to this period as *la Lumière* shows how they saw it generally. Simon tells us that Fourier was particularly moved by the work of Newton, becoming convinced that the equivalent to the law of gravity in the scientific domain also existed as far as society was concerned. If this law could be discovered, we would then be able to fashion a science of society, and thereby, organize society in a rational way, just as others had discovered a science of nature, and made life easier. The purpose of the science of society would be to redesign the basic structure of society building virtue, as Fourier understood it, into its fabric.[49]

Simon tells us that this law of gravity of society was to be discovered by Fourier himself, and he found it in what he called the law of "passionate attraction."[50] The core of his system and of his utopian plans was based on this theory. We might observe that according to Fourier, this was the way God had "given" things. He wrote as follows:

> My theory is limited to utilizing the passions just as nature gives them and without changing anything. That is the whole mystery, the whole secret of the calculus of passionate attraction. The theory does

---

[48] See Simon, *The Definition of Moral Virtue*, 10.
[49] Ibid.
[50] Simon translates Fourier's "passionnelle" as "passional" and thus has "passional attraction" in his works. Jonathan Beecher and Richard Bienvenu prefer "passionate attraction" in their edition and translation of Fourier's work, Charles Fourier, *The Utopian Vision of Charles Fourier*, trans. and ed. Jonathan Beecher and Richard Bienvenu (Boston: Beacon Press, 1971). The idea is the same whether we adopt the one or the other translation.

not ask whether God was right or wrong to endow human beings with particular passions; the societary order utilizes them without changing anything and just as God has given them.[51]

Let us further observe, in addition to what Simon says, that Fourier's argument for his position was based on certain metaphysical premises concerning God and his properties. These metaphysical presuppositions, or what we might call Fourier's theodicy, expressed in different and complicated ways in his many works, were quite simple. They postulated that our understanding of God meant that he necessarily possessed certain properties. Like many of the deists of his time, Fourier believed "that the perfectly harmonious Newtonian universe was itself a proof of an infinitely wise creator." Possessing such qualities as infinite wisdom and universal providence by necessity, he was "bounded by His very nature to have devised a social code for the terrestrial happiness of mankind."[52] Fourier's job was simply to discover this social code, and he was convinced that he had done this in the passions. The passions were meant to be the agents of this social harmony and human happiness.

Putting the theory of universal passionate attraction into place involved practical arrangements which Fourier called the Phalanstery, a term which Simon thinks was coined by Fourier from the Greek word *phalanx* (a military formation), and *monastery*, a kind of common dwelling.[53] Fourier proposed different phalansteries for people of different ages and tastes, such as whether they were young and liked playing in the filth or old and more settled, or whether they preferred monogamy, polygamy, or "free love," or had other likes and dislikes.[54] The idea was to try to make everyone happy according to their preference. I would add that, for Fourier, these new societal

---

[51] Charles Fourier, *Oeuvres Completes de Charles Fourier*, Vol. 5. (Paris: Editions Anthropos, 1966-1968), 157. The above translation is from *The Utopian Vision of Charles Fourier*, 205.

[52] Charles Fourier, *The Utopian Vision of Charles Fourier*, 206-207.

[53] Simon, *The Definition of Moral Virtue*, 11

[54] Yves R. Simon, *Work, Society, and Culture*, ed. Vukan Kuic (New York: Fordham University Press, 1986), 27-29.

structures would constitute the equivalent of moving from "civilized" society and its corrupt nature, to a "harmonious"[55] society. The result would be universal social harmony, the equivalent of a virtuous society.

Simon indicates some of the differences between Fourier's work and that of Rousseau and Emerson in that whereas the latter held man to be good before the genesis of society, Fourier wanted man made good through the refashioning of society. Man was to be made good by society, precisely through appropriate structures. It thus makes sense, as Simon points out, that Fourier would place the achievement of such a society in the future. "Human perfection ... is still in the future, to be found precisely at the term of full rational evolution of society."[56]

Simon mentions that Karl Marx and Friedrich Engels were familiar with Fourier's work.[57] We would add that they mention it, together with the work of Saint Simon and Owen, in *The Communist Manifesto* (1848) as belonging to socialist and communist literature "in the early undeveloped period ... of the struggle between proletariat and bourgeoisie."[58] In their view, since Fourier and the aforementioned, sought to remodel society at a time when the material conditions for a revolt of the proletariat, or working classes, did not yet exist, they tried to create them through new social laws and a new social reality. This constitutes the utopian element in their thought which practically included such measures as, "the abolition of the distinction between town and country, of the family, of the carrying on of industries for the account of private individuals, and of the wage system."[59]

---

[55] To rival his analysis of the different types of financial malfeasance, Fourier names thirteen *species* of adultery adding up to forty nine different *kinds* of adultery in civilized society. All of this would be rectified in a harmonious society. (Cf. Charles Fourier, *The Utopian Vision of Charles Fourier*, 183-88.)

[56] Simon, *The Definition of Moral Virtue*, 11.

[57] Ibid., 9.

[58] Karl Marx and Friedrich Engels, *The Communist Manifesto*, trans. Samuel Moore, ed. Joseph Katz (New York: Washington Square Press Inc., 1965), 109.

[59] Ibid., 111.

Simon believes that Marx did grasp "Fourier's essential idea that the solution to the human problem lies in knowing how to design an appropriate social environment,"[60] but Marx and Engels think that Fourier's efforts were doomed to failure, because he aimed at improving the condition of all members of society without distinction of class, and also because he hoped to achieve his aims peacefully and through small, piecemeal experiments, rather than through revolutionary action.[61] But, whereas Marx and Engels are disenchanted with Fourier for reasons of lack of respect for the canons of dialectical materialism, Simon thinks his efforts wrong-headed for the reasons which we will now expound.

Forms of Sociability or Different Ways of Becoming Socialized

Machiavelli, and those who follow him, would have us believe that politics and morality don't mix.[62] Politics, supposedly, follows its own rules, which might sometimes dictate that an immoral course of action be undertaken if that is what the supposed good of society demands. An often ignored corollary of this view, Simon points out,[63] is that morality is then seen as a strictly individual concern. The presumption is that it is not for society to try to make people good, but rather to ensure their survival, even by immoral means if that is what it takes.

The good news is that Fourier would not have acquiesced to such a view. He answers affirmatively, and rightly so, the question as to whether society has anything to do with morality. After citing numerous examples[64] to show that people behave like wild animals, abandoning the most elementary forms of decency, when law and order break down, as experiences of civil unrest and wars indicate,

---

[60] Simon, *The Definition of Moral Virtue*, 9.
[61] Karl Marx and Friedrick Engels, *The Communist Manifesto*, 109-111.
[62] Simon, *The Definition of Moral Virtue*, 35.
[63]Ibid., 34-35.
[64]Ibid., 34-36. He gives the example of a Serbian student, who speaking from his experiences during the Second World War, related how citizens in his country who were ordinarily law abiding became criminals when societal norms were temporarily suspended.

Simon gives credit to Fourier's basic idea that there is a need for appropriate societal structures since these have a bearing on morals:

> What the available evidence suggests is that society has much to do not only with how individuals actually behave but also with what they believe is moral or immoral. While enforcing different types of conduct, different social arrangements inevitably also produce corresponding ethical beliefs. . . . And so we can see that Fourier was not entirely wrong in his plans for a new society.[65]

Simon reaffirms this need for an ordered society in other works of his, such as *Freedom and Community*. He writes:

> The moral conscience of the common man lends itself to every kind of perversion when it no longer finds, in the daily framework of social relations, a discipline which ensures the protection and promotion of moral truths.[66]

Thus, for Simon, Fourier was right in his plans for a new society since society influences morality. However, the problem is how society assures the task of organizing social relations, and this is where Fourier creates problems for himself, and throws into sharp focus what Simon calls the perennial problem of "forms of sociability" in political philosophy and ethics.

How society and morality interact is an extremely complex question. What is certain, according to Simon, is the fact that various social and political arrangements, amount to different forms of sociability, and these different arrangements affect morality differently, just as morality influences various structures in different ways. By organizing society in phalansteries, Fourier does not so much aim to control the behavior of individuals as to provide a propitious atmosphere in which individuals can pursue their personal desires and instincts, without causing harm to each other and to

---

[65] Ibid., 37.
[66] Yves R. Simon, *Freedom and Community*, ed. Charles P. O'Donnell (New York: Fordham University Press, 2001), 191.

society and thus be happy. He believes that with a clever organization of society, even the oddest of human instincts can be accommodated in a way compatible with the common life of the group.

Fourier's attempt at social engineering, Simon argues, is problematic because it attributes to human beings the social model of the beehive, or the anthill, or the herd of sheep.[67] In this model, no one thinks for himself, but each person has a role to play and is expected to play it. Everything is like clock-work and is smooth-sailing. Virtue, in this model, consists in playing one's part in a set-up.

Indeed, when we look at society today, this is how everything tends to be: predictable and quiet. Simon argues that the model of sociability evidenced by ants in an anthill, or bees in a beehive, and where cattle-like behavior trumps individuality, is reinforced by the regularity and orderliness of technological developments. Simon gives the example of diseases which were deadly in the past but have been conquered in the onward march of science and technology. Trains run on time and are becoming ever more sophisticated. Electricity is regular and cars are ever more reliable in their performance. Simon further speculates that Fourier's model, like totalitarianism, in its various manifestations —Nazism, Fascism, Stalinism, Titoism, and Maoism —seeks to transfer the regularity of the technological environment to society.

But if there is one thing that bucks this trend, he affirms, it is man, who remains unpredictable. Man, Simon thinks, does not always accept a completely regular, predictable pattern of social relations, making it difficult to fit him into known forms of sociability. Simon identifies a form of sociability that best suits man:

> In order truly to understand the human condition, it seems to me that we need to identify at least one other form of sociability, which I should like to call, for lack of a better term, sociability by way of inspiration. Social thinkers and writers have good reasons to avoid looking for this form of sociability because it is extremely difficult to disengage and define. But I do not think that we can just ignore social

---

[67] Simon, *The Definition of Moral Virtue*, 38.

relations in which individuals, far from being depersonalized and made to conform, are actually inspired to be themselves. . . . Thus clearly there is more to human sociability than what keeps the herds of sheep together. If Marx is right, and I think he is on this, there is a form of sociability characteristic of man that promotes his freedom and is indispensable for his becoming a unique individual, that is, a person.[68]

Towards the end of the above quotation, Simon mentions the idea of a form of sociability that respects the person. He is of the view that Fourier's model depersonalizes, robs the individual of the ability to innovate, and thereby, of his uniqueness and freedom.

Simon goes on to give some telling examples of people who were inspired by their societies without being determined by them. He portrays Joan of Arc and the Founding Fathers of the American nation in this light, but adds that one does not have to have entered the history textbooks, to belong to this group of people.[69] A true political society ought to be one that inspires individuals to fulfill their personal destinies rather than one that puts them in a straightjacket. The fact that, "in the process of socialization people (should be) made not only to conform but to be themselves,"[70] gives the lie to Fourier's theories regarding social engineering. We would want to note that it is also in the name of the idea of the involvement of the person in action, even if that argument is different, that Simon ultimately rejects Rousseau's recourse to natural goodness as an adequate substitute for virtue.

Psycho-Technology

Sigmund Freud and the Behaviorists

Simon believes that the challenge of the behaviorists is the most recent challenge to the idea of virtue as traditionally understood, and he thinks that it may well be the most insidious and widespread.[71] He

---

[68] Simon, *The Definition of Moral Virtue*, 42-43.
[69] Ibid., 43.
[70] Ibid., 47.
[71] Ibid., 12.

blames Sigmund Freud (1856-1939) and the behaviorists, not only for its birth, but especially for its extensive propagation.[72]

Whereas Simon presumes such knowledge, a few paragraphs on the basic work and ideas of Freud and his followers might be useful for understanding his critique of their ideas. Sigmund Freud founded the discipline of psychoanalysis, doing pioneering work in the interpretation of dreams as a way to the understanding of the unconscious mind, and thus of human behavior. His work in psychosexual development resulted in his theory of the Oedipus complex, named after the Greek tragedy Oedipus Rex by Sophocles, in which he sought to show that boys have a constant love for their mothers. In 1923, he published *The Ego and the Id*, in which he proposed that the human psyche should be divided into three: Id, ego, and super-ego. He pioneered verbal psychotherapy as a field of treatment of psychic disorders. It is possibly, even if not exclusively, this part of his work that inspired the behaviorists.

B. F. Skinner (1904-1990), whom Simon quotes now and again, is one of the leading lights of the behaviorists, and his theories build on the work of Wilhelm Wundt (1832-1920), Ivan Pavlov (1849-1936), and John Broadus Watson (1878-1958), who are representative of various shades of emphases within this group. The core beliefs of Skinner show us why Simon is disenchanted with him. Skinner distinguishes the pre-scientific view, in which a person's behavior is seen as his own personal achievement (Aristotelianism), from his own scientific view in which "a person's behavior is determined by a *genetic endowment* traceable to the evolutionary history of the species and by the *environmental circumstances* to which as an individual he has been exposed."[73] What Skinner wants to achieve is "the scientific design of culture"[74] through the external manipulation of behavior. He proposes a science or "technology of behavior" which would "adopt the strategy of physics and biology"[75] and which

---

[72] Ibid.

[73] B. F. Skinner, *Beyond Freedom and Dignity* (New York: Knopf, 1971), 101 (our emphasis).

[74] B. F. Skinner, *About Behaviorism* (New York: Vintage Books, 1976), 164.

[75] Ibid., 184.

would more successfully reduce the aversive consequences of the way in which we conduct ourselves. This is possible because Skinner, determined as he is to adopt the ways of science, understands a person in purely materialistic terms. This is his definition of person:

> A person is not an originating agent; he is a locus, a point at which many *genetic* and *environmental* conditions come together in a joint effect. No one else has his genetic endowment, and no one else has his personal history.[76]

He makes the same point elsewhere when he says that all men "are the products of genetic and environmental histories."[77] The autonomous inner man understood as a responsible being is abolished. Wanting to answer the accusation that his psychology devalues the worth of the person, he indicates that he does not question the uniqueness of each individual, but then hastens to add that "the uniqueness is inherent in the sources." These "sources" or components, from which the individual is made, as is clear from the above, are not spiritual but exclusively genetic and environmental.

Man, it should be clear in Skinner's scheme, has no inherent personality, no will, no self-determination, or personal responsibility. He is incapable of self-discipline, chosen moral norms or responsible action since there is no self. Managing oneself is not a manipulation of one's states of the mind but of one's environment.[78] Man can and should be controlled from the outside to behave as we choose. The subject matter of human psychology, therefore, is behavior and not consciousness which is here seen as a legacy of magic and superstition. It is this view that permits Skinner to write as follows:

> We shall not solve the problems of alcoholism and juvenile delinquency by increasing a sense of responsibility. It is the environment which is "responsible" for the objectionable behavior,

---

[76]Ibid., 185 (our emphasis).
[77]Ibid., 247.
[78]Ibid., See, also 195.

and it is the environment, not some attribute of the individual, which must be changed.[79]

Elsewhere, he is equally clear:

> The concept of responsibility offers little help. The issue is controllability. We cannot change genetic defects by punishment: we can work only through genetic measures which operate on a much longer time scale. What must be changed is not the responsibility of autonomous man but the conditions, environmental and genetic, of which a person's behavior is a function.[80]

The behaviorist seeks to limit psychology to what is observable, to behavior, or to what the organism does, and to ask what the stimulus is that gets a certain response. This stimulus is sought in the general environment or the physiological conditions of the organism and its genetic make-up and not in the inner man.

But far from observing after the manner of disinterested spectators, Skinner and his followers seek these stimuli in order to acquire the tools which control man's reactions and are responsible for his behavior. One can then eventually use the observed results to change punishable behavior. For instance one might use hormones to change sexual behavior, surgery to control violence, and tranquilizers to control aggressions.[81] This explains why Skinner performed countless experiments on rats and immediately transferred the results to human society without thought as to the difference between rats and human beings.

Simon observes that it is for these reasons that Skinner and his followers are confident that once their methods are applied to the problems of society, these problems will be resolved immediately and evil eliminated. He quotes Skinner:

---

[79] Skinner, *Beyond Freedom and Dignity*, 74.
[80] Ibid.
[81] Ibid., 71-73.

It is hard to imagine a world in which people live together without quarrelling, maintain themselves by producing the food, shelter, and clothing they need, enjoy themselves and contribute to the enjoyment of others in art, music, literature, . . .and come to know themselves accurately and, therefore, manage themselves effectively. Yet all of this is possible.[82]

From the foregone, Simon rightly concludes that psycho-technology systematically sees the person with emotional problems, or who commits an evil act, or has some destructive tendency, as someone whose problem can only be analyzed scientifically, and a cure provided by the psychiatrist or psychoanalyst.

Simon points to the fact that this way of conceiving human problems is not necessarily new, since there are texts from the Middle Ages showing that a bath was sometimes prescribed as a remedy for sadness, just as an electric shock might have been prescribed as a cure for kleptomania in Simon's day. He even says that, "there is no question that modern psychologists have produced treatments of undesirable human tendencies that often work (and) sometimes result in a complete suppression of undesirable tendencies."[83] He endorses certain aspects of the work of the psycho-technician (even as he gives advice to moralists):

> Moralists who expect even emotionally sick people to act always according to the rules of Ethics are wrong. Before a person can be given moral advice, he or she needs to be emotionally sound. The psycho-technicians definitely have a point here.[84]

---

[82] Simon, *The Definition of Moral Virtue*, 89. Skinner, *Beyond Freedom and Dignity*, 214.

[83] Simon, *The Definition of Moral Virtue*, 13.

[84] Ibid., 22.

The Distinction between Nature and Use.

The above positive note notwithstanding, Simon insists that there are great differences between the techniques of the past and what obtains today in psycho-technology. He explains the difference:

> What is new, however, is . . . their becoming the predominant, if not the exclusive modern approach to problems arising from human tendencies recognized as harmful to either individuals or society or both. Today few people seek moral counsel; most seek medical help.[85]

A little later, he continues:

> People do not expect their psychoanalyst to raise questions of right and wrong, and he is, of course, the last person who would want to do that. But can we be absolutely sure that all those tendencies, inclinations, obsessions, passions, neuroses–not to mention "hang-ups" –that are routinely brought to psychological experts and technicians, are never anything more than psychological tendencies, inclinations, etc.? . . . What is puzzling . . . and deserves our attention, is that so few people seem to realize the very simple and plain fact, namely, that human problems are not limited to the question of soundness of emotional tendencies. Few people stop and think that beyond the problem of diseased emotions, twisted passions, destructive compulsions, and so on, there awaits the real problem of use and abuse of healthy tendencies and sound emotions, which is a problem for everyone, those in need of psychological help not excluded. . . . For me the spread of such moral insensitivity represents one of the most serious problems of our time.[86]

In the above citation, Simon raises the question of use and abuse of our powers, which gives us a clue to his assessment of the widespread use of psycho-technology in our time. While he admits that psycho-technology has its uses, as we have indicated above, he

---

[85]Ibid., 14.
[86]Ibid., 14-15.

denies that it provides the definitive answer to the crisis of morality that afflicts mankind, that is, to a proper understanding of virtue. In the face of "diseased emotions, twisted passions, (and) destructive compulsions," he proposes we raise the moral question, or the "real problem" of the "use and abuse of healthy tendencies and sound emotions." He thus makes an important distinction between nature and use in showing the inadequacy of psycho-technological methods. I will go through Simon's argumentation in three steps.

a) The first step is a threefold distinction Simon makes in the use of a thing. In order to explain the distinction, he alludes to Plato's own distinction "between being good at a particular skill and being good absolutely speaking as a human being."[87] More concretely, he takes the playing of a piano as an example.[88] In this regard, he says that there are three things to be considered. There is first of all the condition or nature of the piano. Is it in a good state or a bad state? Secondly, and assuming that the piano is in excellent condition, he says that there is the question of whether the piano player is a good player or not. Thirdly, and assuming that he is a good player, there is the question of how he uses it. Does he play loud music late into the night unnecessarily keeping his neighbors awake? Simon characterizes these three aspects as 1) the nature of the thing; 2) the particular use to which it is put; 3) the human use of the thing. In particular use we are dealing with whether the piano player is a good or a bad player rather than with his character which concerns the human use.

b) In the second step, it is interesting to see how Simon applies the above distinctions to the internal powers of the human soul. In *The Definition of Moral Virtue* he mentions the following three internal powers of the soul: memory, the will, and the emotions.[89] In *Practical Knowledge* he adds the imagination and intelligence.[90] This does not,

---

[87]Ibid., 21. As for the distinction in the works of Plato one might gainfully consult the following works: *Apology* 22d; *Euthydemus* 288d; *Gorgias* 448b.

[88] Simon, *The Definition of Moral Virtue*, 20-21.

[89]Ibid., 23-29.

[90] Simon, *Practical Knowledge*, 9-11.

however, affect the argument since he gives memory, the will, imagination, and intelligence, summary treatment given that they are not overly involved with the case at hand. In their case, he simply points out that we can use our memory (human use) either to remember the evil that others have done to us, and thereby bear grudges or we can choose to use it for good by remembering the birthdays of others and ours, and other happy events. We can do this whether our memory is good or not so good [91] (particular use). A good or bad memory would thus appear to be neutral concerning its good or bad human use. This is true of the imagination and the intelligence. With regard to the will, he argues that ideally, we need a strong and good will. A strong will alone can be used for evil as the evidence of certain strong willed leaders in history shows. A weak will is like a car without brakes and will more easily lead to trouble.

However, he explains that it is especially our emotional tendencies that are most concerned with the problem at hand. Even our normal emotional tendencies, such as sexual drive, enjoyment of pleasure, and ambition to win, need to be disciplined. They are sound if we have control over them. Therefore, for someone with a strong and good will, the emotions may not be much of a problem.

When this is not the case, we may have one of two situations: that of a destructive emotional tendency which is so strong that it eludes rational control, or that of a destructive emotional tendency which does not take away all rational control. Simon argues that it is only the first instance, which involves irresistible destructive tendencies, and which may mean that the person needs to be locked up for his own good and that of society, which can gainfully be handled by psychiatrists, that is, by the realm of psycho-technology.

The situation of those in the second group is different. The majority of those in this group can be coached into a proper and good management of their emotions and this coaching, which might sometimes require an extended period of time, falls within the realm of moralists. Simon writes:

---

[91] Simon, *The Definition of Moral Virtue*, 23.

Think of the person who has lived, say, fifty years without indulging a tendency of which no right human use can be made. More than likely, controlling that tendency involved a great deal of effort and brought that person considerable suffering. Therefore, if such tendencies could be eradicated once for all by psychological techniques, that would be immensely desirable. But that is not always possible, and we have to realize that there are people who have to spend their lives fighting against all sorts of tendencies which simply do not admit of any good human use. Each of us probably knows several such people, whose secret we do not even suspect, because having succeeded in repressing their urges through the efforts of an enlightened strong will, they lead entirely normal personal and social lives.[92]

c) As for step three, I would like to refer to two questions which Simon raises as to whether the good condition or nature of a thing, which by itself is never sufficient to guarantee good use, may nevertheless favor good use, and conversely, whether the bad condition or nature of something might not favor bad human use?[93]

After examining various concrete examples, Simon answers both questions in the affirmative. In support of this position he points out that it is difficult to envisage a scenario in which, for example, a car without brakes might be put into good use since driving it, even for a good cause such as rushing a sick person to the hospital, constitutes a menace for the driver and other road users. A car without brakes needs to be repaired or sent to the junk yard, not put on the road for whatever reason. If, however, the car is in good condition, while this does not guarantee its good use, it favors it. At least, no one runs the risk of injuring or killing themselves or someone else by simply driving the car.

Transferring these conclusions to the powers of the soul, Simon is of the view that a disposition toward wrong human use can lead to deterioration in the things or powers we use. He tells us he knows a "few people who used to be intelligent, but who have made

---

[92]Ibid., 25.
[93]Ibid., 22.

themselves idiotic . . . just by bad human use of their intelligence."[94] His conclusion:

> Rebellious rejection of fundamental rules of doing things, be that driving a car or studying philosophy, may well lead to the deterioration of the "natural" conditions of the things used, be that a person's intelligence or his car. By contrast, deliberate acceptance of proper particular use of things, supported by a strong tendency toward good human use, may well lead to their improvement especially when these 'things' happen to be the internal powers of the human soul.[95]

By showing that right human use can improve the natural condition of our powers, whereas wrong human use can result in their deterioration, Simon articulates, in addition to b) above, one further reason to avoid purely psycho-technical solutions. In order to clinch the point Simon uses various examples. Let us refer to one. Someone who has a poor memory for names can actually improve on it by repeatedly working at it, using hard and tried rules. The same is true of someone who hates letter-writing. He might improve through persistence. On the other hand, a young, brilliant man who is, lazy or lacking in discipline, runs the risk of failing because he refuses to put his intelligence to proper use. Simon wraps it up beautifully:

> My reservations about "psycho-technology" should . . . be clearer now. Its main fault is that it tends to ignore the notion of use, which is crucial in any realistic understanding of human dependability. Again, modern psychology has made great strides both in treating diseased emotions and in assertive training, that is, in methods for strengthening the will. Yet over and above what psychology can do for the powers of the soul, there looms the vast world of human action proper, consisting of human use of these powers, for whose problems psychology has no answers.[96]

---

[94]Ibid., 27.
[95]Ibid., 28.
[96]Ibid., 28-29.

Here again, as with the other two cases of spontaneous goodness and social engineering, we would point out that the idea of a proper understanding of the person comes to the fore. It is a question of the individual using his inner powers responsibly as a person. Simon refuses to see an individual, as Skinner does, as someone who should in every case of difficulty, be manipulated by drugs or psychoanalytic methods because, supposedly, composed merely of "environmental and genetic" factors. Rather, it is often the case that it is the will and a strong decision of the person that need to be engaged. He captures this element in the following quote in which he has all three modern alternatives in mind:

> In contrast to the modern approaches, all of which appear to want to assure human dependability with the least cost in effort to individuals, in the Aristotelian tradition becoming good and true is primarily a personal achievement. One has to work hard to attain that stable state of character which enables one to remain kind and honest, courageous and truthful in any type of situation.[97]

Having thus dealt with false modern attempts to define virtue, Simon is in a position to move to the preliminaries of a good definition.

II: Towards a Definition of Virtue

As we have seen, Simon explains the basic difference between modern articulations of virtue and the classical view in terms of the neglect of personal effort in the achievement of virtue.

Simon, however, points out that if modern alternative understandings of virtue have been defective on this score, this is also true of some recent explanations of what early philosophers said on the question. He says that given the different shades of emphases that come to us from classical times regarding an understanding of virtue, for instance the fact that Socrates may have hinted that virtue is knowledge, and the fact that Plato's position on the question is not

---

[97]Ibid., 47.

simply reducible to Aristotle's, misinterpretations of these ideas have cropped up. In Part II we will see what these mistaken ideas of virtue are and how Simon corrects them. Specifically, we will examine why *hexis* in Aristotle's definition of virtue, rendered as *habitus* by the Latin translators of Aristotle, cannot simply be translated as habit in English, and why virtue which may resemble habit, opinion, or science, cannot simply be reduced to any of them. In other words, we will see why Simon tells us that in order to understand Aristotle's definition of virtue "it is necessary to keep habit, scientific habit, and opinion separate and distinct."[98]

Problems of Translation Regarding *Hexis*

Aristotle defines virtue in the *Nicomachean Ethics* as a *hexis*.[99] Simon points out that this Greek word was rendered in medieval times in Latin as *habitus*. The problem, however, is that since Aristotle's philosophy was neglected at the dawn of the modern age initiated by Descartes, Bacon and Hobbes, the term *hexis* disappeared from philosophical usage.[100]

But, because of its philosophical importance, Simon believes it is crucial that a proper translation be found —one that does not betray the concept. With regard to such a translation, Simon tells us that he has labored "for the last thirty years trying to do something about it and I keep trying."[101] He mentions the French word *ayance* from *ayant* which was used as a translation for *hexis* in the seventeenth century but which quickly fell into disuse, and concludes that even if it is a useful translation, it would be unprofitable to try to revive it now.[102]

Simon is of the view that W. D. Ross who has done a translation of Aristotle's *Nicomachean Ethics*, is more accurate when he renders

---

[98] Ibid., 66
[99] Aristotle, *Nicomachean Ethics*, 1103b20.
[100] Simon, *The Definition of Moral Virtue*, 56.
[101] Ibid., 55.
[102] Ibid., 56.

hexis as "a state of character."[103] Not the least of the problems with this rendering of *hexis*, though, is the fact that Aristotle also refers to the intellectual virtues—prudence, understanding, art, science, and wisdom—as *hexis*. This translation does not work, Simon argues, when applied to the intellectual virtues since one cannot, for instance, refer to mathematics or architecture as "a state of character." We must, therefore, continue our search for a better translation.

Virtue is not Habit

Simon thinks that there is no worse attempt at translation, than to render *hexis* as habit as some contemporary translations do. Simon feels so strongly on this question that he gives us two examples of action he took to correct this. First, he narrates the story of his sometimes ungentlemanly exchange with Anton C. Pegis who had come up with precisely such a translation in a selection of the works of Aquinas he had edited.[104] Simon tells us that he wrote a review[105] of the work praising the selection and organization of the texts but criticizing the translation of *hexis* as habit. An exchange of views, which progressively degenerated in tone, ensued between him and Professor Pegis, who was President of the Pontifical Institute of Medieval Studies of Toronto at the time.

The second example he gives concerns the surprise that was sometimes expressed when people learnt that he and two of his students were hard at work translating parts of the work by John of Saint Thomas.[106] Why would anyone spend eight years of their life translating an obscure seventeenth century text on material logic, people would ask. Simon tells us that the idea was to put an important

---

[103] Aristotle, *Nicomachean Ethics*, trans. W .D. Ross, in *The Basic Works of Aristotle*, ed. Richard McKeon (New York: Random House, 1941). 957. (2.6.1106b36-1107a3; 2.5.1106a11).

[104] Thomas Aquinas, *The Basic Writings of Thomas Aquinas*, ed. Anton C. Pegis (New York: Random House), 1945.

[105] Yves R. Simon, *Commonweal* 42 (1945): 313-14.

[106] John of St. Thomas, *The Material Logic of John of St. Thomas: Basic Treatises*, trans. Yves R. Simon, John J. Glanville, G. Donald Hollenhorst (Chicago: University of Chicago Press, 1955).

medieval text, written in Latin, "into readable idiomatic English."[107] He adds that one of the reasons "some of the most difficult passages in the volume not just read smoothly but also make good sense," was because they "decided to call *habitus* habitus."[108]

In order to understand why *habitus* should not be rendered as habit, Simon examines four of the main characteristics of habit. These are: i) habit as intermediary potency; ii) habit as requiring stabilization through a repetition of acts; iii) habit as subjective necessity; iv) and habit as excluding voluntariness and freedom. Let us see what Simon says about these qualities of habit which distinguish it from virtue.

Habit as Intermediary Potency.

Simon calls on Aristotle who tells us in the *Metaphysics*,[109] that habit is a disposition to act. It is not the activity itself. This leads Simon to distinguish three phases in every action. There is first simple potency which denotes the capacity to act in a certain way. This refers to a natural ability to do something. Simon gives the example of the capacity to learn and recite a poem. One might remain in this state or decide to act, that is to recite the poem. A third possibility is to learn the poem and just keep it in one's memory which means that one can recite it whenever one wants. Simon writes:

> The ability in reserve, so to speak, this steady and ready disposition to act, if and when called upon, is what Aristotle calls either intermediary potency or an initial act.[110]

Simon holds that habit is a disposition or similar to intermediary potency. It is located between being able to learn the lines of the poem and actually reciting them—that is, learning the poem and keeping it in reserve. As we will see later, this distinguishes habit from *habitus* by a lack of the dynamic character possessed of virtue, since

---

[107] Simon, *The Definition of Moral Virtue*, 58.
[108] Ibid.
[109] Aristotle, *Metaphysics* 5.12.1019a15-b15.
[110] Simon, *The Definition of Moral Virtue*, 51.

here one can only recite what has been committed to memory whereas virtuous action judges the proper course of action in particular situations.

Habit Requires Stabilization through a Repetition of Acts

Simon's second characteristic of habit is related to the first. If habit is a disposition to act, this disposition is achieved through a repetition of acts. Simon recalls Henri Bergson's work, qualifying his "distinction between two kinds of memory (as) one of the best treatments ever of the nature of our habits."[111] He tells us that in his work, *Matter and Memory*, Bergson distinguishes between two kinds of memory: "pure memory"[112] and memory acquired by way of habit, through a repetition of acts.[113] Pure memory has to do with remembering unique events such as where one was when he read a remarkable book for the first time. Memory acquired through a repetition of acts is memory by habituation.

Simon points out that habituation through a repetition of acts is true not only of memory but of habit in general. Disposition is stabilized through a repetition of acts and the number of acts required for a habit to form, varies from person to person.

Elsewhere,[114] Simon links this aspect of habit to natural virtue pointing out that it is not always that acting mechanically is a bad thing. He gives the example of swimming, which once learnt is done mechanically; we no longer think about each stroke we will make in order to stay afloat and continue moving forward. Because of its mechanical nature some have argued that habits lack finality. Simon does not accept this. Automatic as they may be, habits are acquired for a purpose. If there wasn't a reason, we would not acquire them in the first place.

Simon writes that this aspect of habit is like the virtue we find in nature. He points out that before the denial of teleology or final

---

[111] Ibid., 48.
[112] Henry Bergson, *Matter and Memory*, trans. Margaret Paul and W. Scott Palmer (London: Allen, 1912), chap. 3. See Simon, *The Definition of Moral Virtue*, 67.
[113] Ibid., chap.2. See Simon, *The Definition of Moral Virtue*, 67.
[114] Simon, *The Definition of Moral Virtue*, 74.

causality in nature championed by seventeenth century mechanistic interpretations of nature, what a thing was good for, or the way it readily behaved, that is, the presence in it of a certain existential readiness was referred to as its "virtue."[115] After pointing to how Shakespeare uses virtue in this sense in a passage of his play *Romeo and Juliet* (Act II, Scene ii), he concludes that "the virtue habit resembles most is not moral virtue—it is the natural virtue of Shakespeare's rocks and flowers."[116] This then is the problem since a certain mechanical action is implied. As we will soon see, a mere repetitiveness in action is not human if it does not incorporate other qualities such as voluntariness, freedom, and objective necessity.

Habit as Subjective Necessity

The third characteristic Simon mentions goes back to David Hume, and Simon considers it his main claim to philosophical immortality. Simon also tells us that Hume put it at the heart of his work on a theory of knowledge. Hume has become so famous on this score, that Immanuel Kant refers to his work here as jolting him out of his "dogmatic slumber."[117] Simon points out insistently, that for Hume the necessity of habit is a subjective necessity. He refers to the following passage of Hume which contains his argument for this position:

> It appears then, that this idea of a necessary connection among events arises from a number of similar instances which occur of the constant conjunction of these events; nor can that idea ever be suggested by any one of these instances, surveyed in all possible lights and positions. But there is nothing in a number of instances, different from every single instance, which is supposed to be exactly similar; except only, that after a repetition of similar instances, the mind is carried by habit upon the appearance of one event to expect its usual attendant, and to believe that it will exist. This connection, therefore,

---

[115] Ibid.

[116] Ibid., 76.

[117] Immanuel Kant, *Prolegomena to Any Future Metaphysics*, trans. Gary Hatfield (Cambridge: Cambridge University Press, 2004), iii.

which we *feel* in the mind, this customary transition of the imagination from one object to its usual attendant, is the sentiment or impression from which we form the idea of power of necessary connection. Nothing farther is in the case.[118]

Simon draws the following conclusion from the above and similar passages in Hume:

> Thus according to Hume, while we might think that we can discover actual relations of things, all we can ever know for sure are only the habits of our mind. . . . A particular connection between two phenomena, no matter how often observed, remains always a subjective connection, because it exists only in our mind, where it appears so objective and necessary precisely because repetition has turned it into a habit.[119]

Simon adds that no one would deny that there are various degrees of necessity depending on whether the degree of compulsion occasioned by habit is weak, strong, or irresistible. However, whether it is mild or fierce, the necessity of habit brought about through a repetition of acts, is always subjective, that is, created by someone rather than in the nature of things. Nothing could be further from virtue whose necessity is objective as we will see shortly.

Habit excludes Voluntariness and Freedom

Simon cautions that the idea of subjective necessity should not lead us to conclude that when we act under the influence of habit, we always act voluntarily. Acts performed through habit, insofar as they are done solely out of habit, exclude voluntariness.[120] Simon gives the

---

[118] David Hume, *An Inquiry Concerning Human Understanding*, Sect. VII Part ii (Chicago: Open Court, 1909), 77. See Simon, *The Definition of Moral Virtue*, 67.

[119] Simon, *The Definition of Moral Virtue*, 52.

[120] The qualification "insofar as they are done solely out of habit" is important since our reasons for acting are hardly ever simple. Some other motive is usually working together with habit such as indiscreet curiosity in the example given above of checking a different person's mailbox. When that is the case, one's action is no

example of someone who having lived in the same apartment for many years moves house. While he was living in that apartment, he would check his mail box at least once a day. After moving to another house, he returns to that apartment to visit his former neighbor, and his first instinct is to get into the mailbox and check the mail. Should he succumb to instinct and do that, it would be an involuntary act performed from habit and not because he wanted to pry into another person's mail.

To the involuntary nature of such acts, Simon adds that acts performed out of habit are not free. Is this not the same as saying that they are involuntary as we have just done above? In answer Simon points to nuances between the two. He says:

> While freedom and voluntariness are, of course, closely related, I do not think that they should be completely identified. . . . An act may be more free than it is voluntary, that is, desired or wanted, and another act may be more voluntary than free.[121]

An act which is performed merely from habit excludes choice and intention.

Habit and Virtue

Taking the above mentioned characteristics of habit into account, can one say that moral virtue is the same as habit, as Pegis believed at one point when he translated *habitus* as habit? Simon answers the question and tells us that, "if Aristotle's four moral virtues—temperance, fortitude, justice, and prudence—are called "habits," his whole theory of ethics quickly dissolves into nonsense,"[122] because such a translation does not even bring us close to explaining the nature of the virtues.[123]

---

longer purely involuntary and from habit. (See Simon, *A Definition of Moral Virtue*, 54-55).
[121] Simon, *The Definition of Moral Virtue*, 55.
[122] Ibid., 57.
[123] Ibid., 58.

The difficulty arises from the fact that habit shares some of the aforementioned characteristics with virtue. For instance, in both we have to do with a disposition made stable through a repetition of acts. But their similarities end there and their differences which outweigh these similarities are deep-seated. Simon discusses three in particular.

The first is that unlike habit whose necessity is subjective, the necessity present in virtue is objective. It is akin to the necessity present in science. By way of example, Simon points out that personal progress in scientific knowledge would be blocked if the necessity present in mathematics were not objective. One scientist, he says, would not be able to pick up and continue from where another had left off. He quotes the distinguished mathematician Andre Weil, who writes:

> It is certain that few men of our times are as completely free as the mathematicians in the exercise of their intellectual activity . . . (and while) others have to have recourse to the muddy streams of sordid reality (the mathematician is assured that) the very sources of knowledge will always continue to pour forth, pure and abundant.[124]

This grounding in objective necessity makes habit and virtue operate differently. This is how Simon explains this aspect of their difference:

> What we might call their operations are also quite different. For while . . . even as they serve specific ends habits operate automatically or mechanically, the operation of habitus is characterized by unmistakable vitality. Habit relieves us of the need to think; but habitus makes us think creatively.[125]

In order to illustrate this point, Simon compares two teachers: one sticks slavishly to his notes and is dull and predictable, but the other experiments with unrefined concepts, uses metaphors, and

---

[124] Andre Weil, "The Future of Mathematics," *American Mathematical Monthly* 57 (1950): 296. See Simon, *The Definition of Moral Virtue*, 68.
[125] Simon, *The Definition of Moral Virtue*, 60.

seems to run ahead of the demonstration, thanks to his mastery of the subject.[126] This should be taken to mean that whereas habit will operate in exactly the same way in like situations, *habitus* will judge creatively in each situation using especially the virtue of prudence.[127]

An equally important difference concerns the crucial issue of the absence of voluntariness and freedom in actions done from habit and their important role in acts that proceed from virtue. Here, it is useful to recall Simon's disagreement with Pegis since, in the end, what settled the matter was agreement on this issue. Simon narrates the circumstances in which resolution was achieved. Let us follow Simon's interesting account of the incident. Pegis had edited *The Basic Writings of Thomas Aquinas*. Simon writes:

> A student in one of my courses, who had been reading the *Basic Writings* put it to me as follows: "An act done out of habit is involuntary isn't it?" To which I replied: "Yes, sure, insofar as it is done out of habit. It may not be done purely out of habit. But if it is done purely out of habit, I don't see how it could be otherwise." And then came her next decisive question: "Virtue is a habit, is it not?" I did not know whether to laugh or to cry, jump for joy or faint. But as soon as I got back to my office, I took pen in hand and wrote Professor Pegis another letter. . . . *Habitus* translated by "habit," I said again, forces readers to conclude that for Aquinas acts proceeding from virtues are done involuntarily, which is totally absurd.[128]

What this student pointed to brings out a key difference between virtue and habit. While acts performed out of habit are involuntary, like the man who on visiting his old apartment instinctively checks his old mail-box, virtuous acts are free and voluntary. The difference is a radical one. Simon writes that, "a virtuous man acts the way he does, not because he cannot help it, but rather because he wants to act that way and, moreover, he knows exactly what he is doing."[129]

---

[126] Simon, *Practical Knowledge*, 9-11.
[127] Ibid.
[128] Simon, *The Definition of Moral Virtue*, 57.
[129] Ibid., 75.

Virtue Is Not Grounded In Opinion

Having distinguished virtue from habit, Simon makes two further distinctions which are part of the preparation of the grounds for a proper definition of virtue. These concern opinion and scientific knowledge. What is the difference between opinion and virtue? The question needs to be raised because opinion, like virtue, can be a stable source of action.

An examination of opinion, we might observe, could take us back to Xenophanes. He was the first philosopher to raise the question of the fleeting nature of what we know. He was convinced that there actually exists a truth of reality, but human beings are unable to know it and must depend on opinion (*doxa*). Simon tells us that if, however, there was one philosopher concerned to "confirm the mind in unshatterable truth,"[130] it was Plato. Plato, he says, held that an iota of truth (*episteme*) was worth much more than all the opinions on earth. The problem, though, was that he proceeded to situate truth out of this world, in the world of Ideas or Forms. The only way of possessing knowledge of any value in this world was to connect it to the world of Numbers or Ideas. In any case, given that we live in a world of the senses, true knowledge would always be weak.[131]

Aristotle, Simon continues, was aware of Plato's views, and despite his radical departure from major aspects of Platonic thinking on knowledge, agrees with him, that what differentiates scientific knowledge (*episteme*) from opinion (*doxa*) is the objective necessity in the one, and the lack thereof in the other. True science, *episteme*, is the capacity to demonstrate, which *doxa* is not.[132]

To illustrate the difference between the two, Simon takes the example of the Pythagorean theorem, that the square of the hypotenuse (the longest side of a right angled triangle) is equal to the sum of the squares of the other two sides. No matter the lengths of the sides of the triangle taken as an example, the Pythagorean theorem will always be true. This, he says, is not the case with opinion

---

[130]Ibid., 64.
[131] Ibid.
[132]Ibid., 64-65.

which can be defined as what we hold of things that can be otherwise than they are.[133] What are the things of which we can only have opinion? Simon gives numerous examples. For instance, there can be no "science of elections" no matter what pollsters would have us believe, "because everything in the political process can be otherwise than it is without contradiction."[134] Results are sometimes different from the predictions of the pollsters, and then we talk of "upsets." There is no science of accidents. One can take all the precautions that are necessary before a road journey such as, check the tires, fix the brakes, check the oil, abstain from drinking alcoholic beverages, and take a good rest before setting off, and yet have someone run into him and cause an accident. There is no certainty in opinion because its subject matter is itself something indetermined, such as predicting if there will be a recession in the next six months. No one can know the answer because such matters are not subject to any necessity such as that underlying the theorem of Pythagoras.[135]

Simon gives an example of the crucial distinction between opinion and scientific knowledge which regards their subjective and objective necessity. It concerns how error may or may not attach to the person involved. He says:

> We recognize an opinion for what it is every time we admit that we were wrong in our opinion. We were wrong, we say, and our opinion was wrong. We do not talk that way about science. When a working scientist makes an error, we blame him alone, not his science. . . . Normally, we think of his error as due to lack of science; he made a mistake because he was short of knowledge. This is quite different from judging opinion, where we do not hesitate to say that both the man and his opinion were wrong.[136]

But, says Simon, opinion needs to be distinguished from scientific opinion. Whereas the one is subjective, the other has a

---

[133]Ibid., 65.
[134]Ibid., 66.
[135]Ibid., 62-64.
[136]Ibid., 63-64.

certain objectivity. He tells us that scientific opinion is a collective name for "speculative hypotheses, probable judgments, and educated guesses."[137] Simon makes the point that these belong to science in a loose sense, rather than to opinion, playing a substantial role when a leak-proof demonstration is yet to be had, or when a scientist has to accept as provisionally true the results of scientific work he has not performed himself. Simon says that "in their work scientists have no choice but to use reports and formulae of other scientists, which they have not fully checked out themselves and may not fully comprehend."[138] This happens in science all the time and scientific progress would suffer if the scientist had to verify every discovery for himself before accepting or using it.

Besides scientists, Simon says that ordinary people use scientific opinion in the same way, applying discoveries to their daily lives whose truth they could never be able to work out for themselves. Simon gives the example of the upbringing of children in accord with discoveries in child psychology. Parents have taken the experts at their word and abandoned certain harsh methods used in the past.

To show that scientific opinion, like science, is similar to virtue, Simon points out in *Practical Knowledge*, that moralists act in the same way when they act on inclination, which should not be taken as subjective, while deferring proof for their position for later. He writes:

> It is normal that any perfection of man and of mankind, whether in the sciences or elsewhere, be achieved gradually, through a progress that is never unqualifiedly terminated. In such reference to human development, it is normal that a theorem be familiar to geometricians years or generations before it is demonstrated.[139]

Simon stresses one point which opinion shares with habit. Like habit, opinion can be quite stable even if its subject matter is contingent and its necessity subjective. People, he indicates, often

---

[137] Ibid., 64.
[138] Ibid., 65.
[139] Simon, *Practical Knowledge*, 36.

stick to their opinions and one of the reasons for that, may be because we are identified as persons, as we have just seen, with our opinions. Opinion thus shares with habit the qualities of stability and subjective necessity and should be distinguished from virtue.

Virtue is not Science

Aristotle discusses the intellectual virtues, describing them, among others, by the name of *hexis* just as he does the moral virtues. This is on account of the objective necessity of science. In the course of dealing with opinion as different from virtue, Simon mentions aspects of science, particularly the quality of its objective necessity, which distinguish it from opinion. But the fact that science possesses the characteristic of objective necessity just like virtue, does not mean that science and moral virtue are the same. We will now expound Simon's reasoning as to why the two are different, by looking at the practical and philosophical arguments he advances.

The Value-Neutrality of Science

From the time of the Renaissance, science began to record notable advances leading to a fairly widespread conviction that it was good in itself. The onward march of scientific progress would conquer not only ignorance, but all evil as well. Simon tells us, that this faith in the goodness of science (we have seen one example in psycho-technology) and its ability to resolve all human problems in a matter of years, reached its peak towards the end of the eighteenth century.[140]

Simon rather humorously points to a paradox which resulted from this conviction on the part of some people, a paradox which should, ordinarily, have caused people to pause and think. This was the fact that social scientists, and those similarly persuaded, were so fanatical in their conviction in the inevitability of progress that they did not hesitate to kill those who thought otherwise. How could

---

[140] See Simon, *The Definition of Moral Virtue*, 69-70; Simon, *Practical Knowledge*, 115-116, 119, 142.

anyone who believed that mankind, as such, was moving forward be ready to commit murder to prove it? He cites the example of the French Revolution when "not even the ferocious cruelty of these optimistic idealists . . . managed to destroy the myth of human progress through science."[141] Whatever the situation, the triumph of progress was thought to be underway at this time, and there was a heady optimism in the air as to the glorious destiny of mankind that science would guarantee.

This thinking had been inspired by the discoveries of Newton and the fact that science had developed by leaps and bounds thereafter. Inspired by Newton, Descartes' presuppositions as to the inevitability of progress thanks to science were accepted as in the order of things. The presumption was that science was not neutral but good and that scientific progress could only lead to the defeat of darkness in all its forms. Regarding what was expected, Simon writes:

> Servitude, exploitation, destitution, and war would fall under the power of science. Hope for the end of exploitation would have as good a foundation as hope for the end of cancer. A good part of the problem of evil would be virtually solved. Such a vision attained a climax of intensity about a century ago.[142]

However, a change of perspective followed. Simon tells us that, "in contrast with earlier approaches, the social science of modern times generally claims to be independent of ethical concerns,"[143] that is to say, value-neutral. This, it is thought, gives it objectivity and, thus, respectability as a science. He refers especially to Max Weber who argued for *Wertfreiheit* or the irrelevance of value-judgments as essential to social science in a celebrated paper[144] and further points

---

[141] Ibid., 70.

[142] Ibid., 119.

[143] Simon, *Practical Knowledge*, 121.

[144] Max Weber, *On the Methodology of the Social Sciences*, trans. Edward A. Shils and Henry A. Finch (Glencoe, Ill.: Free Press, 1949), 22. See Simon, *Practical Knowledge*, 121-125.

out that, at its inception, a social scientist who questioned this postulate put his reputation in jeopardy.[145]

The idea that science is virtue which remained strong even after the mayhem of the French Revolution, was blown away by the events of World War II and its aftermath. The realization, Simon says, that Curie's discovery of radioactivity in 1898,[146] can be used to treat diseases just as it can be employed in mass murder has had a sobering effect even engendering pessimism regarding scientific progress and human nature. Clearly, scientific progress does not necessarily guarantee the right human use of science, and technical prowess does not determine whether people will employ it for good or for evil. It is now clear from practical experience that science is not virtue.[147]

Qualitative Readiness and Existential Readiness

With regard to the philosophical demonstration of the difference between science and virtue, Simon again utilizes the distinction between nature and use even if now in a different context, that of the kinds of readiness. He indicates that there are two kinds of readiness and calls them qualitative and existential. This is how he illustrates the distinction he is making:

> For instance, don't you know someone who, in your opinion, is wasting his or her talents, whatever these may be? A scientist perhaps, or a writer, or a musician, who has not done anything worthwhile for quite some time? There is no doubt in your mind that he can do it, but he is not doing it. . . . There are people like that in every walk of life, in every science, in every art. While indubitably qualified, they do not use their qualifications. . . . By contrast, if you have a friend distinguished by his prudence, or temperance, or courage, or sense of justice, you are not worried that he may waste his virtues. You confidently expect your friend always to do the right thing at the right time. . . . A just man

---

[145] Simon, *Practical Knowledge*, 121.
[146] Simon, *The Definition of Moral Virtue*, 70-71.
[147] Ibid., 71.

cannot postpone his justice. His readiness is both qualitative and existential.[148]

Basically, the difference here, as Simon explains it, lies in the fact that whereas science has to do with a state of being, on which one may or may not act (qualitative being), virtue has to do with always acting in a certain way thanks to a state of being (existential readiness).

Simon draws our attention to the fact that the name existential readiness corresponds to final causality, or what a thing is good for, or its purpose. There are many things whose finality we know. If, for instance, it was asked what the kidneys are good for, we would answer, and rightly so, that their purpose is to clean the body of waste products resulting from various metabolisms. But, Simon points out, finality is not limited to living things. Rather, it is involved wherever there is movement of any kind. The problem, he continues, is that we do not know what some processes are good for. Why is there gravity in the world for example? True, it ensures that all things fall to the ground rather than into space. Simon doubts that this is a rigorous explanation of gravity. Why should things fall to the ground? Simon says that such questions have led some philosophers, biologists, chemists, and physicists, to regard teleological explanations as irrelevant, and that is why Simon introduces this new terminology of existential readiness. Sidestepping the question of why things act in a certain way (finality), Simon's terminology tells us how they are existentially ready to act.

To further buttress the need for the introduction of this new terminology, Simon draws our attention to an interesting fact of history namely, that going as far back as Aristotle and classical antiquity, the presence of existential readiness was recognized in the things of nature and referred to as their natural "virtues."[149] This is different from a mere qualitative readiness.

---

[148]Ibid., 71-72.
[149]Ibid., 74.

Disposition

The readiness to act is based on a person's disposition. And disposition, is another important area in which science and virtue met and differ. Its importance in both areas cannot be gainsaid, since without a proper disposition neither the one nor the other can exist.

Simon traces the idea of disposition (*diathesis*) back to its source, in Aristotle's fifth book of the *Metaphysics*, where he defines it as "the order of that which has parts."[150] Disposition, from the verb "to dispose," refers to an arrangement "of the parts of a whole with a view to an effect pertaining to the whole."[151] Simon gives the example of furniture in a room or on a display window in a department store before Christmas. If it is jumbled together carelessly, then the room or the window looks unattractive because of a poor disposition of objects. Simon asks us to take note of the fact that it is the whole room which looks bad when the disposition of the furniture is badly done. This is in line with Aristotle who defines disposition not as order of the parts but "the order of that which has parts."

Simon tells us that, there are different kinds of wholes or totality, such as the room with furniture, society, a work of art etc. Whereas the totality of the items of furniture in a room are external to each other, this is clearly not the case with a work of art where the wood and the shape of the statue are clearly not external to each other. A psychological disposition, or the soul, or the disposition of the parts of a person's character, constitute yet another kind of totality. Simon thinks that this "psychological totality" which represents a person's moral character is best described as "dynamic." He describes it as "one whose parts represent a multiplicity of virtualities, potentialities, and real possibilities."[152] To illustrate this, he takes the example of a youngster of about twelve years, who even if of "keen intelligence, good health and looks, excellent memory, artistic talent, (and)

---

[150] Aristotle, *Metaphysics* 5.19.1022b1-3. See Simon, *The Definition of Moral Virtue*, 80.

[151] Simon, *The Definition of Moral Virtue*, 79.

[152] Ibid., 81.

practical sense,"¹⁵³ still has an unformed character. After some fifteen years, when his personality would have achieved some sort of disposition, the multiple talents he has may help him grow in the ways of truth, or leave him with a rotten disposition. Since either way is possible, what the young man needs most in order to be a virtuous human being, is a proper disposition of his qualities. Simon says:

> By a man's disposition we mean precisely the unique arrangement of all his moral traits. And when this arrangement makes him totally reliable and dependable in human affairs, we call both the man and his disposition virtuous.¹⁵⁴

Simon points out that science is a dynamic totality as well. Like virtue it is grounded in dynamic necessity. But unlike it, the qualities which need to be properly arranged in order to constitute this totality, are different. It is not the psychological totality but "the mind that needs to be disposed in order to achieve the most objective order possible."¹⁵⁵ And the right teachers and a willing student are also essential. Simon brings together the elements that lead to scientific virtue as opposed to virtue of the soul thus:

> Take again the virgin intellect of a twelve-year-old. The boy knows some mathematics . . . and he has won the first prize at his school's science fair two years in a row. His parents have thus good reasons to be very proud of him. But since they realize at the same time that none of these achievements, guarantee that the boy will become a great scientist, their main worry now is to find the kind of teachers to whom they can entrust the development of the young genius' mind. . . . Of course, teachers cannot do everything, and in this process the student always remains the principal agent, who if he is ever to acquire the scientific habitus must first of all make himself teachable. . . . (The

---

[153] Ibid.
[154] Ibid., 84.
[155] Ibid., 83.

teachers') help consists in guiding the young mind towards an order among its parts that would match the object known.[156]

Clearly, the scientific *habitus* and moral virtue are different.

III: Understanding Aristotle's Definition of Virtue

Distinguishing Virtue from a False Intention and from Vice

Having shown why virtue is different from all the modern alternatives that are proposed, and why we must further distinguish it from habit, scientific *habitus*, and opinion, Simon makes one last clarification on his way to a definition of moral virtue. He points out that from what has been said about virtue as requiring a qualitative and existential readiness, virtue "is a disposition of the dynamic parts of the psyche that would make us existentially ready to do the right thing at the right time."[157] This means that virtue is a qualitative and existential disposition[158] which, however, needs to be distinguished from two things: i) being rightly disposed and acting in a dependable way but not from virtue and ii) vice, since vice is also a qualitative and existential disposition. Let us take a closer look at these clarifications which Simon makes.

i) In order to make the first point clear Simon gives the example of a business man[159] who is prompt and regular in paying his bills and fulfilling all his contractual obligations. For him, honesty is "the best policy." But, even though he may be dependable, he might not possess the virtue of justice since he might be honest not because he would not steal if someone were not looking, but because he wants to avoid trouble. While such a person might be a good citizen, Simon says, he is not at the same time a good person as such because, "as St. Augustine put it, virtue is the good quality of the soul by which

---

[156]Ibid., 82-83.
[157]Ibid., 93.
[158] Ibid.
[159]Ibid., 91-92.

we live rightly—*qua recte vivemus*—not in pursuit of our various occupations but as human beings."[160]

ii) Simon articulates the second question thus:

> Another problem with defining virtues as dispositions of both the qualitative and existential type is that their opposites, too, are such dispositions. A vice would not be a vice, if it was not a stable disposition, which is why Aristotle himself in several places calls vice a *hexis*.[161]

The question then, is how we might know which dispositions are virtuous, and which are vicious. In order to resolve the problem, Simon points to two factors that differentiate them. First he indicates that the necessity involved in the one and the other is objective or subjective as the case may be. He says:

> Vice is a stable disposition not of the habitus but of the habit type, because the necessity involved in it is subjective rather than objective. Of course, the necessity felt by the person subject to a vice may well appear to him totally irresistible, and in some cases may actually be so—for him. But in the power of vice as such, there is no objective necessity.[162]

But, Simon continues, vices do not result only from the subjective necessity that qualifies them. They also result, he says, from a poor handling of the continuous conflict in man between his senses and his reason.[163] Depending on whether a man handles or resolves this conflict poorly or properly, the result is vice or virtue and a proper resolution of this conflict depends on the will rather than reason. Simon thus brings in the important role played by the

---

[160] Ibid., See Simon, *Practical Knowledge*, 10.
[161] Simon, *The Definition of Moral Virtue*, 92. See Aristotle, *Nicomachean Ethics* 3.5.
[162] Ibid.
[163] Ibid.

will, in determining how this conflict is handled and resolved. He says:

> No one could operate effectively in real life without distinguishing between a person's intelligence and his will. Thus everyone understands perfectly well what is meant when a person is described as "intelligent but unfortunately weak-willed." Likewise, concrete decisions are regularly made, and not only in academe, by finding out that a person's intelligence is not equal to his good will.[164]

If our disposition is to be a good one and we are not to end up in vice, it must be joined to a good and strong will.[165]

The Intellectual and Moral Virtues in Practice

Simon is almost ready to give us a definition of virtue but he reckons that one more exercise is necessary. This consists in seeing how the virtues work in practice. He tells us that "still holding off formal definition, we want to see how these qualities are related to existence."[166]

This demands that the virtues to be treated be identified first. Simon accepts and adopts the list of the intellectual virtues that Aristotle gives and explains in Book VI of the *Ethics* and the moral virtues "on which there is a truly remarkable consensus."[167] He retains Aristotle's list of the five intellectual virtues which are prudence, understanding, science, wisdom, and art.[168] Concerning the moral virtues, he writes:

---

[164] Ibid.

[165] Simon hastens to add that he is not juxtaposing reason and the will in an antithetical way since, "reason, . . . is not excluded from the operations of the will." See *The Definition of Moral Virtue*, 120. See also *Freedom of Choice*, ed. Peter Wolff (New York: Fordham University Press, 1969), 97-98.

[166] Simon, *The Definition of Moral Virtue*, 96.

[167]Ibid., 95.

[168]Ibid., 96.

The list is the same in Plato and in Aristotle, in the Stoics and in an eclectic like Cicero, in the medieval moralists and in the Renaissance moralists, and, insofar as they are interested in such subjects, even in the modern moralist writers. Such a consensus is not often found in the history of philosophy, and it gives this list a special weight. The main moral virtues are: prudence, justice, fortitude, and temperance.[169]

The Intellectual Virtues

Simon begins his brief treatment of the intellectual virtues in *The Definition of Moral Virtue* by noting that prudence is the only virtue that belongs to the five intellectual virtues and the four moral virtues at the same time. He then defines each of the intellectual virtues which besides prudence include understanding ("the ability to perceive self-evident propositions"), science ("the ability to demonstrate conclusions"), wisdom (which "is metaphysics, the supreme science that brings order to the rest of our knowledge"), art (which "is something like carpentry, or painting, or architecture, the knowing of how to make things"), and prudence (which "is practical wisdom").[170]

The Moral Virtues

Prudence

Simon now proceeds to explain how each of the moral virtues works beginning with prudence which he returns to given its importance. He tells us that as an intellectual virtue, "its duty is to utter judgment."[171] As a moral virtue, it is "wisdom in acting, wisdom in practice, wisdom in what we have referred to as human use."[172] He further describes its function as a moral virtue thus:

> The specific duty of prudence is to tell me what to do no matter how unprecedented the circumstances, no matter how unique the

---

[169] Ibid., 95-96.
[170] Ibid., 96.
[171] Ibid.
[172] Ibid.

situation. If the circumstances are common, perhaps I can look up the answer in a manual and do what the book says. But in an unprecedented situation, which may be so constituted by the mere fact that there never has been a person exactly identical with my own self, as well as by the historical uniqueness of the circumstances in which I find myself at that particular moment, there are no answers to be found in any book. To know what I should do here and now, I must rely on the judgment of practical wisdom.[173]

Simon adds that given the fact of contingency, prudence involves "an appropriate inclination and disposition." He says:

> Many people would be happy if they could get a textbook of ethics which would tell them in great detail what to do under all circumstances. But even though it has been tried many times, no such book can ever be written, because the decisive circumstances under which moral judgment has to be uttered are characterized by uniqueness and contingency and an objective response to these circumstances can come only from an appropriate inclination or disposition of the acting subject.[174]

Simon discusses the various ways in which prudence functions. For instance, given the all comprehensive nature of the task it must perform, prudence takes the other virtues into its purview. We will look at Simon's explanation of this heading when we examine what he says concerning the integration of the virtues. Equally noteworthy is the fact that the "readiness of prudence is both qualitative and existential."[175] This, Simon points out, is in contradistinction to the intellectual virtues, of which it is one, which embody only a qualitative readiness. For instance, "when you have art, you still need virtue to make a good human use of it; but if you have prudence, you do not need an extra virtue to make good use of it."[176]

---

[173] Ibid.
[174] Ibid., 97.
[175] Ibid., 98.
[176] Ibid.

Justice

The virtue of justice is traditionally named after prudence, and both Aristotle and the Stoics define it as involving a relation to "another one." This description, he says, is prone to misunderstanding since it implies that "another one" is a person, whereas it might refer also to a community. He gives the example of paying taxes where "one another" refers to the community.[177] Simon explains the three kinds of justice which Aristotle treats in Book V of the *Ethics*, namely general justice, distributive justice and rectificatory or corrective justice, paying particular attention to the last, which students of Aristotle often find hard to understand.[178] After an examination of what Aristotle means by each, Simon gives a resumé of the logic behind the three kinds of justice thus:

> General justice [rules] the relations of the parts of the community to the community itself; distributive justice [governs] the relations between the community and its members; and rectificatory or corrective justice . . . is what the community must enforce when the rule of just exchange is not lived up to by individual citizens.[179]

Fortitude and Temperance

Simon treats the last two virtues, fortitude and temperance, together because, he says, they belong to the sense appetite. "Fortitude," he says, "is relative to the difficult, the arduous, the good which is hard to get and the evil which is hard to avoid."[180] Temperance concerns "the drive towards pleasure and away from pain."[181] It regards sensual pleasure which is normal and good in itself, but can be indulged, that is, done in excess. The reference is to a mean, which as we will see shortly, enters into the definition of virtue.

---

[177] Ibid.
[178] Ibid., 99-100.
[179] Ibid., 100.
[180] Ibid. (Simon notes that Aristotle is more concerned with courage in the battlefield and the fear of death.)
[181] Ibid.

With regard to temperance and fortitude, and still in search of a better understanding of the two, Simon contrasts the positions of Plato and Aristotle. He refers to Plato's treatment of the will and emotions in his well known allegory of the charioteer and the two steeds in the *Phaedrus* (253e). Whereas Plato's description of the two steeds presents the one as spirited (the will) and the other as mean (the sense appetites), in a clear reference to the parts of the soul, Simon thinks that Aristotle is more even handed in his treatment, since he considers the drive towards pleasure as normal and natural if it is well regulated.[182] He thinks Aristotle is also balanced in his view of fortitude which he distinguishes from rash behavior. Even fortitude needs to be regulated, which brings us back again to the mean in virtue.

The Interdependence of the Virtues: The Aristotelian and Stoic Positions

Simon is convinced that a proper understanding of how the virtues are dependent on each other sheds further light on their nature. In order to show how and why they are interdependent, he compares and contrasts the position of Aristotle and his followers with that of the Stoic school.

Aristotle and Aristotelians defend the interdependence of the virtues. Simon refers us to Book VI of the *Nicomachean Ethics* where Aristotle states the position with clarity. In Stoicism, by contrast, "they are treated as aspects of something that is one, solid, and admits of no degrees."[183] He refers us to a classic work on Stoicism, namely, *Stoic Philosophy* by J. M. Rist. In support of Simon's reading of the Stoic position, one might quote the following passage from Rist, which treats of guilt in Stoicism but also goodness, and why there is no middle way:

> From first to last what interests the Stoic is the question: Is it a moral act or not? If it is non-moral, it is, strictly speaking, immoral; and

---

[182]Ibid., 102-103
[183]Ibid., 126.

the Stoics were fond of drawing homely analogies to indicate how they viewed the matter. When a man is under water, he cannot breathe just below the surface of the water any more than if he is lying on the bottom. Similarly a puppy which is just about to open its eyes is no less blind than one which has just been born. Either it sees or it does not. Either one can breathe or one cannot; either one is guilty or one is not. ... A piece of wood is either straight or it is not; there are no degrees of straightness any more than degrees of justice. The wise man differs from everybody else not in degree but in kind. Just as a proposition is either true or not-true, so men are either moral or not-moral. One thing cannot be 'more' true or 'more' false than another; and morality is similar.[184]

Simon wonders whether there ever was or will be a virtuous man (the Stoic wise man) as conceived by the Stoics. It would seem, he says, that the Stoics themselves often doubted that a wise man as they conceived him could ever exist.[185]

Simon gives two Aristotelian arguments for the interdependence of the virtues. The first argument is that "all moral virtues are knotted together in prudence."[186] He gives a telling example:

> Suppose you and your child are starving, and you wonder whether you have the right to take some food that belongs to your neighbor. This is essentially a problem of justice, but in order to make the correct decision you clearly also need both temperance and fortitude. ... To save your life and the life of your child, you have a moral right to appropriate what belongs to your neighbor. But to make that determination, your prudence needs all the other virtues.[187]

The second argument consists in the fact that each of the virtues "needs the modalities procured by the other virtues."[188] What this

---

[184] J. M. Rist, *Stoic Philosophy* (Cambridge: Cambridge University Press, 1969), 83.
[185] Simon, *The Definition of Moral Virtue*, 126.
[186] Ibid., 127.
[187] Ibid.
[188] Ibid., 128.

means, Simon points out, is that one cannot be just without being courageous, courageous without being temperate, temperate without being just and courageous. Simon points out that any virtue will degenerate if temperance is lacking, which is the case when a man possessed of a strong sense of justice goes crusading for a cause without a sense of measure, that is, without exercising temperance.[189]

The reverse side of this argument is that the complete lack of one of the virtues poses insuperable problems for the others. Simon gives the example of a decent person with a good sense of justice who becomes addicted to drugs. That person, he points out, will not long remain just or moderate or courageous.[190]

If this is the case, is not the Aristotelian doctrine ultimately the same as the Stoic, one might ask. The answer is no and Simon indicates the difference between the two. He says that, "while the theory of the interdependence of the virtues requires the presence of all virtues, it does not require that all virtues be possessed in the same degree."[191] It is the complete lack of any of the virtues that would constitute an insurmountable difficulty. Simon points out that society is able to function because most people possess some proportion of all the virtues.[192]

The Definition of Moral Virtue

Having sufficiently cleared the grounds by putting forward a multiplicity of ideas as to what virtue looks like in *The Definition of Moral Virtue* but in other works as well, Simon is now ready to define what "he has been talking about all along."[193] What he proposes to do is to bring all that has been discussed into a definition. Difficult as this might be, he thinks Aristotle does well in his definition which Ross renders thus:

---

[189] Ibid.
[190] Ibid.
[191] Ibid., 129.
[192] Ibid., 130.
[193] Ibid., 104.

Virtue, then, is a state of character concerned with choice, lying in the mean, i.e. the mean relative to us, this being determined by a rational principle, and by that principle by which the man of practical wisdom would determine it.[194]

Simon takes issue with W.D. Ross translating *hexis*, as he does in the above translation, as "a state of character" instead of as *habitus*. He, however, accepts that while it is not the best, it is a much better translation of *hexis* than habit. That this state of character is concerned with choice "lying in the mean" means, Simon explains, that when we choose virtuously we avoid excess or defect. Extremes destroy virtue which lies in the middle. Simon taking the example of our use of money, says that virtue would lie in our being "neither prodigal nor mean but generous."[195] He points out that the phrase "the mean relative to us" might appear subjective. This is in fact not the case since the morality of all action depends also on who we are, and the circumstances surrounding the act, and the prudential judgment that takes these factors into account. He gives the example of Sir Winston Churchill for whom what qualified as temperate, given his great capacity to remain sober after consuming a large amount of alcoholic beverages, might amount to indulging for another person.[196] In any case, Simon explains that the very next phrase removes all traces of subjectivity since Aristotle adds that the mean relative to us "is determined by a rational principle and by that principle by which the man of practical wisdom would determine it." This means that even if it is a person who has to decide, he does this on the basis of an objective rational principle and prudence.

---

[194] Aristotle, *Nicomachean Ethics*, trans. W.D. Ross in *The Basic Works of Aristotle*, ed. Richard McKeon (New York: Random House Inc., 2001), 959. (2.6.1106b36-1107a3).
[195] Simon, *The Definition of Moral Virtue*, 105.
[196] Ibid., 106.

Knowledge of Moral Axioms through Instinct

After giving the definition of virtue and explaining it, Simon points to what he calls a "gap" in Aristotle's ethical theory which, touches on this definition. He argues that "a choice lying in a mean that makes the difference between a good and a bad man clearly requires a general understanding of what makes men good or bad," that is "a system of axioms."[197] Since among the intellectual virtues Aristotle puts understanding in the first place, which as we have seen, he defines as "the ability to perceive self evident propositions" such as the whole being bigger than the part, Simon asks whether Aristotle has any "comparable notion of understanding of practical principles?" He asks whether he has "a theory of how we know the basic premises of the moral order,"[198] or what one might call the self evident propositions of the moral order. In other words, how do we know that it is wrong to steal, lie, or kill? Simon writes:

> There is no point in talking about a wise choice, of choosing rightly in matters of temperance or fortitude, except in relation to what is good or what is bad—for man as man. But how do we know what makes man good as man, and consequently what is right and what is wrong for man to do?[199]

A little later Simon poses the problem in different terms. He says:
> How do we come to know moral axioms? What is the mode of our apprehension of moral principles? Are they known rationally or by inclination? Or both rationally and by inclination? The ancient Greeks were not very explicit on this issue.[200]

The question is how we know natural law. In answer to the question, Simon refers to and agrees with his friend and teacher

---

[197]Ibid., 106.
[198]Ibid., 107.
[199] Ibid.
[200]Ibid., 108.

Jacques Maritain, especially his treatment of the issue in his work *Man and the State*.[201] Simon writes:

> Natural law, Maritain explains, is known first of all by inclination. That does not mean, of course, that it cannot be known rationally, or that rational knowledge of its principles is not desirable. It is simply that primordially, primitively, and primarily, natural law, whose core is constituted by the premises of the moral order, is known by inclination. I think that is indeed the case. We know these things first by a sort of instinct.[202]

If this is true of moral axioms, it is equally true of the decisions we make in contingent circumstances and how we apply principles and maxims to particular situations. Simon explains that the virtue of prudence or practical wisdom comes into play to help us decide what is to be done and this final decision is according to instinct. The decision is taken by instinct and according to Simon this is what Kierkegaard meant by his tantalizing saying, "In der Subjektivität liegt die Wahrheit."[203]

But, Simon emphasizes again the fact that this decision, as well as our knowledge of first principles or axioms, does not lack objectivity because it is instinctive and subjective. If we are trained in virtue, and are always consciously looking to do what is right, our decision in any contingent circumstance will be objectively the right one.[204] This topic of knowledge of moral axioms through instinct or inclination is given a fuller treatment in chapter 4.[205]

When Aristotle defines virtue as "a state of character concerned with choice, lying in the mean, that is, the mean relative to us, this being determined by a rational principle, and by that principle by which a man of practical wisdom would determine it," the complete

---

[201] Jacques Maritain, *Man and the State* (Chicago: Chicago University Press, 1951), 84ff. See Simon, *The Definition of Moral Virtue*, 108.

[202] Simon, *The Definition of Moral Virtue*, 108.

[203] Simon, *The Definition of Moral Virtue*, 110. (The saying translates: Truth lies in subjectivity.)

[204] Ibid., 111-118.

[205] See pp. 393-406.

understanding of this definition, according to Simon, is the discussion contained in Chapter One of this book.

Chapter 2

Virtue in Public Life: Simon's Concept of the Common Good

I: Brief Historical Overview

Introduction

After examining Simon's definition of virtue in Chapter 1, we will now begin an exposition of how he sees virtue as applying to aspects of the public space, beginning, in this chapter, with its relationship to the common good. There are few concepts more central to politics and fundamental to any society worthy of the name than that of the common good. It is, therefore, a respect of good order to begin any consideration of Simon's application of virtue to society at this point.

In the first part of the chapter, I will consider, in very summary fashion, the roots of the idea of the common good as found in ancient Greek philosophy, the evolution of the concept, and a brief description of the present situation of the concept. The idea is to indicate the sources of Simon's work. This introductory segment should open the way to Part II, which will be an exposition of how Virginia Held classifies the various theories of the common good in her book, *The Public Interest and Individual Interests*. I will explain why she calls the three groups "preponderance theories," "public interest as common interest theories," and "unitary conceptions." This explication, which takes in its sweep philosophers from Plato at the dawn of philosophy to Maritain in contemporary times, leads her to a proposition of the elements that should make for an ideal concept of the common good. These elements, which are in fact her own idea of the common good, will close Part II.

We will then be able to see what is distinctive in Simon's articulation of the common good, which will occupy us in the third and final part of the chapter.

The Birth and Evolution of the Concept: Ancient Greek Philosophy to Medieval Times

It is sometimes the case that certain expressions or phrases are so frequently used that we take it for granted that we understand their real meaning. Because of the fact that such terms or expressions are constantly in public discourse we do not take the time to think about them clearly and to ask what exactly they mean. This is the case with words such as "authority," "freedom," and "law." It is also the case with the idea of the common good.[206] As we have just mentioned, it is generally accepted that the idea of the common good is central to the very existence of a political community and to discussions of political action and public policy. The problem is to define the concept properly.

This is part of the reason for its checkered history which begins with ancient Greek philosophy. Even though Herodotus provides good evidence of the activities of Thales as a statesman in Ionia at around 580 B.C.,[207] the first major work of political philosophy, including an exposition of the common good, belongs to Plato (428-347 BC).

At the beginning of the *Laws*[208] Plato eliminates certain ends as not belonging to the common good of the city. He says the city cannot exist to benefit the ruler and his associates. Such a city would not be a *polis* but a "faction city" (*stasiōteia*).[209] Nor, despite the fact that it must defend itself, should it be on a permanent war footing like Crete.[210] Such aims are false.

---

[206] Simon warns against "the Advertising/Public Relations Complex" that tends to transform important concepts into "brand names easily marketed for political wars." Yves R. Simon, *Freedom and Community*, ed. Charles P. O'Donnell (New York: Fordham university Press, 2001), x-xi.

[207] G. S. Kirk, J. E. Raven, and M. Schofield, *The Presocratic Philosophers* (Cambridge: Cambridge University Press, 2003), 78.

[208] Plato, *Laws*, trans. R.G. Bury, ed. Jeffrey Henderson (Cambridge: Harvard University Press, 2004).

[209] Plato, *Laws* 832b; See also 715b.

[210] Ibid., 626c-d.

But, since a city can be defeated also from within through luxury when "individually each man is his own enemy,"[211] the inculcation of virtue, in its complete form, is the goal of the city and all legislation. In the *Republic* he lays it down that the ruler should "establish in this world the laws of the beautiful, the just, and the good,"[212] and that all education in the *polis* must be for molding souls and controlling the appetites.[213] In the *Laws*, his last work, Plato is consistent in identifying the common good with securing both human goods (health, wealth, peace) and divine goods (wisdom, temperance, justice, courage).[214] With regard to the constitution of the new colony of Magnesia which Plato writes about extensively in the *Laws*, Christopher Bobonich tells us that "all are eligible to vote for political offices, to hold most political offices, and participate in the system of the courts. And . . . doing so will require an active exercise of the virtues."[215] From an initial position of proposing rule by a wise philosopher-king in the *Republic*, the common good is, henceforth, to be assured by just laws.

Aristotle (348-322 BC) uses most often the expression *sumpheron koinon* (common advantage) and only rarely *agathon koinon* (common good) in order to emphasize the fact that the good is good for someone and not just in the manner of a transcendent Platonic form.[216] Having read Plato's *Republic* and the *Laws* to which he specifically refers in Book II of the *Politics* (1265a1-4), he agrees with him that the pursuit of virtue is the common good. The end of the individual is a happy life lived in community according to just laws (1179b31-1180a13). Thus "any state that is truly so called and is not

---

[211] Christopher Bruell, "On Plato's Political Philosophy," *The Review of Politics* 56 (1994): 270.

[212] Plato, *Republic*, trans. Paul Shorey in *Plato: The Collected Dialogues*, ed. Edith Hamilton and Huntington Cairns (Princeton: Princeton University Press, 1996), 721. (484c-d).

[213] George Klosko, *The Development of Plato's Political Theory* (New York: Methuen & Co. Ltd. 1986), 101-113.

[214] Plato, *Laws*, 631b-632d. See also 630c; 705d-706a; 707d; 963a.

[215] Christopher Bobonich, *Plato's Utopia Recast: His Later Ethics and Politics* (Oxford: Clarendon Press, 2002), 384.

[216] Michael A. Smith, *Human Dignity and the Common Good in the Aristotelian-Thomistic Tradition* (Queenston, Ontario: The Edwin Mellen Press, 1995), 62-64.

a state merely in name must pay attention to virtue."[217] That is why he also writes that it is more "godlike" (*theiōteron*) to obtain and preserve the good of the whole community for the individual is an integral part of the community.[218]

The nature of the governing regime (*politeia*) of the *polis* determines its common good since the regime is the "form" of the city just as the soul is the form of the body.[219] It makes a difference to the common good whether the ruler knows and has wisdom (aristocracy), or whether he lacks it (tyranny, democracy, oligarchy).[220] Aristotle does not posit any conflict between the common advantage and particular goods because the common advantage includes the interests of particular citizens, but between the common advantage and the private interests of those in power depending on the nature of the *politeia*.[221]

Augustine (354-430), much like Aristotle, gives a rule of thumb by which we can recognize the character of a people. It is determined by their common good or what they agree to love: he says that "the better the object of this agreement, the better the people, and the worse the objects, the worse the people."[222]

He sets out his idea of the common good in chapter 21 of Book 19 of the *City of God*, among others, and does so deliberately in contradistinction to that of Cicero (106-43 BC) who, in his work *De republica*, defines the republic as a multitude "united in fellowship by common agreement as to what is right and by a community of

---

[217] Aristotle, *Politics*, trans. H. Rackham (Cambridge: Harvard University Press, 1932), 205. (1280b5).

[218] Smith, *Human Dignity and the Common Good in the Aristotelian-Thomistic Tradition*, 59.

[219] Mary M. Keys, "Politics Pointing Beyond the Polis and the Politeia: Aquinas on Natural Law and the Common Good," in *Natural Moral Law in Contemporary Society*, ed. Holger Zaborowski (Washington D.C.: The Catholic University of America Press, 2010), 180.

[220] Aristotle, *Politics*, 3.4.

[221] Smith, *Human Dignity and the Common Good in the Aristotelian-Thomistic Tradition*, 59, 66.

[222] Augustine, *The City of God against the Pagans*, ed. and trans. R.W. Dyson (Cambridge: Cambridge University Press, 2006), 960.

interests."[223] Cicero further insists on the endurance of the republic. By way of a reaction, Augustine stresses the spiritual side of the common good pointing out that "what is right" flows from "justice." He argues that without justice, without order in the souls of the citizens, without the rule of reason over vices, without virtue, there can be no true republic.[224]

Augustine names peace ("ordered concord"), in the individual and in the city, as this common good. Peace is the fruit of justice, that is, respect for divine law. It results from the disposition of the souls of the ruler and the ruled.[225] The republic, in which there is an inordinate desire for pleasure, power, gain, glory, and honor, cannot be at peace. Augustine's description of the common good is "as close to communion with God as one can imagine on this earth."[226]

Thomas Aquinas (1225-1274) is mainly indebted to Aristotle and Augustine for his ideas on the common good. The main difference between him and Aristotle is that whereas for the latter the common good does not transcend the temporal sphere, for Aquinas, like Augustine, society is ordinated to the heavenly city and to God.[227] Aquinas goes beyond the civic and political good of Aristotle to insist that the common *telos* of society must include moral virtue. After laying down the principle that "everything is called good from the divine goodness, as from the first exemplary, effective and final principle of goodness,"[228] he concludes that the common good must reflect this highest good through a communion of all under God, and tend towards God through love of Him and of men. That is why society needs virtue to flourish. This is also the meaning of Aristotle's remark that men form communities, not just for the purpose of living

---

[223]Ibid., 950. (See *On the Commonwealth* 1.25.).

[224]Ibid., 950-951.

[225] Herbert A. Deane, *The Political and Social Ideas of St Augustine* (New York: Columbia University Press, 1963), 119.

[226] J. Brian Benestad, *Church, State, and Society: An Introduction to Catholic Social Doctrine* (Washington D.C.: The Catholic University of America Press, 2011), 110.

[227] Smith, *Human Dignity and the Common Good in the Aristotelian-Thomistic Tradition*, 71-72; 81-82.

[228]Thomas Aquinas, *Summa Theologiae* 1a 6. 4., Vol. 1., trans. Fathers of the English Dominican Province (Notre Dame, IN: Christian Classics, 1948), 30.

but of living well.²²⁹ But coming together for the purpose of living well has a material component as well, since a virtuous life would be difficult if the ordinary necessities of life went unfulfilled. The common good, therefore, must take into consideration the need for sufficiency in material goods.

He proposes a new foundation for political virtue based on natural law.²³⁰ For Aquinas, natural law reveals important truths about life and political action and thus about the common good by making people "aware of their citizenship in a universal community under God," or "the ethical requirements of human sociality."²³¹ Mary Keys points out that this is Aquinas's answer²³² to the dichotomy between being a good citizen and being a good human being or between human and political virtue,²³³ a question which arises in *Politics* 3.4, within the context of the merits and demerits of the various kinds of regimes or the tension between human and civic virtue.

Aquinas also sees this priority of the ethical as "the chief nexus"²³⁴ between the personal good of individuals and the common good and affirms that a personal good can be more important than the common good if the two are not in the same genus. However, whenever they are in the same genus, the common good holds priority. This principle, together with the idea of distributability, that is, the sharing of the *bona communia*, which fosters political friendship,²³⁵ and is another important component of the common good, will be of value to Simon.

As we conclude this section, the point that needs to be underlined, and that distinguishes this period from modern thinkers

---

²²⁹ Aristotle, *Politics*, I.2.1252b29-30; 3.6.1278b17-24; 7.2.1325a7-10

²³⁰ Keys, "Politics Pointing beyond the Polis and the Politeia: Aquinas on Natural Law and the Common Good," 185.

²³¹Ibid., 184.

²³² Aquinas, *Summa Theologiae*, I, II, q. 113 a. 1; See also I, II, q. 94 a. 2. See Keys, 184.

²³³ Keys, "Politics Pointing beyond the Polis and the Politeia: Aquinas on Natural Law and the Common Good," 172.

²³⁴Ibid., 170.

²³⁵ Gerald B. Phelan, "Justice and Friendship," *The Thomist* 5 (1943): 157.

who follow it, is that the doctrine of Augustine and Aquinas respects the nature of man and takes cognizance of his intrinsic worth. In the period of the Enlightenment that follows, society is seen as the result of a contract rather than of nature, and instead of having a divinely ordained end, the reason for its existence is conceived in terms of a harmonious resolution of conflicting interests.

The State of the Concept in Modern and Contemporary Thought

A decisive shift in thinking takes place with Machiavelli (1469-1527). He breaks with the classical view, but it is Thomas Hobbes (1588-1679), to whom we now turn, who brings this change into the mainstream. Hobbes initiates the era of natural rights doctrines later made even more acceptable by Locke.[236] He is the first to advance the theoretical construct of a state of nature, a device which he then uses to demonstrate that government is established to act as a cure, in practical terms, for fallen human nature.

Hobbes writes that the state is established in order "to defend (citizens) from the invasion of foreigners, and the injuries of one another, and thereby to secure them in such sort, as that by their own industry, and by the fruits of the earth, they may nourish themselves and live contentedly."[237] The *locus classicus* where he states his doctrine of contract also specifies the end of the commonwealth. It is in *The Elements of Law*:

> In the state of nature, where man is his own judge, and differeth from other concerning the names and appellations of things, and from these differences arise quarrels, and breach of the peace; it was necessary there should be a common measure of all things that might fall in controversy; as for example: of what is to be called right, what good, what virtue, what much, what little, what *meum* and *tuum*, what a pound, what a quart, etc. for in these things private judgments may

---

[236] Leo Strauss, *Natural Right and History* (Chicago: University of Chicago Press, 1949), 243

[237] Thomas Hobbes, *Leviathan*, ed. Michael Oakeshott (New York: Macmillan Publishing Company, 1962), 132.

differ and beget controversy. This common measure, some say, is right reason: with whom I should consent, if there were any such thing to be found or known in *rerum natura*. But commonly they that call for right reason to decide any controversy, do mean their own. But this is certain, seeing right reason is not existent, the reason of some man, or men, must supply the place thereof; and that man or men, is he or they, that have the sovereign power.[238]

In the above passage, Hobbes calls for "a common measure" to be decided by "the sovereign power" in order to avoid a "breach of peace." The common good consists in an avoidance of a breach of the peace, and the promotion of "the security of man's person in his life and in the means of preserving life"[239] or "the procuration of *the safety of the people*."[240]

Hobbes explains his idea of public safety very broadly, going beyond the mere avoidance of harm. He writes:

> But by safety here, is not meant a bare preservation, but also all other contentments of life, which everyman by lawful industry, without danger, or hurt to the commonwealth, shall acquire to himself.[241]

It should be noted that no matter how wide Hobbes defines safety, the bottom line is always the security of the citizens of the commonweal. What this means is that Hobbes reduces the common good to its basic material expression, and sees it as an aggregate of private goods. These ideas set the pattern for those who come after him.

John Locke (1632-1704), born half a century after Hobbes, theorizes that value is produced by private individuals through their labor. Since its genesis is private, he defines the common good in terms of an aggregation of private interests. For him "unlimited

---

[238] Thomas Hobbes, *The Elements of Law: Natural and Politic* (London: Frank Cass & Co. Ltd., 1969), 188

[239] Hobbes, *Leviathan*, 105.

[240] Ibid., 249 (his emphasis).

[241] Ibid. See also *De Cive or The Citizen* (New York: Appleton-Century-Crofts, 1949), 142-145.

appropriation with no concern for the needs of others"[242] is a good thing, and by pursuing their selfish goals people automatically contribute to the common good.[243] Through his work *A Letter Concerning Toleration* (1689), he is at the origin of the liberal contention that religion should be a private affair and should be kept out of the business of the state.[244]

Jeremy Bentham (1748-1832) is adamant that it is futile to talk about the good of the community apart from that of the individuals who make it up.[245] For instance he says:

> The interest of the community then is, what?—the sum of the interests of the several members who compose it. It is vain to talk of the interests of the community, without understanding what is the interest of the individual. A thing is said to promote the interest or be *for* the interest of an individual, when it tends to add to the sum total of his pleasures: or, what comes to the same thing, to diminish the sum total of his pains.[246]

Since we will examine his work in greater detail in the next part, it should be sufficient to mention here that he is the most radical of those who propose private interest as the reason for the existence of the state.

Nemetz and Massaro give a beautiful summary of the picture that emerges of the 19th century leading up to our times thus:

> The 19th century inherited and advanced the doctrine that the main business of government was to do for the multitude what no one citizen could do for the corporate person, viz, defend the nation from attack and maintain domestic order. The notion that government . . . should provide the social conditions for universal self-fulfillment was unthinkable. The notion of the common good and its priority over

---

[242]Strauss, *Natural Right and History*, 243.
[243]Benestad, *Church, State, and Society*, 25.
[244]Ibid., 427.
[245]Jeremy Bentham, *An Introduction to the Principles of Morals and Legislation* (New York: Hafner, 1948).
[246]Ibid., 3. (1.IV-V) (his emphasis).

private interests had completely disappeared, and its loss involved the denial of the belief that every man has intrinsic worth and dignity.[247]

In contemporary discourse, the concept of the common good is marked by confusion, a welter of opinions, and the inability of theorists to arrive at any kind of consensus. Even the terminology is the subject of quarrels. From Aristotle who speaks of the "common advantage" to the "common good" in medieval times, there is a switch today to "public interest," or "general welfare" or "common interest." As we will see these phrases are not necessarily synonymous, even if henceforth we will take the "common good" and the "public interest" as meaning the same thing and use them interchangeably.

The philosophers Wayne A. R. Leys and Charner M. Perry have made a detailed study of the meaning of the term in contemporary thinking. After consulting some seventy five philosophers, lawyers, and social scientists, they conclude, among others, that the state of theorizing on the concept is "unsatisfactory"[248] and that it "can have several radically different meanings"[249] which they go on to explain. From this study and others, it is clear that contemporary scholars reflecting on the public interest fall into three different groups:

i) Those who think that the concept exists but is vague and mired in confusion.

ii) Those who think that the concept is vacuous and unnecessary and, therefore, reject outright the very idea of the public interest as real and worthy of study.

iii) Those who think that it is a necessary and extremely important concept even if it is differently characterized by various authors.

---

[247] A. Nemetz and T. Massaro, "Common Good," in *New Catholic Encyclopedia*, 19.

[248] Wayne A. R. Leys and Charner Marquis Perry, *Philosophy and the Public Interest* (Chicago, Ill.: Committee to Advance Original Work in Philosophy, 1959). See Virginia Held, *The Public Interest and Individual Interests* (New York: Basic Books Inc., 1970), 203-204; 5.

[249] Ibid., 44.

i) Regarding the first category, one might point to an article on the public interest by Anthony Downs, in which he arrives at the following conclusion:

> The term public interest is constantly used by politicians, lobbyists, political theorists, and voters, but any detailed enquiry about its exact meaning plunges the inquirer into a welter of platitudes, generalities, and philosophic arguments. It soon becomes apparent that no general agreement exists about whether the term has any meaning at all, or if it has, what the meaning is, which specific actions are in the public interest and which are not, and how to distinguish between them.[250]

In support, Frank Sorauf points out that "not only do scholars disagree on the defining of the public interest, they disagree as well about what they are trying to define: a goal, a process, or a myth."[251]

ii) Given the confusion surrounding key aspects of the concept of the public interest, some of those who allude to this confusion, go on to reject the concept as unnecessary. That is, they deny "that there *ought* to be a theory of the public interest."[252] This is the case of Glendon Schubert and Frank Sorauf just mentioned above. Schubert argues that since the concept "makes no operational sense, notwithstanding the efforts of a generation of capable scholars . . . political scientists might better spend their time nurturing concepts that offer greater promise of becoming useful tools in the scientific study of political responsibility."[253] Frank Sorauf suggests that "perhaps the academicians ought to take the lead in drawing up a list of ambiguous words and phrases which never would be missed. For

---

[250] Anthony Downs, "The Public Interest: Its meaning in a Democracy," *Social Research* 29 (1962): 1-2. See Held, *The Public Interest and Individual Interests*, 2.

[251] Frank Sorauf, "The Conceptual Muddle," in *The Public Interest*, Nomos V, ed. Carl J. Friedrich (New York: Atherton Press, 1962), 186. See, Held, *The Public Interest and Individual Interests*, 2.

[252] Glendon Schubert, *The Public Interest* (Glencoe, Ill.: The Free Press, 1960), 223-224. (his emphasis) See Held, *The Public Interest and Individual Interests*, 1.

[253] Ibid., 224. See, Held, *The Public Interest and Individual Interests*, 9.

such a list," he continues, "I would have several candidates but it should suffice here to nominate the 'public interest.'"[254]

iii) However, despite all the problems one encounters in an effort to circumscribe the idea of the common good, it does not seem that it is an idea that can easily be dispensed with. Many writers argue that the concept is so fundamental to society that we would have to invent a replacement if we got rid of it.[255] Gerhard Colm writes that "it is difficult to imagine that politicians, statesmen, judges, and officials concerned with the formulation of government policies could do without this concept,"[256] and Julius Cohen points out that decision makers would be "tongue-tied" if they were deprived of the concept.[257]

This consensus as to its importance does not mean that scholars who accept its indispensability define it the same way. Schubert, whose study surveys thirty years of thinking on the common good leading up to the 1960s, sees a chronological progression, within that time frame, from rationalist thinking through idealist thinking to realism. He thinks that rationalist elements dominated in the 1930s and that realist ones are in the ascendancy today. This is his summary of the key points each of the groups attributes to the common good:

> The Rationalists are propublic, proparty, and anti-interest group. They postulate a common good, which reflects the presumed existence of various common —frequently majoritarian —interests. The common good . . . finds expression in a popular will (public will; will of the people); the common obligation of all public officials is faithfully to execute the popular will.

---

[254] Frank Sorauf, The Conceptual Muddle," in *The Public Interest*, Nomos V, ed. Carl J. Friedrich, 190.

[255] Richard E. Flathman, *The Public Interest: An Essay Concerning the Normative Discourse of Politics* (New York: Wiley, 1966), 1-2.

[256] Gerhard Colm, "In Defense of the Public Interest," *Social Research* 27 (1960): 306-307.

[257] Julius Cohen, "A Lawman's View of the Public Interest," in *The Public Interest*, 160. See Held, *The Public Interest and Individual Interests*, 11.

> The Idealists are propublic, anti-party, and anti-interest group.... Idealists support the true interests of the public, which do not necessarily coincide with the interests of the public as perceived by the public itself. Idealists believe that the public interest reposes not in the positive law made by men, but in the higher law, in natural law.... The public interest becomes whatever the still, small voice of conscience reveals to each official.
>
> The Realists are pro-interest group.... Political parties become merely a special kind of interest group, and "public" becomes segmented as "publics," in which form it, too, merges in the concept of "interest group." The Realists, in other words, do not oppose the public and political parties; they devour them.[258]

What the above quote means is that the Rationalists see the public interest as coinciding with the values already held and shared by the citizens, or a majority of the citizens of a society (propublic). The public interest equals the public will. Rationalists are for political parties and against special interests. The Idealists see the common good as transcending the opinions of the citizens. Each official ought to follow his conscience, and because political parties and interest groups may not have the real interest of the state in mind, decision making ought to be left to a wise statesman or official who must rise above partisan considerations to his best understanding of the public good. For the Realist, there is no such thing as the "public" interest. Rather there is the interest of the various groups in society, and the role of government is not to decide but to arbitrate, and to take decisions "based upon a synthesis of many conflicting group interests."[259]

By way of conclusion, it should be remarked that this characterization and others[260] refer to "conscience" (Schubert) or "a normative conception" (Leys and Perry), thus indicating that the

---

[258] Schubert, *The Public Interest*, 198-201. See Held, *The Public Interest and Individual Interests*, 212.

[259] Schubert, *The Public Interest*, 160.

[260] This is the case of another classification of Wayne A.R. Leys and Charner Marquis Perry, *Philosophy and the Public Interest*, 44. See Held *The Public Interest and Individual Interest*, 205-206.

moral element has continued to be part and parcel of some conceptions of the common good in our times. After World War II, which showed the bankrupt nature of materialist totalitarian ideologies, Jacques Maritain, (1882-1973) perhaps the most influential philosopher of the period, sought to inject this spiritual and moral aspect into the debate on the common good, within the context of a wholesome philosophy of personalism.[261] He laid out his vision in numerous works, most especially in *The Person and the Common Good*,[262] *Man and the State*,[263] and *The Rights of Man and Natural Law*.[264] We will explore certain aspects of his thinking on the common good which influenced Simon's work and were adopted by him on this question.

Maritain takes as his point of departure the metaphysical distinction between the individual and the person, a distinction which he says has the potential to cause endless trouble when ignored.[265] Maritain explains the difference between the individual and the person in clear metaphysical terms. The individual, he says, is a member of a species[266] and as such is individuated by matter. The diversity of individuals depends on the quantitative division of matter. Designated quantified matter (*materia signata quantite*)[267] is crucial to individuality in such a way that individuality has its first ontological roots in matter.[268] On the other hand, a person is a spiritual whole. Maritain quotes St. Thomas Aquinas, who says that "person signifies what is most perfect in all nature –that is a

---

[261] Given the many philosophies of personalism which developed after World War II and because of it, Maritain distinguishes his version of personalism, which avoids the excesses of liberal individualism and totalitarian ideologies, by rooting it in the philosophy of Thomas Aquinas.

[262] Jacques Maritain, *The Person and the Common Good*, trans. John J. Fitzgerald (Notre Dame, Indiana: University of Notre Dame Press, 1966).

[263] Jacques Maritain, *Man and the State* (Chicago: University of Chicago Press, 1998).

[264] Jacques Maritain, *The Rights of Man and Natural Law*, trans. Doris C. Anson (London: Geoffrey Bles, The Centenary Press, 1971).

[265] Maritain, *The Person and the Common Good*, 11.

[266] Ibid., 38.

[267] Ibid., 37.

[268] Ibid., 36.

subsistent individual of a rational nature."²⁶⁹ Personality refers to the spiritual, to liberty, to the bountiful in man. The person is such because of the presence of the spiritual soul, which is the principle of independence, creative impulses and charity.

He argues that since as St. Thomas says, "the person is that which is most noble and most perfect in all nature,"²⁷⁰ and since personality tends by nature to communion,²⁷¹ the common good must be personalist and communalist at the same time. The common good must be the good of the person in community and not just the good of the individual.

On account of the spiritual connotations attached to personality which are completely lacking in individuality, "the adage of the superiority of the common good is understood in its true sense only in the measure that the common good itself implies a reference to the human person."²⁷² He thus links the common good closely to the good of the human person who is superior to the individual, demonstrating that one cannot grasp the true nature of society and the common good dissociated from that of the person.

In working out the practical consequences of the above metaphysics, Maritain concludes that the common good cannot be understood simply in terms of providing public services such as roads, schools and military power for the protection of the state, but above all in terms of justice, friendship, truth, beauty, and the promotion of moral rectitude. Because of the spiritual element in the person, the common good must transcend the conditions of temporal society.²⁷³ In a classic passage Maritain writes:

---

²⁶⁹Ibid., 32. See Thomas Aquinas, *Summa Theologiae*, 1a, q. 29, a. 3.

²⁷⁰ Maritain, *The Person and the Common Good*, 33; Thomas Aquinas, *Summa Theologiae*, 1, 29, 3.

²⁷¹ Maritain explains that persons need society in response to the law of superabundance inscribed in the depths of their being, and also because of the deficiencies which derive from material individuality. See Maritain, *The Person and the Common Good*, 47-48.

²⁷² Maritain, *The Person and the Common Good*, 29-30.

²⁷³Ibid., 52.

Thus, that which constitutes the common good of political society is not only: the collection of public commodities and services—the roads, ports, schools, etc., which the organization of common life presupposes; a sound fiscal condition of the state and its military power; the body of just laws, good customs and wise institutions, which provide the nation with its structure; the heritage of its great historical remembrances, its symbols and its glories, its living traditions and cultural treasures. The common good includes all of these . . . and above all the sum of these; . . . It includes the sum or sociological integration of all the civic conscience, political virtues and sense of right and liberty, of spiritual riches, of unconsciously operative hereditary wisdom, of moral rectitude, justice, friendship, happiness, virtue and heroism in the individual lives of its members.[274]

Maritain concludes his description thus:

Only on condition that it is according to justice and moral goodness is the common good what it is, namely, the good of a people and a city, rather than of a mob of gangsters and murderers. For this reason, perfidy, the scorn of treaties, political assassination and unjust war, even though they be useful to a government and procure some fleeting advantages for the peoples who make use of them, tend by their nature as political acts . . . to the destruction of the common good. The common good is something ethically good.[275]

Linking the common good to man's eternal destiny is only a last logical step for Maritain, since the individual as person is made for God and eternal life, before he is constituted a part of the city.[276] As the human person is ordained directly to God as its ultimate end, every social institution must work in this direction.

---

[274] Ibid.
[275] Ibid., 53.
[276] Ibid., 74-75.

II: The Threefold Classificatory Scheme Of Virginia Held As Outlined In *The Public Interest And Individual Interests* And Her Concept Of The Public Interest

Preliminary Considerations

In the broad examination of the history of the idea of the common good touched on above, I have shown the changes from one philosopher to another, and the historical shifts in the understanding of the common good. Is there a comprehensive matrix for classifying these theories?

Mark C. Murphy[277] has attempted such a task in our times and has formulated three candidate conceptions of the common good: the Instrumentalist Conception, the Distinctive Conception, and the Aggregative Conception. However, Murphy does not engage in a thorough historical analysis but rather has a limited focus. He briefly examines the concepts that he says are currently being used, in order "to exhibit the strength of the credentials of the aggregative conception for filling the role assigned to the common good by the natural law account, and to argue that the instrumentalist and distinctive good conceptions gain their plausibility only by way of the aggregative conception."[278] In other words, his aim in discussing the various conceptions he details, is to show that the aggregative conception best captures the normative appeal of the common good. Little wonder that he does not mention a good number of the main philosophers who have theorized on the common good.

Virginia Held's[279] account, which is more comprehensive, has remained a highly influential analysis of the literature on the subject, and will therefore be the focus of our attention. I would like to begin with the preliminary issues Held treats by way of clearing the grounds before tackling the substantive questions.

---

[277] Mark C. Murphy, *Natural Law in Jurisprudence and Politics* (Cambridge: Cambridge University Press, 2006).

[278] Ibid., 63, 85.

[279] Virginia Held, *The Public Interest and Individual Interests* (New York: Basic Books, Inc., 1970).

1) She indicates some of the numerous questions one might ask in an effort to understand the common good and identifies those relevant to her discourse. Thus she names eight groups of questions[280] and eliminates seven. She retains the following group of questions as of interest to what she intends to do:

> What are the meanings of:
> X is in the public interest,
> X is not in the public interest,
> X is more in the public interest than Y,
> X is more in the public interest than Y or Z?[281]

She eliminates, as outside of her purview, such questions as who should determine the answers to the above questions; how and by whom such judgments should be implemented; and the validity of possible alternatives to those retained above.[282] All questions are considered to the extent that they relate to or clarify the four questions in the citation above. Much confusion, she affirms, results when what is to be attempted is not clearly circumscribed.

2) She thinks that the question is best expressed in terms of the relations and tensions between the public interest and various configurations of individual interest and group interest. She writes:

> My attempt to classify various theories concerning the concept of the public interest will be in terms of the relations taken to hold between assertions of public interest and assertions of individual interest—whether of single persons or of groups.[283]

She thus proposes to examine the relations, in logic and in fact, that are thought to exist, according to the theories of different thinkers, between the four questions indicated in No. 1 above.

---

[280] Ibid., 12.
[281] Ibid.,
[282] Ibid., 12-13.
[283] Ibid., 36.

3) Held seeks to clarify the meaning of the word "interest" in the context of individual and group interests, since the word receives a welter of definitions. In other words, when it is said that X is in the interest of Y individual or group, what does the word "interest" mean?

She examines the responses given in the relevant literature and, not only refers to, but elaborates on three of the responses[284] contained in the book *Political Argument*[285] by Brian Barry. The first she refers to is a view that Barry attributes to C. B. Hagen and that she herself associates with Roscoe Pound.[286] According to this view, "X is in the interest of Y" is taken by some to mean that X wants Y. Both Held and Barry discount this understanding of interest, because what someone wants may not necessarily be in their interest. She gives the example of a child who wants to put his hand into a fire, whereas not doing so is what is in its interest.[287]

The second explanation, attributed to John Plamenatz,[288] makes the phrase "X is in the interest of Y," "equivalent to X would be a justifiable claim on the part of Y."[289] This idea of interest is also problematic, because something might be in someone's interest without the person being justified in claiming it. She gives the example of individuals who might correctly claim that a tariff levied elsewhere is in their interest because their businesses would otherwise die, arguing that this does not settle the question as to the moral justification of their claim.[290]

The third explanation which Held quotes Barry as referring to, concerns those who equate "X is in the interest of Y," with "X will give Y more pleasure than any alternative open to him."[291] Whereas

---

[284] Ibid., 21-29.

[285] Brian Barry, *Political Argument* (New York: Humanities Press, 1965).

[286] Roscoe Pound, "A Survey of Social Interests," *Harvard Law Review* 57 (1943-1944): 1-39.

[287] Held, *The Public Interest and Individual Interest*, 21.

[288] John Plamenatz, "Interests," *Political Studies*, Vol. II. (Oxford: Clarendon Press, 1954).

[289] Held, *The Public Interest and Individual Interest*, 21.

[290] Ibid., 28.

[291] Ibid., 21, 28.

Barry associates Bishop Butler and Hume with this position, Held sees Bentham as its principal advocate. She quotes Bentham, who says that "a thing is said to promote the interest or to be *for* the interest of an individual, when it tends to add to the sum total of his pleasures; or what comes to the same thing, to diminish the sum total of his pains."[292] Held agrees with Barry's objection to this definition of interest when he points out that a person might find pleasure in advancing the interests of others rather than his own.[293] Such is the case when X has an interest in seeing Y enacted into law because it is in the public interest even if it will cause him more pain than pleasure.[294]

After criticizing these three attempts at a definition of interest, Held says that the statement X is in the interest of Y means more than Y wants X, or Y demands X. "What it claims in addition," she says, "is that there are some, though perhaps not conclusive, good reasons for enacting or effecting X."[295] She then goes on to quote the following passage of Benn, with which she agrees:

> An account of the interests of a (group) of people is not simply a list of actual wants and aspirations which are widely held by members of that class (though it might be based on such a list), but refers to a paradigm whose wants would correspond to certain socially accepted standards, and be limited to what was reasonable by those standards. But once wants are referred to standards, they are already claims, i.e., demands backed by reasons for satisfying them. They may be defeated by counter-claims or the standards themselves might be questioned; but they are no longer simply wants.[296]

This means that, if certain questions are clarified, such as the fact that interest involves a claim and a justification and not just a

---

[292] Bentham, *An Introduction to the Principles of Morals and Legislation*, 3. See, Held, *The Public Interest and Individual Interests*, 28.

[293] Held, *The Public Interest and Individual Interests*, 22.

[294] Ibid., 29.

[295] Ibid.

[296] S. I. Benn, "'Interests' in Politics," *Proceedings of the Aristotelian Society* 60 (1960): 127-128. Quoted in Held, *The Public Interest and Individual Interests*, 29-30.

demand, Held can be said to lean towards the second definition. She refers approvingly to Charles Fried who regards wants in terms of "bare demands for satisfaction" and interests in terms of "appeals to some scheme (or justification) for satisfying wants."[297] She eventually states her position thus:

> On my analysis, a judgment that "X is in the interest of I" is more than a factual statement that I wants X or that I claims X or that someone claims X for I. It is a judgment that X is being claimed as *justifiable* by or for I, although it does not have to represent more than an *assumption* that the justification appealed to is normatively sound. . . . The explication which I have proposed . . . provides a conception of interests which places them somewhere between wants, on the one hand, and rights, on the other. . . . To say on this analysis, that I have an interest in X, or that X is in his interest, is to say that a case can be made for X, by or on behalf of I; it is not to say that the case can be won. I shall, then, henceforth take my explication as given.[298]

4) In her effort to understand the various theories of the common good, beginning from early Greek philosophy to the present time, Held develops a threefold classificatory scheme. She names these as "preponderance theories," "the public interest as common interest" theories, and 'unitary conceptions."

The "Preponderance Theories" of Thomas Hobbes, David Hume, and Jeremy Bentham

Held makes it clear she is thinking here of aggregationist conceptions in which the public interest is the side on which there is a preponderance or a greater sum of individual interests. This preponderance might, however, be calculated in different ways. She says:

---

[297] Charles Fried, "Two Concepts of Interests: Some Reflections on the Supreme Court's Balancing Test," *Harvard Law Review* 76 (1963): 755-778. See Held, *The Public Interest and Individual Interests*, 30.

[298] Held, *The Public Interest and Individual Interest*, 32-34.

The judgment that an action or state is or is not in the public interest must coincide with the claim of the side with a preponderance of individual interests. Some of the theories in this group base preponderance upon a greater amount of power, others on the votes of a majority of individuals, others on the forces of contending interest groups, others on calculations of preference or utility.[299]

Elsewhere, and in line with the above citation, she writes that "preponderance" in the theories that follow is taken to be a magnitude of some kind, either a degree of force, or a greater amount of sentiment, or a stronger level of opinion."[300]

Held associates Hobbes, Hume, and Bentham, with this position and shows the precise way in which preponderance shows itself in each of them. Let us now examine the essence of each of their theories as she sees it.

Hobbes's Preponderance of Force

Held is of the view that Hobbes's theory is a classic example of a preponderance theory. According to her, Hobbes places the public interest in a situation of conflict with individual interest. This is the meaning of the state of nature. Held points out that one of Hobbes's assumptions is that men are equally vulnerable in the state of nature because even the weakest can harm the strongest. She quotes the following passage from *De Cive*:

> If we look on men full-grown, and consider how brittle the frame of our human body is . . . and how easy a matter it is, even for the weakest man to kill the strongest, there is no reason why any man trusting to his own strength should conceive himself made by nature above others; they are equals who can do equal things one against the other.[301]

---

[299]Ibid., 43.
[300]Ibid., 49.
[301] Hobbes, *De Cive or The Citizen*, 25. See, Held, *The Public Interest and Individual Interests*, 52.

From these words she draws the relevant conclusion for her thesis. She says:

> In view of this, the establishment of government is seen by Hobbes as justifiable, in his sense, because it is in the preponderant interests of a preponderance of men, and those in whose interests it might not be at its theoretical beginning would be at the mercy of all the rest. Thus once a preponderance of individual interests would be better served by the existence of a common power than by a reliance of each upon his own strength, then acquiescence in its creation may come to be in the interests of all. It is in discussing this transition from a state of nature to a state of civil society, that what may be interpreted as Hobbes's theory of the public interest is most apparent.[302]

For Hobbes, therefore, individual interests precede all others, logically and empirically in a state of nature. Since this engenders a permanent condition of war, men realize that it is in their interest to confer "all their power and strength upon one Man, or upon one Assembly of men, that they may reduce all their Wills, by plurality of voices, unto one Will."[303]

Held points out that once people come together to hand over power to a Sovereign and accept that he represent them, his decrees become identical to the public interest. As long as the Sovereign continues to keep the peace and do his work, his declarations of what is in the public interest are taken as in the interest of a preponderance of individual subjects.[304] Held explains how this view differs from the second category of theories that of the public interest as the common interest, by making the point that it is only after a preponderance of individual interests develops that *some* interests may become common ones such as the interest in some government rather than none.[305]

---

[302] Held., *The Public Interest and Individual Interests*, 52-53.
[303] Hobbes, *Leviathan*, 89. See, Held, 53-54.
[304] Held, *The Public Interest and Individual Interests*, 54.
[305] Ibid., 54-55.

Hume's Preponderance of Opinion

Even if unlike Hobbes, Hume "almost" presupposes the existence of government, like him, he sees "the public interest served by government as being to the advantage of a preponderance of individuals who submit to it."[306] If a preponderance of those affected by an action or policy benefit from it, it is in the public interest. How does Hume go about demonstrating his position that what is of public interest is what is *considered* as having utility by a preponderance of the individuals of a nation?

Held indicates that Hume, in his treatment of the public interest, takes us into the field of morality, interpreting the public interest as "judgments of moral virtue."[307] Since for him morals can only be derived from sentiment rather than reason, Philippa Foot argues that "this theory of Hume's about moral sentiment commits him to a subjectivist theory of ethics."[308] Held contests this interpretation of Hume, pointing out that he repeatedly draws an analogy between having a moral feeling and perceiving something.[309] She quotes the *Treatise on Human Nature* where he writes:

> When you pronounce any action or character to be vicious, you mean nothing, but that from the constitution of your nature you have a feeling or sentiment of blame from the contemplation of it. Vice and virtue, therefore, may be compared to sounds, colours, heat and cold, which according to modern philosophy, are not qualities in objects, but perceptions in the mind.[310]

But looking at the above passage, we would be more inclined to side with Philippa Foot's interpretation. However, this does not seem

---

[306] Ibid., 57.

[307] Ibid., 58.

[308] Philippa R. Foot, "Hume on Moral Judgment," in *David Hume: A Symposium*, ed. D. F. Pears (London: Macmillan, 1963), 71. See Held, *The Public Interest and Individual Interest*, 59.

[309] Held, *The Public Interest and Individual Interests*, 59.

[310] David Hume, *A Treatise of Human Nature* (Garden City, N.Y.: Doubleday Dolphin, 1961), 423. See Held, 59.

to affect the essence of the argument, since Held then continues by saying that "just as a preponderance of opinion gives us some confidence that snow is white, it enables us to be satisfied that certain actions are wrong and that certain policies are in the public interest."[311] Held goes on to conclude as follows:

> The central element in Hume's theory of the public interest is his assertion that for something to be in the public interest it must be considered as having utility by a preponderance of individuals.... The preponderance upon which the public interest depends is for Hume not the preponderance of force it was for Hobbes, but a preponderance of opinion.[312]

This conclusion is in accord, she says, with Hume who declares that "as force is always on the side of the governed, the governors have nothing to support them but opinion. It is, therefore, on opinion only that government is founded."[313]

Bentham's Superior Sum

After treating Hume, Held turns to Bentham and begins her explanation of his theory of the public interest with his description of three realities: individual interest, the community, and the public interest. Bentham says that "a thing is said to promote the interest, or to be *for* the interest, of an individual, when it tends to add to the sum total of his pleasures: or what comes to the same thing, to diminish the sum total of his pains."[314] As for a community, he says that it is no more than a collection of individuals. Thus he defines it as "a fictitious body composed of the individual persons who are

---

[311]Held, *The Public Interest and Individual Interests*, 59.
[312]Ibid., 62.
[313] David Hume, "Of the First Principles of Government," in *Hume's Moral and Political Philosophy*, ed. Henry Aiken (New York: Hafner, 1948), 307. See Held, *The Public Interest and Individual Interests*, 62.
[314] Bentham, *An Introduction to the Principles of Morals and Legislation*, 3. See Held, *The Public Interest and Individual Interest*, 63-64.

considered as constituting as it were its members."[315] If we should consider that the public interest and "the interest of the community" are the same thing for him, then this would be his definition of the public interest: "The interest of the community then is, what?—the sum of the interests of the several members who compose it."[316] If individual interest is what causes happiness and diminishes pain, since according to Hume nature is governed by the two sovereign masters of pleasure and pain,[317] and if the public interest is the sum of the interests of several members, then it is logical that the public interest be that which "augments the happiness of the community."[318]

Held goes on to point out that as part of calculating the sum of individual interests, Bentham introduces the requirement that every person is "to count for one and no more than one." That is why Held says elsewhere that for Bentham "the process of determining preponderance is seen as a mathematical operation, rather than as a physical (Hobbes) or psychological (Hume) process."[319]

But Bentham complicates matters for himself somewhat by adding to the numbers the intensity of feeling (which is an intangible) in determining preponderance. Held writes:

> Since the degrees of interest which a measure can have for different individuals can in Bentham's view vary indefinitely, the intensely and lastingly felt interest of even a small minority might constitute a preponderance. Bentham offers a procedure for calculating a preponderance of interests: for every action under consideration as being in or not in the public interest, account should be taken of the number of persons affected, and of the way they are affected. The value of an action to an individual, Bentham argues, will vary according to the intensity, duration, certainty or uncertainty, propinquity or remoteness, chance of being followed by similar sensations (fecundity)

---

[315]Ibid. See Held, *The Public Interest and Individual Interests*, 64.
[316]Ibid. See Held, *The Public Interest and Individual Interests*, 64.
[317]Ibid., 1.
[318]Ibid., 3.
[319]Held, *The Public Interest and Individual Interest*, 63.

and chance of not being followed by opposing sensations (purity) of the pleasure or pain produced.[320]

In confirmation of the above summation, Bentham recommends that every individual "sum up all the values of all the *pleasures* on the one side, and those of all the pains on the other. The balance, if it be on the side of pleasure, will give the *good* tendency of the act upon the whole, with respect to the interests of the *individual* person; if on the side of pain, the *bad* tendency of it upon the whole."[321]

We would be right in seeing the difficulty of bringing the intensity and duration of sensations of pleasures and pains together in an ordered whole, but Bentham is not oblivious of the problem. Held points to how Bentham brings it all together with this prescription:

> Take an account of the *number* of persons whose interests appear to be concerned; and repeat the above process with respect to each. *Sum up* the numbers expressive of the degrees of *good* tendency, which the act has, with respect to each individual, in regard to whom the tendency of it is *good* upon the whole; do this again with respect to each individual, in regard to whom the tendency of it is *good* upon the whole:[322] do this again with respect to each individual, in regard to whom the tendency of it is *bad* upon the whole. Take the *balance* which, if on the side of pleasure, will give the general *good tendency* of the act, with respect to the total number or community of individuals concerned; if on the side of pain, the general *evil tendency*, with respect to the same community.[323]

---

[320] Ibid., 65.

[321] Bentham, *An Introduction to the Principles of Morals and Legislation*, 31. See Held, *The Public Interest and Individual Interests*, 65.

[322] In a footnote, Held discusses Bentham's repetition at this point and speculates as to how this might be explained. Her explanation and the further problems it raises cannot be explored here. (Held, *The Public Interest and Individual Interests*, 95).

[323] Bentham, *An Introduction to the Principles of Morals and Legislation*, 31. See Held, *The Public Interest and Individual Interests*, 66.

Even though Bentham was exceedingly sure of his "political arithmetic"[324] for calculating the public interest, it has caused nothing but trouble for his followers seeking to explain the logical aspects of aggregation. The basic problem has been how one puts a figure on or calculates such imponderables as intensity of feeling, level of fecundity, degree of opposing sensations and measuring one man's pleasure against the pleasure of another man.

Held indicates that Bentham seemed to be aware of these problems since he says himself that comparing one man's happiness with that of someone else is like adding "20 apples to 20 pears."[325] But whatever the problems in determining the public interest, Held is convinced that "Bentham's view bases it clearly upon a superior sum of individual interests."[326]

The "Public Interest as Common Interest" Theory

Held begins her explanation of this theory with its general characteristic. She writes that "this view may be seen in the equation of the public interest with those interest which *all* members of a polity have in *common*, their common interest, perhaps, in a system of government, or in a particular decision method for settling their differences, or their common interest in maintaining some arrangement that benefits every single individual or group."[327] She adds that whereas this conception, like the first, might not rule out conflicts of individual interest, it defines "the public interest in terms of unanimity and compatibility."[328] What this means is that those in this group define the public interest in terms of individual interests held in common by all the members of a community. Held gives as examples the defense of the state, minimal standards of health, or even a governmental system as a whole.[329] Based on unanimity or

---

[324] Ibid.

[325] Jeremy Bentham, *Works*, Vol. IV, ed. John Bowning (Edinburgh: William Tait, 1843), 540. See Held, *The Public Interest and Individual Interests*, 67.

[326] Held, *The Public Interest and Individual Interests*, 67.

[327] Ibid., 44.

[328] Ibid.

[329] Ibid., 99.

non-conflicting interests, the theories of those in this group avoid problems having to do with aggregation.

Rousseau: The Common Good and the General Will

She names Jean Jacques Rousseau as the clearest example of a theory in this group. In Held's view, Rousseau set out to correct what he saw as problematic in the preponderance theory of Hobbes, especially what Hobbes says with regard to the obligation to obey authority. In order to prove this opinion, she quotes Rousseau, who says:

> If it is necessary to obey by force, there can be no occasion to obey from duty; and when force is no more, all obligation ceases with it. We see, therefore, that this word "right" adds nothing to force, but is indeed an unmeaning term. If in saying "Let us obey the powerful," they mean to say, "Let us yield to force," the prospect is good, but it is superfluous, for it never is or can be violated.[330]

Held offers the following revealing commentary to this text of Rousseau's:

> Applied to the public interest, Rousseau's argument suggests that if an action or measure merely accords with the interests of those individuals with a preponderance of force or opinion or preference on their side, to say that it is in the public interest is "unmeaning" unless something more is claimed than such a fact or set of facts. What more this may be, in the case of obligation, is for Rousseau moral authority.[331]

She cites Rousseau in support of this interpretation:

---

[330] Jean Jacques Rousseau, *The Social Contract*, ed. Charles Frankel (New York: Hafner, 1947) Book I, Chapter III, 8-9. See Held, *The Public Interest and Individual Interest*, 100.
[331] Held, *The Public Interest and Individual Interest*, 100.

> Force is a physical power: I do not see what morality can result from its effects. To yield to force is an act of necessity, not of inclination, or it is at best only an act of prudence. In what sense then can it be a duty?[332]

What this means, Held continues, is that the public interest is the result of moral authority rather than the result of a preponderance of force or opinion.

Held then explains Rousseau's doctrine of the public interest as the general will. She begins with an important distinction between what Rousseau refers to as "the will of all," a sort of sum total of conflicting interests, and the general will, which is the will of all in common, or the will in which all interests coincide.[333] Rousseau writes that "the Sovereign, being formed only of the individuals who compose it, neither has nor can have any interest contrary to theirs."[334] On a particular issue, an individual will may coincide with the general will, but it is "impossible that such agreement should be regular and lasting; for the private will is inclined by its nature to partiality, and the general will to impartiality."[335] Rather the aim of government is, according to Rousseau, to cater for those interests held in common by all, that is, those interests which all individuals share.

Does this mean that a decision taken by majority vote as in preponderance theories is null and void? Not necessarily, Rousseau would answer. After the original contract which establishes the polity by unanimous consent, a majority vote might be taken, but this vote would indicate only that "which is in accord with the general will." Held points out that for Rousseau majority vote should never be a mechanism used by the majority or anyone to impose their will on others, since majority or preponderant interest does not constitute

---

[332] Rousseau, *The Social Contract*, 8. See Held, *The Public Interest and Individual Interests*, 100.

[333] Held, *The Public Interest and Individual Interests*, 100-102.

[334] Rousseau, *The Social Contract*, Book II, Chap. VII, 17. See Held, *The Public Interest and Individual Interests*, 101.

[335] Rousseau, *The Social Contract*, Book II, Chap. 1, 23. See Held, *The Public Interest and Individual Interests*, 102

the public interest.[336] Held concludes that for Rousseau, "a valid judgment of public interest rules out a valid judgment of individual interest in conflict with it, for the public interest is equivalent to the interests which all members have in common."[337]

Pareto's Criterion of Optimality.

Some of Rousseau's followers have sought to apply his theory to other areas of community life. Held mentions Vilfredo Pareto's[338] (1848-1923) work in the economic field, where he seeks to develop "optimal" situations that benefit the public interest. His famous criterion of optimality for economic changes appeals to the principle that if one person is better off without anyone being the worse for it,[339] the common good is assured through an improvement in the welfare of society

This means that even if a particular government cannot be reestablished on the principle of unanimity, every governmental action can at least be measured by the yard stick of whether it benefits at least one person and harms no one. Held mentions Kenneth Arrow[340] (b. 1921) and William Baumol[341] (b. 1922), as thinkers who have weighed in on Pareto's criterion of optimality. Held briefly explains what is referred to as the decision method of James M. Buchanan (b. 1919), and Gordon Tullock[342] (b. 1922) authors who seek to show how choice can be in the interest of all the members of a community. She concludes with Brian Barry[343] (1936-2009), another scholar of similar persuasion.

---

[336] Held, *The Public Interest and Individual Interests*, 105.
[337] Ibid., 107.
[338] Vilfredo Pareto, *Manual of Political Economy* (London: Macmillan, 1972).
[339] Held, *The Public Interest and Individual Interests*, 107-109.
[340] Kenneth Arrow, *Social Choice and Individual Values* (New York: Wiley, 1964).
[341] William J. Baumol, *Economic Theory and Operations Analysis* (Englewood Cliffs, N. J.: Prentice Hall, 1961).
[342] James M. Buchanan and Gordon Tullock, *The Calculus of Consent: Logical Foundations of Constitutional Democracy* (Ann Arbor: University of Michigan Press, 1965).
[343] Brian Barry, *Political Argument* (New York: Humanities Press, 1965).

The "Unitary Conception"

Held begins, her explanation of the philosophers she brings under this heading, as she does with the other two categories, with a general expression of what she believes to be distinctive about this group. She states their general position in a straightforward way. According to her, belonging to this group are various idealist theories, and all philosophers who appeal to a single, ordered and consistent scheme of values. In addition, they characterize as unjustifiable, all other theories that contradict it in any way. She writes:

> On this conception, there can never be justifiable conflict either between the interests of some individuals and others, or between any individual interests and the public interest. What is a valid judgment for one is a valid judgment for all and consistent with the public interest. There is, on theories in this category, only one legitimate source of validity for social and political and any other interests, and it cannot allow both a claim for X and a claim against X to be valid.[344]

This is so because "they assert a frankly normative position for the public interest and expect that claims concerning it can be as valid as moral claims generally, which they see as capable of judgment in terms of a unitary, coherent system of values."[345] She continues:

> According to the theories in this group, the public interest is a moral concept, there is a unitary scheme of moral judgments which should guide every individual at a given time and place, although these individuals may be unaware of it. And a *valid* judgment that a given measure, decision, or arrangement is in the public interest rules out the possibility that conflicting individual claims of interest, . . . may be *valid*. On a unitary conception, what is genuinely of moral worth is so

---

[344]Ibid., 45.
[345]Held, *The Public Interest and Individual Interests*, 135.

universally. Hence, individual interests cannot *justifiably* conflict with the public interest or with each other.[346]

Held, considers Plato and Aristotle as the philosophers at the origin of this theory of the common good. She sees Hegel and Marx as eminent disciples of Plato in this regard, and Thomas Aquinas as being inspired by Aristotle. Jacques Maritain is a contemporary protagonist.[347] We will now examine how she describes what these philosophers have to say.

Traditional Theories: i) Plato

Plato, she points out, hardly ever uses the phrase translated as "the public interest" in his writings, which is not to say that the concept is lacking in his writings. In support of its presence in his thought, she says:

> Plato speaks frequently of what has been translated as "the interests of the community" (Lee) or "the interest of the state" (Jowett). Those who govern should be those most devoted to it: "If we want to pick the best guardians, we must pick those who have the greatest skill in watching over the interests of the community."[348]

The concept is thus not lacking in Plato. On the contrary, she thinks he is the first to articulate it clearly. One of the ways he does this, Held contends, is through the idea of the good. She quotes Plato who says that "good is the end of all endeavor, the object on which every heart is set, whose existence it divines, though it finds it difficult

---

[346]Ibid., 135-136.

[347] As Vukan Kuic and Clark E. Cochran point out, the philosophers Held brings together under this category make strange bedfellows. See Vukan Kuic, "Yves R. Simon on Liberty and Authority," in *Acquaintance with the Absolute: The Philosophy of Yves R. Simon* (New York: Fordham University Press, 1998), 132; Clarke E. Cochran, "Yves R. Simon and the Common Good: A Note on the Concept," *Ethics* 88 (1978): 230.

[348]Held, *The Public Interest and Individual Interests*, 138. Held draws the concluding quote from Plato's *Republic*, trans. H. D. P. Lee (Baltimore: Penguin, 1955), 354.

to say just what it is."³⁴⁹ She gives the following interpretation of this and similar passages:

> Since an assertion that something is in the public interest is a claim that it is right or good, and since an assertion that something is in the interest of an individual is, also, a claim that it is right or good, if the two are both true, and hence valid, they cannot conflict. For Plato, it is fundamental that genuine values are in harmony, not in conflict. All men seek the good.³⁵⁰

She clinches the point by indicating that, for Plato, since judgments concern human values, or are capable of being true or false, they assert something which is either true or false for the individual and the society. The values of the individual and the public cannot be different.³⁵¹

In order to further demonstrate this thesis, Held presses into service Plato's ideas regarding unity and justice. She says that the main reason for social organization in Plato's view is to consolidate the unity of the society which is a common good. It is not achieved at the expense of individual interests, and what is in the interest of the community is in the interest of all its members. She quotes Plato, who says:

> Is there anything worse for a state than to be split and disunited or anything better than cohesion and unity? ... And is not cohesion the result of the common feeling you get when all members of a society are glad or sorry at the same successes and failures? ... The best run state is one in which as many people as possible use the words "mine" and "not mine" in the same sense of the same things.... Our citizens, then, are devoted to a common interest, which they call their own; and in consequence entirely share each other's feelings of joy and sorrow....

---

³⁴⁹ Plato, *Republic*, trans. H. D. P. Lee, 506. See Held, 137.
³⁵⁰Held, 137.
³⁵¹Ibid., 136.

We agreed that this unanimity was the greatest good a society can enjoy.[352]

Sharing each other's feelings of joy and sorrow is not only a concrete expression of unity, but of justice. Plato says that, "our purpose in founding our state was not to promote the happiness of a single class, but so far as possible, of the whole community. Our idea was that we were most likely to find justice in such a community."[353] Held argues that this is the main reason Socrates refuses to escape from prison after his sentence of death, as some his friends urge him to do. He is convinced it would be unjust to belong to a state, benefit from its laws, and escape from it when there is an unfavorable situation. Thus for Plato, "the solution to actual problems of conflicting interests is to apply correct philosophical conceptions of both individual interests and the public interest.[354]

Traditional Theories: ii) Aristotle

Like Plato, Aristotle does not use the term public interest, but he does talk of the common advantage (good) of society, and there is no doubt that their meaning is the same. Since he defines the good as "that at which all things aim," the common good as a part of the good as such, will be sought by the political community.[355] In this regard, Held points to the following passage at the beginning of the *Politics*:

> Every state is as we see a sort of partnership, and every partnership is formed with a view to some good (since all the actions of all mankind are done with a view to what they think to be good). It is therefore evident that, while all partnerships aim at some good, the partnership that is the most supreme of all and includes all the others does so most of all, and aims at the most supreme of all goods.[356]

---

[352] Plato, *Republic*, 462-464.
[353] Ibid., 420. See Held, 139.
[354] Held., 140.
[355] Ibid., 141.
[356] Aristotle, *Politics*, trans. H. Rachkam (Cambridge, Massachusetts: Harvard University Press, 2005), 3. See 1252a.

It is not difficult to see why Held places Plato and Aristotle together in this category since she compares their theories at various points and finds similarities. She writes that "like Plato, Aristotle thinks (that) the common interest of a society is that which is best for all men of that society."[357] The one difference, she says, is that whereas Plato places the structure of values in the realm of Ideas, for Aristotle, it is found in Nature.

What then, one might ask, is this common good of the *polis* as Aristotle discerns it? For him, like for Plato, the objective of the polis is moral goodness, or virtuous living.[358] Even if Held does not actually do so, we would corroborate this view with the following passage from the *Politics*:

> If men formed the community and came together for the sake of wealth, their share in the state is proportionate to their share in the property.... But if on the other hand the state was formed not for the sake of life only but rather for the good life.... and if its object is not military alliance for defense against injury by anybody.... All those who are concerned about good government do take virtue into their purview. Thus it is clear that any state that is truly so called and is not a state merely in name must pay attention to virtue.[359]

For Aristotle, the state exists to further the virtuous activities of the individual and of the state, and the two are, in his estimation, not to be seen as incompatible. Held quotes John Herman Randall Jr. according to whom "the good is the same for the individual citizen and for his city or *polis*."[360] Political good embraces all other goods and is good for each individual as well as the state.

Held does mention significant differences between Plato and Aristotle concerning what the public interest actually is. She mentions two questions in particular: the question of private property and a

---

[357] Held, *The Public Interest and Individual Interests*, 141.

[358] Aristotle, *Nicomachean Ethics*, 1094b. See Held, 142.

[359] Aristotle, *Politics*, trans. H. Rackham, 213-215. (1280a25-1280b5).

[360] John Herman Randall Jr., *Aristotle* (New York: Columbia University Press, 1962), 250.

"private sphere." Aristotle remarks that those who own property in common are more often at variance with each other[361] and that the communal arrangements favored by Plato conflict with a public interest demand for a private sphere.[362] These disagreements notwithstanding, Held holds that "they are basically in accord on the position that if a judgment of public interest is valid, a judgment of individual interest cannot validly conflict with it."[363]

Medieval and Modern Representations: Aquinas, Hegel, and Marx

After explicating how the original protagonists of the unitary conception articulate this position, Held explains the contributions of Thomas Aquinas (1225-1274), Hegel (1770-1831), and Karl Marx (1818-1883), whose theories she identifies with this group. She traces the sources of the medieval doctrine sanctioning sedition in certain circumstances to Cicero who declared that "true law is right reason in agreement with nature," concluding that, "it is of universal application, everlasting (and) valid for all nations and all times."[364] On the basis of the above principle of Cicero, Aquinas is of the view that occasions can arise in which citizens understand better what natural law demands, and this may include the need to rebel against a tyrannical regime.[365] Aquinas argues that it is for civil governments to help citizens follow their "ultimate interests which coincide with the norms of natural law."[366] Because positive law, which by definition is ordained to the common good, has its sources, among others, in natural law, a conflict between judgments as to what constitutes public interest and individual interest is unthinkable.[367]

Held contends that just as Aquinas was mainly influenced by Aristotle, Hegel's views go back to Plato. In addition, what Hegel

---

[361] Aristotle, *Politics*, 1263b.

[362] Ibid., 1261a, See Held, 142-143.

[363] Held, 143,

[364] Cicero, *Republic*, Book III, trans. C. W. Keyes (Cambridge: Harvard University Press, 1928), 33. See Held, *The Public Interest and Individual Interests*, 143.

[365] Aquinas, *Summa Theologiae.*, II-II, Q. 42, a. 2.

[366] Held, *The Public Interest and Individual Interests*, 144.

[367] Ibid.

says on the question of interests must be understood within the context of his philosophy of history. Held writes that Hegel holds that there is "a coherent order of values such that all individual interests are ultimately compatible with it."[368] She alludes to this passage from Hegel's *Philosophy of Right*:

> The state is the actuality of the ethical Idea. . . . Since the state is mind objectified, it is only as one of its members that the individual himself has objectivity, genuine individuality, and an ethical life. Unification pure and simple is the true content and aim of the universal, and the individual's destiny is the living of a universal life.[369]

According to Hegel, the fact of individuals pursuing their selfish interests is only a temporary stage to be overcome, in the development of the state which knows its universal will.[370]

Karl Marx follows Hegel, Held maintains, in defending the position that true interests must be one in a global social order.[371] The modern representative state based on self interest is a tool of the bourgeoisie.[372] This situation can only be redressed if the proletariat or working class seizes power, as eventually it will, and acts as the movement for the attainment of the common good as distinct from the exercise of political power over others. The free development of each will lead to the free development of all, [373] social classes will disappear as well as "the furies of private interest," leading to the withering away of the state. When class struggle comes to an end, the

---

[368] Ibid.

[369] G. W. F. Hegel, *Philosophy of Right*, trans. T. M. Knox (Oxford: Clarendon Press, 1942), 257-258. See Held, *The Public Interest and Individual Interests*, 144-145.

[370] G. W. F. Hegel, *Philosophy of Right*, 270.

[371] Held, *The Public Interest and Individual Interests*, 148.

[372] Karl Marx and Friedrich Engels, "Manifesto of the Communist Party" in *Basic Writings on Politics and Philosophy*, ed. Lewis S. Feuer (New York: Doubleday Anchor, 1959), 9. See Held, *The Public Interest and Indivdual Interests*, 148.

[373] Ibid., 29.

government of persons will be replaced by the administration of things.[374]

Contemporary Advocates: Jacques Maritain (1882-1973)

Held's mention of Maritain is worthy of note since Maritain's approach is quite different from that of the other philosophers in this group. Her treatment of Maritain is very brief but, we have already looked at him in some detail in Part I of this chapter and will return to relevant aspects of his thought in Part III.

According to Held, Maritain disagrees with Hegel, and insists that it is persons who are timeless and immortal, rather than states which are not.[375] Persons have the spark of the divine in them. Maritain thus reverses the equation, arguing that it is the public interest that needs to be brought into line with true personal interests and not the other way round, even if both are subject to eternal principles.[376] As to the kind of society Maritain wants us to strive for, Held says:

Maritain's objective is a community of men giving themselves to each other and thus to God. "The man of Christian humanism knows that political life aims at a common good which is superior to a mere collection of the individual's goods and yet must flow back upon human persons."[377] Conflict is to give way to love.[378]

Virginia Held's Proposed Constituent Elements of the Common Good

i) Critique of the Three Groups of Theory

After explaining the theories of the common good in each of the three categories by looking at the representative philosophers of each group, Held gives us her assessment of their strong and weak points.

---

[374] Karl Marx and Friedrich Engels, "Socialism: Utopian and Scientific" in *Basic Writings on Politics and Philosophy*, 106. See Vukan Kuic, "Yves Simon's Contribution to Political Science" in *The Political Science Reviewer* 4 (1974): 70.
[375] Jacques Maritain, *The Range of Reason* (New York: Scribner, 1952), 147.
[376] Ibid., 151.
[377] Ibid., 197.
[378] Held, *The Public Interest and Individual Interests*, 151.

Held sees the strength of preponderance theories as residing in the fact that they allow for valid individual interests of the members of a community to diverge with each other and with the public interest, which the other two do not allow. In addition, unlike theories in the other two categories, there is no presumption that if a government decision or program is in the public interest, it must be in the interest of every member of the community.[379]

But preponderance theories present two kinds of problems, Held explains. These are logical or naturalistic. With regard to the question of logic, Held points out that if a society decides to resolve an issue or issues by majority vote (preponderance), the question as to whether majority vote equals the public interest is not thereby resolved.[380] Elsewhere, in an effort to save the idea of public interest from "indiscriminate use", she makes a clear distinction between the concepts of public interest, common interest, and majority interest. She says:

> If a discussion concerns "what the majority of a given population declares it favors," or if it concerns "the interests which all members of a community have in common," the terms "majority interest" and "common interest," respectively, might well be used instead of "public interest."[381]

Preponderance theories speak more to majority interests rather than the public interest.[382] Using a second type of argument which flows from the first, Held shows that the argument of superior group strength does not thereby resolve ethical questions about normative judgments. She says:

> If we want to know whether a given X is in the public interest, we want to know something else than the empirical fact that it is in the interests of a preponderance of individuals, although being in the

---

[379] Ibid. 82.
[380] Ibid., 83.
[381] Ibid., 163.
[382] See p. 190.

interests of a preponderance of individuals may well be among the possible good reasons for believing that such an X is in the public interest.[383]

This brings us to what Held has to say about theories belonging in the second group, namely, those that look at the public interest as referring to those interests which all have in common. Held begins with the weak points of the theory and argues that, besides the fact that few decisions would meet the requirement of being in the interest of all, which would often lead to deadlock and anarchy, the main problem with this approach is that it "rewards egoism." She quotes Buchanan and Tullock:

> With the most inclusive decision rule, unanimity, each voter is a necessary party to any agreement. Since each voter, then, has a monopoly of an essential resource (that is his consent), each person can aim at obtaining the entire benefit of agreement for himself. Under these circumstances, it seems highly likely that agreement would normally be almost impossible. Certainly, the rewards received by voters in any such agreement would be directly proportionate to their stubbornness.[384]

If individual advantage is to be the principle for action, then action would be impossible in large collectivities. On this assumption, one might say that "the larger the group, the less likely it will further its common interests."[385] Held concludes her criticism of this model by referring to the game-theoretical situation known as Prisoner's Dilemma,[386] which shows that mutual trust is more beneficial than individual interest.

---

[383]Ibid., 84.

[384] Buchanan and Tullock *The Calculus of Consent*, 69. See Held, *The Public Interest and Individual Interests*, 118-119.

[385] James S. Coleman, "Foundations for a Theory of Collective Decisions," *The American Journal of Sociology*, 81 (1966): 616. See Held, *The Public Interest and Individual Interests*, 121.

[386] Virginia Held, "Rationality and Social Value in Game-Theoretical Analyses," *Ethics* 76 (1966):215-220; "On the Meaning of Trust," *Ethics* 78 (1968):

With regard to unitary conceptions of the public interest, Held has recourse to the critique of Karl Popper[387] which, in her estimation, is generally true if hyperbolic, and which regards Plato and his ideas as the harbinger of totalitarianism. She quotes Popper, who says of Plato's theory that it "worships the state, history, and the nation,"[388] and insists on "the absolute moral authority of the state, which overrules all personal morality, and conscience."[389] She brings in Ernest Baker who contends that this theory sacrifices the individual and his personal development to the state seen as a higher end.[390]

Held thinks that at a practical level, the unitary conception can lead to intolerance toward individual interests and demands. In this atmosphere, anyone involved in a conflict with the state might tend to be seen as misguided or evil, and victimized on that account.

A question that might be asked is whether conflict in such a state would be a thing of the past since according to Marx, material needs which are the sole cause of conflict would be a thing of the past? Held answers in the negative since, as Hobbes has demonstrated, conflicts in society can be generated by any of three factors: competition, diffidence and glory. The first makes men fight for gain, the second for safety, and the third for reputation.[391]

ii) Proposed Ethical System

Following on her critique of the three categories of theory on the common good, Held sets forth, in the last chapter (Chapter 6) of her book, what she considers as a "minimal content which the term must have in order to do the jobs which we should want it to do."[392] It is

---

156-159. There has been a lot written in recent times on the centrality of the topic of the Prisoner's Dilemma —See Anatol Rapoport and Albert M. Chammah, *Prisoner's Dilemma* (Ann Arbor: University of Michigan Press, 1965).

[387] Karl Popper, *The Open Society and Its Enemies*, 2 Vols. (New York: Harper Torchbooks, 1962).

[388] Ibid., 11, 13.

[389] Ibid.

[390] Aristotle, *The Politics of Aristotle*, ed. Ernest Baker, Introduction, 1.

[391] Hobbes *Leviathan*, Chapter 13. Held., *The Public Interest and Individual Interests*, 156.

[392] Held, *The Public Interest and Individual Interests*, 8.

nothing remotely resembling a system, but rather consists of a series of distinctions, principles, and recommendations.

Held begins her considerations with the question as to who is best able to choose interests. She says that whereas, in general, individuals should have the right to choose their interests,[393] in certain instances, it is best done by others. She gives the example of a doctor who might be the best placed to decide if an operation is opportune.[394] The right of individuals to choose is thus not absolute, and implies an "internally consistent"[395] validating system which need not be rigorous in any sense, but which children and the mentally incompetent might not easily understand. As for judgments of public interest, their validity presupposes a political and legal system since it might otherwise be difficult to sort out rival claims. No public interest can be valid outside of its political and legal system which provides a decision making procedure as to what is or is not in the public interest.[396]

However, a political and legal system cannot stand on its own. It needs a normative grounding outside of itself, a *Grundnorm*. She quotes Dennis Lloyd, who writes:

> Any system of rules must come to a point beyond which you cannot go. Ultimately you will come to a rule which is the outer limit of the system, and it is really senseless to look for *legal* justification, though there may be some other type of justification such as the will of God, morality, or *de facto* obedience.[397]

Held summarizes her argument up to this point in the following way:

---

[393] Julius Stone, *Human Law and Human Justice* (Stanford: Stanford University Press, 1964), 341. See Held, *The Public Interest and Individual Interests*, 166.

[394] Held, *The Public Interest and Individual Interests*, 166

[395] Ibid., 167.

[396] Ibid., 168-174.

[397] Dennis Lloyd, *Introduction to Jurisprudence*, (New York: Praeger, 1965), 195. See Held, *The Public Interest and Individual Interests*, 183.

On the explication of the public interest which I am proposing, no judgment concerning the public interest can be valid outside the political system whose decision procedures validate claims about it, although judgments concerning individual interests may be independent of judgments concerning the public interest, and the political system can itself, be judged in moral terms.[398]

Having made the above points, which are of a general nature, Held examines in greater detail the relationship between individual interest and public interest with particular emphasis on the question of norms. She returns to the fact that the declaration of an interest is always an assertion that what is claimed is justifiable. This, she says, is a normative claim.[399] Anyone therefore, asserting that something is in the public interest or the private interest, is asserting that it is justifiable. Thus she can conclude that "a valid judgment that X is in the public interest does not, on my analysis, imply that judgments of individual interest in conflict with it are invalid."[400] How is this possible?

In answer, Held introduces the idea of moral norms at this juncture. She writes:

> A settlement between rival claims that something is or is not in the public interest on the basis of the political authority of the claimants does not amount to a position that whatever a political system decides is therefore morally justified, since such assertions, even if *valid* upon the political system, may be invalid upon other systems, such as the moral systems of individuals.[401]

From Held's point of view, therefore, "an individual may validly claim that a given decision, policy, law, or arrangement is or is not justifiable, and a polity may validly claim the contrary."[402] When this

---

[398] Held, *The Public Interest and Individual Interests*, 183.
[399] Ibid., 184. (Preponderance theories fail to take this into account).
[400] Ibid., 186.
[401] Ibid., 187.
[402] Ibid., 188.

happens and both parties have evidence supporting their positions, disputes can only be settled by a mechanism beyond the systems of both.[403]

In order to achieve success in this task, Held proposes the construction of ethical systems shared by all. She admits that such a task would challenge the resources of moral philosophers but she is optimistic that it can be done. She says:

> It is not inconceivable that the development of effective ethical systems could proceed in ways analogous to those in which scientific systems have grown since the 16th and 17th centuries. Within the sciences, decisions are reached according to agreed upon methods, and these decisions are accepted as authoritative. It might not be unreasonable to hope that secular ethical enquiries, in such fields as social ethics and political ethics, conducted by independent and impartial scholars, on the bases of assumed principles and ascertainable tests could begin to make comparable progress.[404]

Considered in this way, what is in the public interest may or may not be advantageous to the majority of citizens, nor gain unanimity, or the consent of all of the citizens. In the end the assertion that the action of a state is or is not in the public interest is a normative claim requiring a normative justification in a political system.

III: Simon's Concept of the Common Good

In the process of explaining the three categories into which she classifies theories concerning the common good, Held remarks of the third category that it has "fewer contemporary defenders than the other approaches."[405] But, could the problem be that she does not look hard enough? For instance, even though she gives Maritain a brief hearing, she does not mention Yves Simon at all, whom Clarke

---

[403] Ibid.
[404] Ibid., 190-191.
[405] Ibid., 151.

E. Cochran puts forward as an eminent representative of this group.⁴⁰⁶ Cochrane says of Simon's work in this regard:

> I intend to suggest how a "unitary conception" of the common good, such as Yves R. Simon's, avoids the theoretical pitfalls to which other theories are subject.... I wish to suggest... that Yves R. Simon's conception of the common good is a unitary theory which, despite certain lacunae which I will try to fill, resolves the dilemma posed by Held.⁴⁰⁷

In this final section of chapter 2, we will seek to redress this lacuna in Held by looking at Simon's quite considerable contribution on this question.

This contribution, in my estimation, concerns precisely an area of the common good to which Held cannot find a clear solution. As we have just seen, Held attempts to resolve the dilemmas thrown up by her analysis by proposing an ethical system that achieves a reconciliation between individual and public interests. Whereas for her this system is still to be elaborated by moral philosophers, it would seem that it already exists in the work of Yves Simon.⁴⁰⁸ It only needs to fleshed out, which is what we propose to do here.

What then is Simon's contribution to this question? Simon did not write a treatise on the common good but rather treated it in a number of works⁴⁰⁹ as the occasion presented itself and within the

---

⁴⁰⁶ Clarke E. Cochran, "Yves R. Simon and 'The Common Good': A Note on the Concept," *Ethics* 88 (1978): 229.

⁴⁰⁷Ibid., 229-230.

⁴⁰⁸ This is also the persuasion of Clarke E. Cochran. See Cochran, "Yves R. Simon and 'The Common Good': A Note on the Concept": 230.

⁴⁰⁹ The works concerned are the following: *Philosophy of Democratic Government* originally published by the University of Chicago Press, 1951. (Notre Dame: University of Notre Dame Press, 1993), 47-50, 62-66; "Common Good and Common Action," *Review of Politics* 22 (1960): 202-244. This article has been reprinted with slight changes, as Chapter 2 of *A General Theory of Authority* (Notre Dame: University of Notre Dame Press, 1980), 23-79; *The Tradition of Natural Law: A Philosopher's Reflections*, ed. Vukan Kuic (New York: Fordham University Press, 1965), 86-109; *Freedom and Community*, ed. Charles P.O'Donnell (New York: Fordham University Press, 1968), 103-108, 130-144.

context of other questions. He thus examines the idea within the context of civil society, of authority, and of the law. When we bring together what he says in his works, we can begin to piece together the elements constitutive of the common good and its place in his philosophy as a whole.

Two Misconceptions of the Common Good.

A good place to start an examination of Simon's contribution is with what he regards as the two counterfeit ideas of the common good. He begins his treatment of the common good with these two erroneous ideas in *A General Theory of Authority*[410] and *The Tradition of Natural Law: A Philosopher's Reflections*.[411]

i) Concerning the first false conception, Simon says that "the most frequent [misconception] is the myth of the common good as external to man."[412] This error perceives the common good as "something to be constructed and admired, but not something which touches the hearts of individuals."[413] Here, the common good is represented as something external to the members of a state, and the example that Simon gives is that of the pyramids of Egypt.[414] It is the temptation of political leaders who conceive of the human community after the pattern of perfection supplied by a beautiful artwork. To explain what he means, Simon says:

> The myth which identifies the common good with the perfection of a work of art and thus represents it as something nonhuman is constantly strengthened by the assumption that society, or at least the temporal, as distinct from the spiritual society, is concerned only with external actions, such as digging, orderly conduct in the street,

---

[410] Simon, *A General Theory of Authority*, 26-31, 157.
[411] Simon, *The Tradition of Natural Law*, 92-107. (Simon gives a summary of these false ideas on page 107).
[412] Ibid., 92.
[413] Cochran, "Yves R. Simon and "The Common Good": A Note on the Concept," 232.
[414] Simon, *A General Theory of Authority*, 27.

marching, charging and retreating according to orders, paying taxes, fulfilling contracts, etc. Political society in this view, would have nothing to do with what goes on in the heart of man.[415]

In his consideration of what Simon is here referring to, Vukan Kuic writes that "insidious instances are found in the theories of the transcendent state from Plato to Hegel."[416] He continues:

> In this model, the state is conceived as a kind of masterwork of art, and because there is special satisfaction in handling its "material," that is, beings endowed with intelligence and freedom, both men of action and political thinkers are attracted to it. . . . What we have to recognize is that the good of the city so conceived is exclusively its own good which not only permits but requires that the lives, liberties, and the pursuit of the happiness of its members be sacrificed to it. Indeed, with all the qualifications that would have to be added, Plato's *Republic* may be said to be the original example of such a false common good and Machiavelli's *Prince* its best modern version.[417]

What, one might ask, is the problem with this idea of the common good? We have started hinting at it already in the above quotes. Simon is of the view that this idea is completely irrelevant to the common good. Whereas an artwork is good as something to be admired, whereas it captivates the imagination of politicians because of the joy they get in creating and managing something as difficult to manage and as noble as man,[418] it has nothing to do with the common good. This is the meaning of the following passage:

> In all domains of art, whether relative to beauty or not, there is perfection if the thing worked out is perfect, and the good of man is completely irrelevant. Gauguin probably would not have produced his

---

[415] Simon, *The Tradition of Natural Law*, 95.

[416] Vukan Kuic, "Yves R. Simon on Liberty and Authority," in *Acquaintance with the Absolute: The Philosophy of Yves R. Simon* (New York: Fordham University Press, 1998), 132.

[417] Ibid.

[418] Simon, *The Tradition of Natural Law*, 93.

admirable paintings if he had not deserted his family: his desertion was bad for his people and for himself but did not affect the quality of his painting.[419]

In addition to seeing man as something to be manipulated, this idea of the common good is untenable because the common good itself is presented in material terms. However, social and political life and, therefore, the common good, is not made up of just such facts as "men engaged in digging a canal, clearing a jungle, building a railroad (and) the reclaiming of swamp land."[420] These are not the only examples of "social facts." There are others of another nature:

> But when men are aware of their unity in knowing and loving or hating, we speak with entire propriety of their communing in acts of cognition and love and hatred. Here are immanent actions which, because of the awareness of unity, assume a social character. Clearly, these communions are the most genuine and the most profound of all social facts, and the good condition of whatever pertains to acting together in these immanent actions, is the deepest and the most precious part of the common good.[421]

The idea of the common good as a beautiful work of art is false, therefore, because it neglects the fact that immanent actions, or actions of the spirit, are constitutive of the common good. Simon gives the example of prisoners watching a play on television first in their separate rooms and then together in a common hall. Whereas there is silent watching when they are by themselves, once they are together, there is communion of interest in what they are watching. They now express suspense, pity, and admiration together. The most important part of community life takes place in the heart of man.[422]

---

[419]Ibid., 92.
[420]Ibid., 95.
[421]Ibid., 96.
[422] Ibid.

ii) If the idea of the common good as a work of art is an error, it does happen that by way of reaction, and in a bid to defend the rights of the individual, social and political thinkers sometimes go to the other extreme. The second example of a mistaken view of the common good is the idea that the common good is a means to the good of the individual[423] or an aggregation of individual or particular interests.[424] Simon refers to Harold Laski, a member of the British Labour Party, as representative of this position. Accusing Laski of nominalism, he says that, "the nominalist mind is as unable to grasp the reality of a community as it is unable to grasp the meaning of a universal nature."[425] Laski himself writes as follows:

> The surrender we make is a surrender not for the *sake* of the society regarded as something other than its members, but exactly and precisely for men and women whose totality is conveniently summarized in a collective and abstract noun.[426]

Kuic explains this citation as follows:

> Laski lets individuals trade with each other in surrenders rather than contributions. And in order to quash all possible claims on its behalf, Laski, a socialist, not only denies that the good of society has an independent existence but does not hesitate to reduce "society" itself to a convenient abstraction.[427]

Kuic gives another example of an adherent of this position in the person of Friedrich A. Hayek. By way of illustration, he points to the following passage in which Hayek is answering the question as to

---

[423] Simon, *A General Theory of Authority*, 26-27.
[424] For those who defend this position see Howard R. Smith, *Democracy and the Public Interest* (Athens: University of Georgia Press, 1960); E. Pendleton Herring, *Public Administration and the Public Interest* (New York: McGraw-Hill Book Co., 1936).
[425] Simon, *The Tradition of Natural Law*, 106.
[426] Harold Laski, *Liberty in the Modern State* (New York: The Viking Press, 1949), 39. See Simon, *The Tradition of Natural Law*, 106.
[427] Vukan Kuic, *Yves R. Simon: Real Democracy*, 54.

whether a government should use taxes to pay for projects such as care for the disabled:

> It is not to be expected that there will ever be complete unanimity on the desirability of the extent of such services, and it is at least not obvious that coercing people to contribute to the achievement of ends in which they are not interested can be morally justified. Up to a point, most of us find it expedient, however, to make such a contribution on the understanding that we will in turn profit from similar contributions of others towards the realization of our own ends.[428]

This thinking accords with that of Christian Bay,[429] whom Kuic also names as belonging in this circle, since for Bay "man himself is the only end, (and) maximization of every man's and woman's freedom—psychological, social, and potential—is the only proper first-priority aim for the joint human effort that we call political."[430]

What, one might ask, is the problem with individualism? Any assessment of those who conceive the common good in this way would have to acknowledge that this position is not completely without merit. It is understandable that some scholars should be extremely cautious of endorsing a common good independent of that of the citizens in the light of recent history. The quest for a classless society, as evidenced in various shades of totalitarianism, the modern version of Plato's transcendent state, has led to awful crimes and a denial of individual rights that is still fresh in our memories.

But individualism creates more problems than it resolves. If one were asked what the problem is with individualism, one would immediately point to its egoistic connotation, and one would be right. It conceives of society almost entirely in terms of what is useful for the individual. Simon articulates this concern when he says that, "the philosophy of individualism implies that whatever is called common

---

[428]Friedrick A. Hayek, *The Constitution of Liberty* (Chicago: The University of Chicago Press, 1960), 144.

[429]Kuic, "Yves R. Simon on Liberty and Authority," in *Acquaintance with the Absolute: The Philosophy of Yves R. Simon*, 133.

[430]Christian Bay, *The Structure of Freedom* (Stanford, California: Stanford University Press, 1958), 390.

good is merely useful, that things common are but means, and that the character of end belongs exclusively to the individual."[431]

If society exists only for the sake of satisfying individual desires, is this not a recipe for grabbing everything for oneself with the potential for chaos that this can cause? Clarke E. Cochran articulates this legitimate critique in a number of works,[432] his basic position consisting in the fact that "their most fundamental flaw is the failure to see anything to politics beyond the encounter of interests: that is, wants, desires, or preferences. In the "politics of interest"" he continues, "there is no public to possess an interest, let alone any criteria according to which an interest's moral or political worth might be assessed."[433]

Simon goes even further in his philosophical argumentation to counter the idea of the common good as the sum of particular goods. He argues that individualism is a fundamental misreading of human needs. This is how Vukan Kuic explains Simon's argument:

> True, we need others to survive, and we use others as they use us for our own ends. But we also need our fellow human beings gathered in society in order to become what is in us to be, and that ultimately means giving to others, not taking from them. The philosophy of individualism grossly underestimates what Simon calls our other-centered needs. For instance, what other use is there for love, strength of character, wisdom, or any other real and lasting human accomplishment, except to give it freely?[434]

Simon himself presents and develops this argument in especially three of his four writings on the common good, namely, *A General*

---

[431] Simon, *A General Theory of Authority*, 68.

[432] Clarke E. Cochran, "Political Science and "The Public Interest,"" *Journal of Politics* 36 (1974): 327-355; and "The Politics of Interest: Philosophy and the Limitations of the Science of Politics," *American Journal of Political Science* 17 (1973): 745-766.

[433] Cochran, "Yves R. Simon and "The Common Good": A Note on the Concept," 229.

[434] Kuic, "Yves R. Simon on Liberty and Authority," in *Acquaintance with the Absolute: The Philosophy of Yves R. Simon*, 134.

Theory of Authority, *The Philosophy of Democratic Government*, and *The Tradition of Natural Law: A Philosopher's Reflections*. His opening and, indeed, basic premise is that "among the tendencies which make up the dynamism of a rational being, some are self-centered and some are generous. All," he continues, "admit of a state of need, and the need to give is no less real than the need to take."[435]

He then takes the example of someone who is a "firm and accomplished person" possessing virtue and not in any material need. Even such a person, he says, needs to give in order to achieve his completion. This is the argument:

> He (the accomplished person) does not depend on the help of friends for food or shelter; he is not in the least motivated by expectation of physical care in case of disease; neither does it occur to him that he may need friendly attention to soothe him in case of emotional disaster, for his nervous balance is well assured; . . . We are describing a distinguished instance of mature development, strength of character, soundness, dominating indifference, freedom. . . . His very state of accomplishment intensifies in him every generous trait and every tendency to act by way of superabundance. He needs to give. True, the center of the act of giving is found in the beneficiary of the gift. Yet the gift satisfies also a need in the giver.[436]

In *The Tradition of Natural Law: A Philosopher's Reflections*, Simon refers to this characteristic as "disinterested sociability."[437] In fact, he insists, the desire to give is so pervasive that even "people of debased conduct and skeptical judgment still find it natural to die for their country or for such substitute for a country as a gang." He continues that, during the golden age of individualism the conscience of men, in spite of what the theorists said, often recognized the common good and served it with devotion under such improper names as "general interest" or "greatest good of the greatest number."[438] That

---

[435] Simon, *A General Theory of Authority*, 24.
[436] Ibid., 25-26.
[437] Simon, *The Tradition of Natural Law*, 90.
[438] Simon, *The Philosophy of Democratic Government*, 50.

is why "in case of frustration the tendency to act generously becomes the most redoubtable of antisocial drives."[439] It is also the reason why "men would rather stand physical destitution than be denied the opportunity for disinterested love and sacrifice."[440] This is the meaning of the saying by Aristotle that "the common good is greater and more divine than the private good."[441]

Simon gives this argument another slant when he points out that one of the "limitations of individual plenitude"[442] is the fact that individuals are limited in what they possess and can give, a limitation that is completed by society. Even highly accomplished people are wanting in some gift that is completed by what others bring to the table. He says:

> The rule to which all men are subjected in varying degree is one of specialization for the sake of proficiency. . . . A man highly successful in his calling accomplishes little in comparison with the ample virtualities of man. He has failed in a hundred respects. Only the union of many can remedy the failure of each. But of all the restrictions inflicted upon the boundless ambition of our rational nature, the most painful concerns the duration of individual achievements. Within the temporal order we would feel hopeless if the virtual immortal life of the community did not compensate for the brevity of individual existence. Death is known to be particularly hard and surrounded with anxiety for those who end their days in individualistic loneliness.[443]

Simon means that individuals are necessarily limited in their achievements. They depend on society and achieve immortality therein. Kuic captures this aspect beautifully when he says:

> Considering the other-centered needs of individuals, also helps us see more clearly how intrinsically social is all human achievement. Even

---

[439] Simon, *A General Theory of Authority*, 26.
[440] Ibid.
[441] Ibid., 27; See Aristotle, *Nicomachean Ethics*, 1. 2. 1094b7.
[442] Simon, *A General Theory of Authority*, 28.
[443] Ibid.

the greatest man or woman, besides living but a short time, can excel at best in two or three fields of endeavor out of an indefinite number required by society to produce what we call civilization and culture. Without society there would be no "common heritage of mankind," no science, no mathematics, no art, no morality, and probably no mankind. That is why all theories to the contrary notwithstanding the common good of society is greater than any individual good.[444]

As Simon says, "beyond the satisfaction of individual needs the association of men serves a good unique in plenitude and duration."[445]

Simon even thinks that adherence to a common good, and a desire to contribute to it, and the sense of communion it engenders, not only give the lie to the philosophy of individualism, but is the antidote to alienation. Contrary to the analysis of Karl Marx, whom we would add, sees alienation in purely economic terms as resulting from the appropriation by some of the fruits of the labor of others, Simon gives us a different and all round analysis. Solitude results from individualism, and the mere partnership as opposed to communion and common action cannot help the situation since partners in a deal look to their individual interests. Common action which is "conditioned by immanent actions of knowledge and desire in which members commune,"[446] results in communion, a communion that relieves solitude, anxiety, and loneliness. Simon writes:

> Communions in immanent actions make up the most profound part of social reality; theirs is a world of peace where ennui is impossible. . . . There alone the individual is freed from solitude and anxiety. Mere partnership, on the other hand, does not do anything to put an end to the solitude of the partners. They may be better off as a

---

[444]Vukan Kuic, "Yves Simon's Contribution to Political Science," *Political Science Reviewer* 4 (1974): 69. See also Kuic, *Yves Simon: Real Democracy* (Lanham, MD: Rowman & Littlefield Publishers Inc. 1999), 57.

[445]Ibid., 29.

[446] Simon, *Philosophy of Democratic Government*, 64.

result of their contract, but their contract will not relieve their lonesomeness. Mere partnership . . . would be a major cause of the anxiety prevalent in our societies.[447]

Simon also touches on this question in this sense in his book, *Work, Society, and Culture*.[448]

Simon's Concept of the Common Good

Preliminary Considerations and Definition

If the two counterfeit conceptions of the common good examined above do not give us an accurate idea of the concept, Simon's task is to lay out an understanding of the common good that avoids both errors, and goes to its essence. We think that in answer to the concerns of Virginia Held such a theory must do at least two things: i) correct the errors in the counterfeit explanations of the common good; and ii) give a proper account of how private goods are to be reconciled to the public interest by resolving clearly the questions that lead Held to propose the elaboration of an ethical system by moral philosophers or even flesh out the details of such a system.

Our thesis is that Simon fills the void that Held detects, by giving a clear description of the common good, by showing how valid particular goods may be reconciled with the common good, and by alluding to a moral principle that should guide us in the reconciliation of conflictual interests.

Let me begin with something which is fundamental to Simon's political theory, namely the twin concepts of community or communion and the common good.[449] The two are linked by inescapable and mutual ties in such fashion that a proper understanding of the one leads to a right understanding of the other.

---

[447]Ibid., 65; See 307-318.
[448] Yves R. Simon, *Work, Society, and Culture*, 83-86.
[449] Cochran, "Yves R. Simon and "The Common Good": A Note on the Concept," 231.

We have already seen how Simon shows the deficiency in individualism by using the contrast between a partnership which promotes individualism, and community, the other basic form of association.[450] Let us pursue the difference here a little further. Those engaged in a partnership pursue their common interests or their private interests which might be interdependent, but not the common good. In order to illustrate what he means by partnership he gives the example of the collaboration that might exist between a money-lender and a merchant,[451] or what we would call today an investor and a businessman. The money-lender puts money into the merchant's business with the understanding that the profits will be divided according to an agreed ratio. He then waits for the merchant to do the work. One of the protagonists might get ten percent, which is a private good, and the other twenty percent depending on the agreement, a private good as well. The relationship is purely contractual. There is no common action or common desire here since the money-lender is a silent partner. There is only common interest or a pseudo-common good.[452] Held thus distinguishes common interest from common good.[453]

Following on from the above, Simon points out that those who see government as a partnership will necessarily have an idea of government as "involving no common existence, no common life, no common love, and no common action" but "(as) produced by our wants."[454] He refers to the famous saying of Thomas Paine that, "society is produced by our wants and government by our wickedness."[455] The first part of this saying, namely, that society is the result of our wants implies the idea of government as a partnership to resolve a lack. The corollary of this is the "tendency

---

[450] Ibid.

[451] Simon, *A General Theory of Authority*, 29-30; *Philosophy of Democratic Government*, 48-49.

[452] Simon, *Philosophy of Democratic Government*, 49.

[453] Held., *The Public Interest and Individual Interests*, 163.

[454] Simon, *Philosophy of Democratic Government*, 63.

[455] Thomas Paine, *Common Sense in the Writings of Thomas Paine* (New York: G. P. Putnam's Sons, 1894), 1, 69. See Simon, *Philosophy of Democratic Government*, 4. 61.

to substitute a sum of particular goods for the common good of civil society."[456]

In contradistinction to the partnership and individualism as described above, there is the common good which Simon is now ready to define.[457] He does so by saying that a common good calls for communion in action. It is the activity of achieving something in common.[458] It calls for common action and common desire. In this light, when there is no common good in the hearts of the members of a community to hold them together, the community has long fallen apart and is dead. Thus Simon describes a common good as follows:

> In order that a good be common, it does not suffice that it should concern, in some way or other, several persons; it is necessary that it be of such a nature as to cause, among those who pursue it and in so far as they pursue it, a common life of desire and action. Whenever the good interesting several persons or groups causes such common life, it is a genuine common good.... If, on the other hand, a good interesting several does not call for a common life of desire and action, ... it is the sum of particular goods.[459]

Simon gives his idea of a common good a number of qualities that sharpen it, and further distinguish it from defective notions of it. A key attribute which he mentions again and again is that of "distributability." If a common good is not to be confiscated by a group of individuals, it calls for constant distribution to society's members. This quality would seem for him and for Maritain, as we will see below, to be the biggest antidote to individualism. When common goods leak out of society for the exclusive use of a few, they

---

[456] Simon, *Philosophy of Democratic Government*, 63.

[457] Commentators note that Simon does not explicitly define the common good and is sometimes loose with his terminology, switching between a common good and the common good as if the two are synonymous. See Cochran, "Yves R. Simon and "The Common Good": A Note on the Concept," 232.

[458] Simon, *A General Theory of Authority*, 27.

[459] Simon, *Philosophy of Democratic Government*, 49.

are denatured and become, by that very fact, private goods.[460] Simon writes:

> A thing which has the appearance of a common good, inasmuch as it cannot be realized without common desire and common action, is not a genuine common good and may amount to sheer destruction if it is kept apart from the persons who make up the community. Because society does not exist except in individuals (connected by definite relations), the good of society demands, by nature and not by accident, a constant distribution to individuals.[461]

Simon is at one with Maritain on this head. In a remarkable passage, in which he combats the twin errors of totalitarianism and individualism, Maritain writes:

> The end of society is the good of the community, of the social body. . . . The common good of the city is neither the mere collection of private goods, nor the proper good of a whole which, like the hive with respect to its bees, relates the parts to itself alone and sacrifices them to itself. It is the good human life of the multitude, of a multitude of persons; it is their communion in good living. It is therefore common to both the whole and the parts into which it flows back. . . . It requires by its very essence . . . redistribution to the persons who constitute society.[462]

In the same vein, Maritain argues elsewhere that the good of the whole is "superior to the private good, only if it benefits the individual persons, is redistributed to them and respects their dignity."[463] The importance of distributability cannot be gainsaid since it strengthens both the community spirit and the individual. A winner-takes-it-all society destroys itself by distorting the common

---

[460] Simon, *The Tradition of Natural Law*, 98-100. See Cochran, "Yves R. Simon and "The Common Good": A Note on the Concept," 232.
[461] Simon, *The Tradition of Natural Law*, 98.
[462] Maritain, *The Person and the Common Good*, 40-41.
[463] Ibid., 50-51; 66.

good. That a common good or the common good demands distribution belongs to its essence and a common good or the common good that does not possess this essential quality is not a common good or the common good.

Besides the question of redistribution in the above quote, Maritain mentions two other qualities of the common good, namely, the benefit to persons and respect for their dignity, which Simon deals with at various points in his own work, and which we might summarize as the spiritual element of the common good. He deals with this spiritual component by arguing that the common good is rational. But he goes further to demonstrate that this rationality is not based on reasoning alone but on affective communion. This is the full meaning of the idea of common desire and is necessary if common action is to be fruitful and stable. For instance, the family would cease to exist as a community if each member did not judge it opportune to stay in a particular house, just as a factory could not operate if a fixed schedule was not observed by the personnel.[464]

But this is not the only sense in which the spiritual and the moral are integral to the common good. The very essence of the common good is eminently a spiritual good. It is often believed erroneously, Simon says, that while the physical and material needs of the body such as the search for food and security are better satisfied through collaboration among men, "the goods of the spirit are altogether individual and that their pursuit is an entirely individualistic concern. Thus, human life would be split into a part socialized by material needs and a nobler part distinguished both by spirituality and individual independence."[465] Simon disposes of this construct by pointing to the role of society in the passing on of and growth in knowledge, and the fact that people, as a fact of who they are, are ready to give of their talents to human society and sacrifice for it.[466] We are wont to pursue and benefit from the spiritual as community.

A common good is not just attained in any transitive action or communication but in common aversion to evils, in dedication of

---

[464] Simon, *A General Theory of Authority*, 32.
[465] Ibid., 24.
[466] Ibid., 24-26.

lives to what is held to be right and good, and in common fidelity to plans for a better society and a better world.[467] We are here reminded of Maritain's beautiful description of this point in a passage which we have already quoted in Part I of this chapter,[468] and with which Simon must have been familiar given that it resonates in his writings.

The Individual Good and the Common Good

The above definition of the common good notwithstanding, we still have to explain its relations with the particular good of the members of society. In other words, how are we to reconcile the common good with particular goods which one might legitimately choose in contingent circumstances, since both Held and Simon accept that such conflicts can arise, and for Simon even in a society of virtuous people?[469]

Simon gives the example of a wife who would be in the right if she did all in her power to save her husband justly condemned to death for a serious crime. Whereas the common good called for capital punishment, her personal good would dictate that she should support her husband.[470] Clarke E. Cochran adds the example of the building of a highway, a common good, which might require that an individual cede some of his private land.[471] The individual concerned here would be right to defend his personal good. In fact Simon says that, *"that particular goods be properly defended by particular persons matters greatly for the common good itself,"*[472] and the emphasis is his.

In working out an answer to the question of conflicts between the particular and the common good, Held proposes the elaboration of an ethical road map to be fleshed out in the future by specialists of moral philosophy. Simon's resolution of the problem is a mosaic that can only be discerned through a close reading of his works. We

---

[467] Simon, *A General Theory of Authority*, 125-126.
[468] See p. 150-151.
[469] Simon, *Philosophy of Democratic Government*, 26.
[470] Ibid., 41-42.
[471] Cochran, "Yves R. Simon and "The Common Good": A Note on the Concept," 233.
[472] Simon, *Philosophy of Democratic Government*, 41.

are convinced it involves a proper working out of the following relationships:

i) The distinction between the individual and the person as the fundamental basis for thinking about the common good;

ii) The relationship between the individual good (interest) and the personal good (or relations within the particular good);

iii) The relationship between the individual good and the common good;

iv) The relationship between the personal good and the common good;

v) The personal good as ethically superior to the common good in matters concerning the supernatural order.

i) The Distinction between the Individual and the Person as the Fundamental Basis for Thinking about the Common Good

Clarke E. Cochran writes that this is an extremely important classical metaphysical distinction which underlies Simon's thinking on the question of the common good. Whereas Simon does not go into a detailed analysis of the distinction in the way that Maritain does, it is clear that he has his friend's work, *The Person and the Common Good*, at the back of his mind. In fact, he specifically cites this work in his article, "Common Good and Common Action."[473] We have already explained in some detail Maritain's metaphysics of the difference between the individual and the person.[474] Simon takes this metaphysics as given.

ii) The Relationship between the Individual Good (Interest) and the Personal Good (or Relations within the Particular Good)

The terms particular good, private good, individual good, and personal good can confuse us if we are not particularly attentive to their use. The particular good may be private or functional

---

[473] Yves R. Simon, "Common Good and Common Action," *Review of Metaphysics* 22 (1960): 202-244. It is a matter of regret that this citation was left out when this article was reprinted as chapter 2 of *A General Theory of Authority*.

[474] See 153-156.

(special).[475] As private it refers to the good of a subject, and as functional to the good of an agency such as the good of the advertising department of a company. The particular good may also be individual or personal. Let us look at this distinction between the individual and personal good in some detail.

When Simon talks of individual goods, he has in mind goods of a material nature such as income, health, and occupation. These are the same as interests. Personal goods on the other hand, refer to the soul and would include rationality, freedom, charity, the life of virtue, and one's relationship to God.[476] This is consonant with and a follow up of Maritain's distinction between the individual and the person. For Simon (as for Maritain), whereas the individual is a member of a species, the person is rational, a distinctive way of being a whole. As rational, the person breaks out from being a mere member of a species and shows himself as possessing virtually limitless possibilities for goodness and an adherence to the truth. The person is autonomous in a way the individual is not and for this reason the individual is a part in a way the person is not.[477]

We would indicate, even though neither Cochran nor Simon actually says so, that this distinction mirrors the distinction of Plato between human goods and divine goods. In the *Laws*, Plato names the human goods in order of importance as health, beauty, strength, and wealth; and the divine goods, which correspond to the cardinal virtues, as wisdom, moderation, justice and courage.[478] Let me add that Plato sees a relationship of dependency between the human goods and the divine goods such that "he who receives the greater (divine) acquires also the less (human), or else he is bereft of both."[479] Simon talks rather, of individual goods being of service to personal goods. Thus, regarding what Simon thinks about priority between individual goods and personal goods, Cochran writes that, "personal

---

[475] Simon, *Philosophy of Democratic Government*, 56.

[476] Cochran, "Yves R. Simon and "The Common Good": A Note on the Concept," 233.

[477] Simon, *A General Theory of Authority*, 67-74.

[478] Plato, *Laws*, 361b-d.

[479] Plato, *Law*, trans. R. G. Bury, Loeb Classical Library (Cambridge: Harvard University Press, 1926), 56.

goods are of higher value than individual goods, for individual goods are essentially means to personal goods."[480]

Simon accepts the principle of subsidiarity, such that for him the pursuit of individual and personal goods should be left to the smallest possible unit, that is, to the individual or the small group and not to the nation as such. This is a demand of the twin principles of autonomy and authority.[481] Simon writes:

> The progress of society and of liberty requires that at every given moment in the evolution of a community the greatest possible number of tasks should be directly managed by individuals and smaller units, the smallest possible number by the greater units.[482]

It should be remarked also that for Simon, whereas people can have divergent individual goods, this is not the case with personal goods since "these have an objective transcendent goal which is full human development and autonomy which is the same for each," and "the full development of one does not detract from the full development of others."[483] Persons, therefore, do not differ as to end but the means which are the goods to this end might differ.

iii) The Relationship between the Individual Good and the Common Good

In the same way as individual goods are supposed to be of service to personal goods, and cede precedence to personal goods, they are called upon to give way to the common good when so demanded by legitimate authority. This is in line with Simon who writes:

> Insofar as the individual has the character of a part, the principle of the primacy of the whole signifies not only that the common good

---

[480] Ibid., 233.

[481] Cochran, "Yves R. Simon and "The Common Good": A Note on the Concept," 235.

[482] Simon, *Philosophy of Democratic Government*, 140.

[483] Cochran, "Yves R. Simon and "The Common Good": A Note on the Concept," 234.

is greater, but also that the private good may have to be sacrificed to the greater good of the community.[484]

The common good which, as Simon shows, includes elements of a spiritual nature, clearly takes pride of place over individual goods which are of a material nature. Even when a common good is material like the provision of roads and portable water, it is still more important than an individual good because a common good is the good of the whole community and thus of a higher value.[485] The person pursuing his individual good must formally interiorize the goods of the society to which he belongs if he will remain a good citizen, and promote them before his own, if there is divergence from his own. Such action, therefore, demands virtue on the part of the individual.

iv) The Relationship between the Personal Good and the Common Good

Simon acknowledges that situations of conflict do arise between personal goods and a common good or the common good. We have already seen the case of a wife who has to defend her husband condemned to death for committing a crime. In this case, it is legitimate for the wife to choose the personal good of her family which is threatened by the proposed execution of her husband because, as Simon says, she wills the common good formally but her personal good materially.[486] That is, she supports the general common good of her society, yet is materially committed to the welfare of her family which is a part of the common good. Elsewhere, Simon gives another example, drawn from the universal dominion of God. He points out, that even if by some special revelation which was absolutely certain, God told me that my father would die tomorrow, it would still be my responsibility to continue to do everything in my power to save his life.[487]

---

[484] Simon, *The Tradition of Natural Law*, 91.

[485] Cochran, "Yves R. Simon and "The Common Good": A Note on the Concept," 233.

[486] Simon, *Philosophy of Democratic Government*, 41-42.

[487] Ibid., 42

Simon argues that even if the common good itself takes precedence formally, it demands that personal goods be defended in this way.[488] But it is not always that the common good takes precedence formally. This is the case when the good in question concerns the supernatural order. Let us see what Simon says about it.

v) The Personal Good as Ethically Superior to the Common Good in Matters Concerning the Supernatural Order

Simon presents a series of poignant quotations from Blaise Pascal (*Pensées*), in which he contrasts the body and the mind. Two examples will suffice to give us his drift:

> All bodies, the firmament, the stars, the earth and its kingdoms, are not equal to the lowest mind; for mind knows all these and itself; and these bodies nothing.
>
> All bodies together, and all minds together, and all their products, are not equal to the least feeling of charity. This is of an order infinitely more exalted.[489]

These two quotations, which refer to the sublimity and exalted nature of the soul and of charity vis-à-vis the material order, lead Simon to the following conclusion:

> What is significant is that Pascal expresses, with his unique power of words, the great metaphysical and ethical truth that all good of a lower order falls short of any good of a higher order, "The good of grace in a single soul is greater than the good of nature in the whole universe" (Sum. Theol. i-ii.113, 9 ad 2). The primacy of the common good holds only so long as the goods under comparison belong to one and the same order, for as Thomas Aquinas and Pascal say, any good of the higher order is greater than the totality of the good that the lower order admits of.[490]

---

[488]Ibid., 41.

[489]Blaise Pascal, *Pensées*, (New York: E.P. Dutton, 1958), 235. See Simon *The Tradition of Natural Law*, 102.

[490] Simon, *The Tradition of Natural Law*, 102.

What this means is that for Simon, "the common good enjoys primacy over the private good of the individual when both are of the same order,"[491] which is in accord with Maritain, who says that just as "the human person, as a spiritual totality referred to the transcendent whole surpasses and is superior to all temporal societies, . . . a single human soul is worth more than the whole universe of material goods."[492]

Drawing the Threads Together

It does seem that for Clarke E. Cochran, Simon's philosophy of the common good as advanced above fails to resolve two questions: aspects of the complicated relationship between the particular good and the common good; and the question as to whether the common good can be captured in a given policy and thus be attainable, or whether it is an ideal and can, therefore, only be aspired to but not achieved.

As far as the first question is concerned, Cochran accepts all that Simon says about the relationship between the particular good and the common good. We have sought to outline the different facets of this relationship above. He returns to the dictum that the fact of persons pursuing their particular goods is necessary for a proper understanding of the common good itself. But he points to the fact that an individual who occupies public office might sometimes have to decide on an issue in which he is an interested party. Simon, he rightly says, works out the following principle to resolve such cases: "As a private person, he must will the common good formally and his own particular good materially. As a public person, he must be concerned with both the form and the matter of the common good."[493] However, the question that arises might be framed thus: Even if as Simon says he must pursue his particular good materially, how far can he go, as a public servant, without the two goods

---

[491] Ibid., 107.
[492] Maritain, *The Person and the Common Good*, 51.
[493] Cochran, "Yves R. Simon and "The Common Good": A Note on the Concept," 235.

colliding or entering into conflict at some point? Cochran thinks that Simon neglects to fully account for a resolution of such inevitable conflicts.

In answer, we would like to suggest that a way out is to be found in what Simon says, in his definition of virtue which we have considered in Chapter 1, specifically, the impossibility, and the futility of trying to legislate for every occasion. Let us recall what Simon says:

> Many people would be happy if they could get a textbook of ethics which would tell them in great detail what to do under all circumstances. But even though it has been tried many times, no such book can ever be written, because the decisive circumstances under which moral judgment has to be uttered are characterized by uniqueness and contingency and an objective response to these circumstances can come only from an appropriate inclination or disposition of the acting subject.[494]

As we have seen, the process of practical wisdom, or what might be called decision-making to use everyday language, presupposes right reason and good will. But it depends also on an indefinite number of other factors besides these formal qualities which one cannot always foresee. The acquisition of the virtues is the best training for action in existentially unique situations. It suffices to have what Simon calls "affective knowledge" and then to leave the application of the virtues, in contingent circumstances, to individuals who are presumed to be virtuous. If they are possessed of moral virtue, they will end up doing the right thing.

Cochran expresses his second concern, a problem which he sees also in Maritain,[495] thus:

> Does Simon consider the common good to be a normative standard by which the life of a political society is to be oriented and judged but which can never be fully actualized, or does he consider it

---

[494] Simon, *The Definition of Moral Virtue*, 97.
[495] Maritain, *Man and the State*, 11-12 & 54. See Cochran, "Yves R. Simon and "The Common Good": A Note on the Concept," 236.

to be a policy or a set of policies or a particular set of social realities which, when actualized, constitute the whole of the common good?[496]

While admitting that Simon generally sees the common good as an ideal to be aimed at, Cochran thinks he fudges and confuses the issue by sometimes referring to common goods being "procured" and "pursued,"[497] implying that they are attainable. The problem here is, I think, more apparent than real since an ideal has to be pursued and can be procured in steps that move progressively towards it, even if it can never be completely attained by human beings who are subject to sin. It can in fact be attained in keeping with the particular circumstances of the moment.

This, in my estimation, is the sum of Simon's resolution of the conundrum posed by Held when she questions whether in unitary conceptions a/the public interest can ever be successfully reconciled with justifiable individual interests. Simon's answer consists in a series of metaphysical distinctions in which—without neglect of the material good—virtue, rationality, the spiritual order, and the good of the soul ultimately triumph. It is a masterful bringing together of the insights of Plato, Aristotle, Thomas Aquinas and Jacques Maritain. It disqualifies the idea of the common good understood either as a coming together of individual interests or ideas (preponderance theories), or as corresponding with the general will, affirming instead the unitary conception, if certain factors, especially the preeminence of ethical values, are given their proper place. This is what Simon means when he says that "every problem relative to the meaning . . . of the common good . . . deserves to be treated with elaborate instruments."[498]

---

[496] Cochran, "Yves R. Simon and "The Common Good": A Note on the Concept," 236.

[497] Simon, *The Tradition of Natural Law*, 91. See Cochran, "Yves R. Simon and "The Common Good": A Note on the Concept," 236.

[498] Simon, *The Tradition of Natural Law*, 105-106.

Chapter 3

Virtue in Public Life: The Virtue of Theoretical Truth and the Virtue of the Ruler and the Ruled

Introduction

In the last chapter, we began the examination of virtue in public life by explaining how it relates to the important question of the common good. Our conclusion was that, for Simon, the common good cannot be understood mainly in terms of material and individual interests. Rather, because of the fact of human personality, it has a strong spiritual and moral component both as reality (normative standard) and project (ideal to be pursued).

After treating of the common good and common action in chapter 2 of *A General Theory of Authority*, Simon informs us at the beginning of chapter 3 (The Search for Truth), that "so far our discussion has been entirely relative to action and practical judgment."[499] In other words, the discussion of the common good is relative to action and concerns practical rather than theoretical cognition. This is how Simon distinguishes the two realms:

> Every practical cognition is designed to answer, directly or indirectly, the questions "What ought we to do?" "What should we have done?" "What shall we do?" The ultimate answer to the practical question is a command. . . . Just as practical cognition is an answer to the question "What ought we to do?", so theoretical cognition is defined as an answer to the question "What are the things?" By definition, any judgment whose perfection consists in conformity to a real state of affairs is theoretical.[500]

---

[499] Simon, *A General Theory of Authority*, 81.
[500] Ibid., 81-82.

The conclusion to a practical judgment is, "do this!" It has the character of a command.[501] As Vukan Kuic says, here "thought and action are fused together in a synthesis of realization."[502]

The conclusion to a theoretical question tells us how the thing is constituted. It answers to the question, "what are the things?" Whereas theoretical cognition signifies primarily contemplation, it might refer to contemplation of practically anything: a picture, an idea, an event etc. Simon makes the point though, that it should be contemplation of a "theoretically relevant" question and not just a "theoretical" question or speculation for its sake such as finding out "the number of pebbles in the bed of a river."[503]

In this chapter, we will continue our exploration of virtue in public life first on a theoretically relevant virtue and then on a practical question. Our reflections, therefore, will take us in the following two different directions:

i) In so far as the virtue of explanatory knowledge or theoretical truth is concerned;

ii) With regard to the virtue of the ruler and the ruled: that is, how and why each party is supposed, in his own way, to do what the common good demands if he is to act virtuously.

This gives us the two parts into which this chapter will be divided. In Part 1, we will look at the truth value of witness, science, and what results from creative freedom. This should lead us to the topical question of whether truth can be tested and confirmed by the market place of ideas as some would have us believe. If, as Simon shows, transcendent truth cannot be shifted out in the market place of ideas because of a deficit in its communicability, what role might authority play in the search for and proclamation of such truth? The answer to this question will close Part 1.

In Part II, still concerned with virtue in public life, but shifting from theoretical to practical cognition, we will look at the

---

[501] Simon, *Practical Knowledge*, 4.
[502] Vukan Kuic, "Yves Simon's Contribution to Political Science," 91.
[503] Simon, *A General Theory of Authority*, 83.

philosophical arguments Simon adduces for the virtue of the ruler. Why is a Machiavellian vision of the ruler inadequate? In addition, since experts sometimes tend to usurp the place of the statesman, we will look at Simon's reasons for opposing this trend. We will close this chapter with the flip side of the virtue of the ruler, namely the call to exercise the virtue of obedience on the part of the ruled. Simon says that obedience, like authority, has been given a negative value. It will be a question of understanding why anyone should obey and why a certain kind of obedience is virtuous.

I: The Virtue of Theoretical Truth

i) The Truth Value of Witness

Simon treats of a number of sources of theoretical truth. Let us begin with that of witness. He says that we tend to regard this source of truth with diffidence and suspicion, probably because "witnesses do not enjoy, in human relations, a position superior to ours."[504] Unlike our leaders, they cannot issue commands to make us accept or refuse what they say. But, according to Simon, the authority of the witness is much more pervasive in scholarly life as in everyday life than we imagine. He points to the fact that society continually uses the authority of one scholar rather than another as model in various disciplines. It is the case that in some fields of study "social influence supports the authority of Descartes and Kant, elsewhere that of Aristotle and St. Thomas, elsewhere that of Hume and Mill, elsewhere that of Karl Marx."[505] He continues:

> Until the beginning of the 19th century, Hippocrates was commissioned by all Western societies to teach medicine to physicians. For more than one century the same societies commissioned Newton to teach physics to physicists. Closer to us, several generations of biologists have been subjected to the teaching authority of the theorists of evolution. In spite of common pronouncements against "the

---

[504]Ibid., 84.
[505]Ibid., 98.

method of authority" modern societies are very anxious to designate the teachers that students and professors will have to listen to.[506]

The fact that this authority has sometimes been misused does not take anything away from its basic value. Its necessity and truth-value should not, therefore, be downplayed. In fact Simon praises the role of witness when it is judiciously used:

> (In order) to realize that it is a thing normal and necessary, it suffices to consider the insuperable difficulties that the choice of a guide would involve if society remained silent. . . The young man does not know where to go and his parents would not be less embarrassed if society did not tell them, through the voice of persons whose dependability it certifies, that in anatomy Grant is better than Aristotle and that in philosophy Plato is better than Herbert Spencer. Throughout his life (every scholar) is confronted with the necessity of trusting those who, on such and such a subject, know more than he does.[507]

Simon gives the example of a theoretical physicist who must accept at face value the conclusions of an experimental physicist and use them in his work.[508] The fact of scientists presuming the correctness of each other's work is common and is based on the fact that life is short and one man cannot be everything at the same time.

This, Simon says, is also true of the facts of history which are unique and unrepeatable. Even when we are helped in our analysis by concrete findings such as artifacts, these are few and far between and the testimony of witnesses is often all that stands between us and complete ignorance. Such testimony helps us achieve certitude, which may be complete or of varying degrees, depending on the credibility of the witnesses.

Since the reason for confidence is the authority of the witness, Simon argues that authority is here used as a substitute for objectivity.

---

[506] Ibid.
[507] Ibid., 99.
[508] Ibid., 85.

Here "the function of authority is substitutional."[509] But the fact of authority playing such a role makes sense since we would otherwise remain in darkness. Simon writes:

> The simple consideration that the role of authority in theoretical matters is entirely substitutional makes it easy to understand both how docility to reliable witnesses proceeds from the love of truth, and how the love of truth stirs an indefatigable eagerness for a cognition in which authority no longer plays any part. If truth is loved, the main thing is to know it. If truth cannot be known obviously, it is good to know it by way of belief. . . . Only those who do not love truth would prefer ignorance to belief, since belief is able to preserve, no matter how imperfectly, the union of the mind with truth.[510]

To further illustrate the importance of witnesses in the search for truth, Simon takes the example of friendship. The ideal friendship is one of common life and common action. But if this, for some reason is impossible, a union in thought and affection can substitute for when common life is again possible.[511]

ii) The Truth Value of Science

The most perfect kind of theoretical knowledge has to do with demonstration. Simon defines demonstration as "a discursive operation designed to show, through the power of obvious principles, that there exists a relation of conformity between the interconceptual synthesis and the real world."[512] Taking as an example a subject S and a property P that belongs to the subject, he continues:

> I have understood the demonstration and I have understood that it holds when I have come to perceive that the object designated by S

---

[509] Yves Simon, *Nature and Functions of Authority* (Milwaukee: Marquette University Press, 1948), 11; See, *A General Theory of Authority*, 93.
[510] Simon, *A General Theory of Authority*, 93-94.
[511]Ibid., 94.
[512]Ibid., 86.

would not be what it is—that it would be both identical with itself and different from itself—if it were not united with the object P. Then the synthesis "S is P" is no longer merely enunciated; it is asserted. It has received the assent of the mind and by this assent has been promoted from a state of weakness and potency to a state of firmness and actuality. Judgment is entirely formed when the mind, by perceiving the truth of a proposition, i.e., its conformity with the real assents to this proposition.[513]

Unlike the truth from the authority of witnesses which can have varying degrees of certitude depending on the credibility of the witnesses, the truth of the demonstrated proposition necessitates assent. It is the triumph of objectivity rather than of authority. Simon implies that this discursive work is the highest form of theoretical knowledge and truth that a man can attain through his efforts. But he throws in two caveats.

1) It should be noted, he says, that while such knowledge has objectivity on its side, this is not the same as exhaustiveness. Simon thinks that this limitation speaks to human nature itself:

> Human knowledge is never exhaustive. In exhaustive knowledge, the object is, from any conceivable or imaginable point of view, identical with the thing known, but in man, the most true, the most thorough, the most exact knowledge never succeeds in conferring the state of object upon more than some aspect of the thing known. No matter how clearly this aspect is attained there remains behind it something that may be designated, with equal propriety, as a transobject or as a mystery and which calls for new acts of cognition and for indefinite progress in an apprehension never equal to the knowability of the thing.[514]

2) The second note of warning concerns the question of objectivity. Simon recalls that there are different forms of objectivity

---

[513]Ibid., 86.
[514]Ibid., 87-88.

which affect both the reality and necessity of the thing known. This means that the thing will be known in different ways depending on whether the subject under consideration is logical or mathematical. Whereas an object which is logical is grounded in reality, the necessity of mathematical conclusions may be postulational.[515]

iii) The Truth Value of Creative Freedom

Simon considers another kind of knowledge, which is current, but which, unlike the above two examples, must disavow all links with truth. It is the creative freedom of the mind which some posit as an alternative to demonstrative knowledge.[516] In order to better explain what he means, Simon contrasts this idea of knowledge with knowledge as understood in mathematics and logic. Beings of reason, which exist thanks to the activity of the mind, may constitute the entire subject matter of logic and may "crowd the science of mathematics," and they may "impose their forms upon the mind," but it still remains that beings that are freely created by the mind such as chimerae and undines "belong to literature" and not to reality.[517] Beings of reason should not displace beings that truly exist.

It is true that all knowledge is constructed piecemeal by adding fact to fact. Simon is, however, adamant that "whenever research ends in a free construction, the theoretical intellect has undergone a setback."[518] If, however, a determinate piece of research continually replaces one postulate by another through the accumulation of knowledge, we are dealing with genuine scientific knowledge and not a free creation of the mind.

Simon explains why some people might want to replace scientific knowledge with what is freely created by the mind. The problem is with our language, which seems to give priority to the object rather than the mind. Our language inclines us to say that the mind is "forced" to assent to the object when it is engaged in the process of knowing things. According to this way of thinking, when the mind is

---

[515]Ibid., 87.
[516]Ibid., 88.
[517] Ibid.
[518]Ibid., 89.

confronted by an object or an axiom, it cannot but assent. Simon points out that putting things this way confuses two kinds of passivity that are completely different from each other: that of material things and that of the soul. When material things are acted upon, they lose some determination and acquire another through the instrumentality of an external agent. In this case we might say the mind is forced to assent.

But this is different from the passivity of the soul which receives "forms and perfections without undergoing concomitant losses."[519] Simon writes:

> There is no constraint in the necessity that obvious truth brings about in the mind, for constraint is a necessity from without and a violence done to the spontaneity of the subject. When the intellect assents to obvious truth, it acts according to what is most intimate in its own nature. *The victory of objectivity is also a victory of intellectual vitality.*[520]

He cites Aristotle's work *De Anima* in support of this position:

> For this reason Aristotle (*On The Soul*, 2.5.41765-8) denies that the knower is changed or altered in any ordinary sense; rather there takes place a development into his true self. Objective knowledge far from being an alienation (alteration) of the knower from his true self, is the only remedy (soteria, 417b2) for the alienation which is ignorance, error, doubt.[521]

Those, therefore, who champion the cause of "pure truth" do so on the basis of a false premise. Even from a pragmatic point of view, Simon adds, it is impossible to live one's life from one day to the next on the basis of what the mind itself creates. The proof of this is that advocates of this theory are prepared to accept and live by the testimony of witnesses in their daily lives.[522]

---

[519]Ibid., 91.
[520]Ibid., 90 (his emphasis).
[521]Ibid., 91.
[522]Ibid., 93-94.

iv) Freedom of the Intellect: The Trouble with the Position of the Liberals

The topic of creative freedom of the mind leads Simon to raise the question of freedom of the intellect in general and the quest for truth as seen especially by what he calls 'liberals.' Simon gives us a definition of liberalism while tracing the links between it and democracy in *Philosophy of Democratic Government*. Before doing this he gives a couple of examples of its manifestation in economic and civil life: the liberal prefers that market forces rather than the government determine the prizes of goods and the amount paid out in wages; he prefers that in matters of public decency everyone be left to decide for themselves rather than a recourse to censorship; he would rather high-ranking persons be treated like everyone before the law.[523] He then describes liberalism as follows:

> A systematic tendency to adopt liberal attitudes evidences *the belief that the good of the social whole, or, as they generally put it, the greatest good of the greatest number, is best procured by the spontaneous operation of elementary energies.*[524]

This means that, basically, liberals detest that their thinking and actions be directed from outside of the person. Classical liberalism takes freedom as primary given originally as a natural right that the social contract ought to protect.

Little wonder, therefore, that liberals should promote freedom of the intellect. Simon indicates that he has no quarrel with freedom of the intellect understood as "the defeat of the forces of error and ignorance, blind traditions and unreasonable fashions, the imperialism of the schools and the arbitrary dogmatism of their programs."[525] If this, and all that works against truth, is what is meant by intellectual freedom, Simon is all for it. So understood, freedom of intellect would transcend the programs of all schools of thought.

---

[523] Simon, *Philosophy of Democratic Government*, 119-122.
[524] Ibid., 122 (his emphasis).
[525] Simon, *A General Theory of Authority*, 100.

But there are movements that militate against freedom of the intellect even as they pretend otherwise. Simon tells us that "in the historical reality of the liberal movements, the freedom of the intellect is the subject of several interpretations."[526] Some are radical and others less so. He distinguishes two groups of radical liberals and names Charles Renouvier (1815-1903)[527] as the founder of the more radical of these two groups. He believes that Charles Renouvier saw as his mission the systematic extension of the domain of voluntary assent. But he pushed it to extremes, and "since necessity is really and logically prior to freedom,"[528] he sought to do away with all rational determination, positing axioms and first principles as objects of free belief.[529]

According to Simon, while only a few adherents hold on to this extremist position, the problem is the extensive influence this theory of "a free dominion over obviousness"[530] has enjoyed. For instance, in the field of mathematics, "the term axiom, which used to convey the inflexible necessity and absolute primacy of the self-evident propositions, has come to be taken as a mere synonym of postulate."[531] He continues as follows:

> From the point of view of the history of culture, what is decisive is that the idea of a *choice* among principles, of a human initiative in matters of first premises, of a *control* over primary determinations, is active precisely in the area which, for so many centuries, has been reputed to supply the ideal pattern of determination by objective evidence.... It is easy to detect, in the common discussion of the most important subjects, the underlying theory that, since the first premises of mathematics from being axioms have become postulates, there can be no domain of thought where principles escape the condition of mere

---

[526]Ibid., 101.
[527]Ibid., 102.
[528] Ibid.
[529] Ibid.
[530] Ibid.
[531]Ibid., 103.

assumptions selected by the human mind with some degree of arbitrariness.[532]

Simon mentions a second tendency in liberalism which connects it with agnosticism. Those who make this link draw inspiration from Auguste Comte, the father of positivism.[533] Pushing to the side the main thrust of Comte's work, they are more interested in his efforts to free man from any reference to the transcendent and dependence on the absolute. They also downplay the possibility of theology and metaphysics as important fields of study. They thus divide knowledge into the *positive* system, which is that of experience organized by logic, and the *transcendent* system which is beyond experimental verification.[534]

Whereas the positive system and its usages are held in high esteem, this is not the case with the transcendent system. Simon points out that "any assent to transcendent propositions is treated with disdain, as if it were expressive of intellectual debasement."[535] Any reference to the absolute as the guide for living is seen as the worst servitude.

But agnostic liberalism cannot be logical since as soon as one begins to define it with exactitude cracks immediately appear. Simon writes:

> The transcendent system comprises all propositions relative to the divine mysteries and the mysterious history of the relations between God and man. It comprises propositions relative to metaphysical objects, such as the first cause of the world and its last end. Consistency would require that it comprise also the great epistemological problems, e.g., the relation of universal ideas to reality and the significance of scientific theories—but then science would prove impossible. It should also comprise the supreme principles of morality, viz., views relative to

---

[532]Ibid (his emphasis).
[533]Ibid., 104.
[534]Ibid., 104-105.
[535]Ibid., 105.

human destiny, to the meaning of human life, to genuine happiness, to the origin of obligation, etc.—but then would ethics still be possible?[536]

Having given a sketch of these two branches of liberalism, Simon gives the common denominator that brings them together as far as intellectual freedom is concerned in terms of a "sociological agnosticism."[537] He points out that everyone agrees, without even giving it a second thought that society can and should legislate on a number of issues regarding its welfare such as marriage, property rights, and vaccinations to control infectious diseases, etc. While people might question a particular piece of legislation for the prevention of road accidents or certain provisions in a contract, no one questions society's right to legislate on such matters. The paradox, he says, is that "on the contrary, society is commonly denied the right to have ideas in transcendent matters. It is often denied the right to take stands on metaphysical issues and on issues pertaining to the ultimate vindication of legal and ethical rules. The transcendent system "is held to be the domain of private conscience and of the spiritual power if there is such a thing."[538]

This "sociological agnosticism" leads Simon to circumscribe the liberal in relation to freedom of thought in this way.

> Whoever holds that society must refrain from any act relative to transcendent truth, and that the search for such truth must be neither directed nor helped in any way by society, is a liberal. And whoever holds that society normally should be concerned with transcendent truths, or some of them, has rejected the liberal notion of intellectual freedom.[539]

---

[536]Ibid., 105-106.

[537] In the *Philosophy of Democratic Government* (119-122), Simon deals with liberalism within the state as such and characterizes it as "the belief that the good of the social whole is best procured by the spontaneous operation of elementary energies." (122) What this means is that the market be allowed to take care of itself. This question is treated immediately after.

[538] Simon, *A General Theory of Authority*, 107-108.

[539]Ibid., 108-109.

Simon articulates the justification given by liberals which on the surface appears reasonable. They argue that society is made up of a motley collection of people with diverse beliefs. If one disagrees with his Church one can look for another one. But this is not the case with the society in which one lives and which one cannot leave at will. It is, therefore, necessary for society to choose the least common denominator with which all can agree. This means that positive truths which are immediately demonstrable have the upper-hand vis-à-vis transcendent truths, which are a source of continuous and strong disagreements.

Simon asserts a link between the argument for giving priority to positive rather than transcendental truths and the more general problem of the communication or "intersubjectivability"[540] of truth. He writes:

> Whereas the conditions required for the understanding of mathematics and biology seem to be well assured by our schools and other learned organizations, the conditions necessary to understand the most fundamental theories of metaphysics have never been commonly satisfied in any society.[541]

Simon shows that positive truths are easier to communicate *de jure* and *de facto* than transcendent ones which are only so *de jure*.[542] This is the case because positive thinking is particularist in a way that philosophy cannot be. For instance, positive truths leave out of consideration the qualitative aspects of things preferring to concentrate on what is measurable. In the ethical domain things cannot be calculated just in terms of their economic value. In *Nature and Functions of Authority*, Simon gives the example of a family man who has to decide whether to take his family on summer vacation to

---

[540] Simon often uses the awkward word "intersubjectivability in his *Nature and Functions of Authority* (17-19; 59-60), but replaces it later by the simpler term "communication."

[541] Simon, *A General Theory of Authority*, 112; See *Nature and Functions of Authority*, 17.

[542] Simon, *A General Theory of Authority*, 115. See, *Philosophy of Democratic Government*, 20-21.

the mountains or by the seashore. The state of his finances will certainly come into play but other unquantifiable factors, such as the health of his family, must also be considered.[543]

Positive truth will more easily make itself known because of its communicability. The problem is that not only is this factor lacking as far as transcendent truth is concerned and in philosophy, but rather "the powers at work in the processes of communication do not give truth any promise of help."[544] The situation can even sometimes be worse since, according to Simon, "the proliferation of philosophic theories is often determined, more or less consciously, by the desire to ease situations which would remain intolerably difficult if no alternative were offered to the ways of truth."[545] In addition, many hold that there is no such thing as philosophic truth, and the function of philosophy is seen as not the search for truth but the stimulation of the mind.[546] This explains the fact that though some philosophy schools are better than others they do not necessarily receive any public recognition. Clearly as far as the transcendent is concerned, truth will not take care of itself in the market, because though *de jure* communicable, *de facto* this communicability is often limited to "a group of kindred minds."[547] In *The Tradition of Natural Law*, where Simon again talks of truth being limited to "kindred minds," he speaks in terms of contingent events influencing our ability to know. He gives the example of a plant whose growth is determined by such contingent factors as the nature of the soil, the amount of rainfall, the presence of insects that might destroy some of the leaves,[548] and concludes as follows:

> The popular belief—shared by a great variety of philosophical thinkers—that a genuinely demonstrated consensus is perfect evidence of failure to attain demonstrativeness, ignores the unpleasant fact that contingency affects intellectual life as certainly as it does the growth of

---

[543] Simon, *Nature and Functions of Authority*, 22.
[544] Ibid., 120; *Philosophy of Democratic Government*, 271-272.
[545] Simon, *A General Theory of Authority*, 120-121.
[546] Ibid., 121.
[547] Ibid., 100, 113; *Philosophy of Democratic Government*, 20.
[548] Simon, *The Tradition of Natural Law*, 55-56.

plants in our forests and in our cultivated fields. There are departments of knowledge where demonstration, no matter how flawless, is unlikely to entail factual agreement except within small circles of kindred minds.[549]

It is in this context that we are to understand the objections of Simon to the position of Justice Oliver Wendell Holmes (1841-1935), a moral skeptic, who would have truth decided by the market place of ideas. Since Holmes remains one of the most cited and influential U.S. Supreme Court justices in recent times, it would help our understanding to give a little background to him and his ideas in order to understand what he says and Simon's reaction to it.

Holmes, who was an Associate Justice of the Supreme Court from 1902-1932, developed his views consequent on the pragmatism and social Darwinism that dominated intellectual life after the American Civil War. He then transferred these 'scientific' attitudes to morality and the law which he studied in Harvard. After defining morality as "a body of imperfect social generalizations expressed in terms of emotion,"[550] and denying the existence of natural law, he wanted to eradicate both from judicial reasoning. Legal decisions should be taken with a view to the practical effects of such decisions and the needs of the time.

Holmes was thus led to debunk the quest of the philosophers for absolute truth, suggesting that truth is a function of the outcome of our endeavors. For instance he says of World War 1:

> I used to say, when I was young, that truth was the majority vote of that nation that could lick all others. Certainly we may expect that the received opinion about the . . . [First World] war will depend a good deal upon which side wins (I hope with all my soul it will be mine), and I think that the statement was correct in so far as it implied that our

---

[549]Ibid., 64.
[550] Oliver Wendell Holmes, "Ideals and Doubts," *Illinois Law Review* 10 (1915): 3.

test of truth is a reference to either a present or an imagined future majority in favor of our view.[551]

Holmes transferred this thinking to other spheres of life such as the economic sphere writing the piece that Simon uses in his work about ideas being true by getting themselves accepted "in the competition of the market," in his dissent to a judgment argued on October 21 and 22, 1919, in the case of Abrams v United States. The case concerned five defendants charged with printing and publishing anti-U.S. leaflets during the First World War in violation of the provisions of the Espionage Act of Congress of June 15, 1917. In his dissenting position following their conviction Holmes writes:

> The ultimate good desired is better reached by free trade in ideas . . . The best test of truth is the power of the thought to get itself accepted in the competition of the market.[552]

Simon's explanation of the difficulty in the de facto communicability of transcendent truths shows the inaccuracy of the reasoning of Justice Holmes. Let us explore the issue a little further in the next question concerning truth and the market place of ideas.

v) Truth and the Market Place of Ideas

In addition to the above explanation as to why Justice Holmes is mistaken, Simon subjects his dictum to a rigorous philosophical examination. He refers to Aristotle, since he thinks that an examination of the conditions for the spontaneous production of order will resolve the problem at the philosophical level. While order sometimes results from disorder, the question is how this happens. For an answer, Simon uses Aristotle's treatment of chance in the *Physics*.[553] Aristotle distinguishes two kinds of chance for which he

---

[551] Oliver Wendell Holmes, "Natural Law," *Harvard Law Review* 32 (1918): 40.

[552] Oliver Wendell Holmes, *The Essential Holmes: Selections form the Letters, Speeches, Judicial Opinions, and Other Writings of Oliver Wendell Holmes*, ed. Richard A. Posner (Chicago: The University of Chicago Press, 1992), 320. (Holmes, Abrams v. United States, List of United States Supreme Court Cases, volume 250, n. 616 (1919)).

[553] Simon, *A General Theory of Authority*, 116-117; Aristotle, *Physics* 2.4-6.

uses two different words. There is the chance event (*automaton*) which results from the obviously unintended actions of a non-rational cause and the chance event (*tyche*) which results from the unintended actions of a rational cause. These, Simon tells us, are rendered in Latin by the words *casus* and *fortuna*. It is the former that concerns us here since our subject is the market place of ideas.

In order to get to the heart of the matter, Simon uses the example of a box with black and white balls in it. Continually shaking the box might at some point result in all the black balls going to one side and all the white balls to the other.[554] So understood, things can take care of themselves spontaneously. However, this is a random event that happens by accident. Simon writes:

> The end-like event which happens automatically has no ground in any essential unity: accordingly it is a rare occurrence.[555] A desperate person may jump out of the window precisely at the time when a truck loaded with mattresses passes by. The landing is smooth, but this should not be expected to happen twice.[556]

The person falling on the mattress, as well as the black and white balls congregating by themselves are fortuitous happenings which result from accidental rather than essential causes and do not prove any law of statistical regularity.[557] It should be remarked that this is true of economic affairs as well. Even if the liberal mind is confident that order will spontaneously result from disorder in economic affairs, and that truth will impose itself and defeat error, this is not necessarily the case because order cannot result from disorder as a necessary and consistent cause.[558] This is Simon's conclusion from Aristotle's analysis in the *Physics*.

---

[554] Simon, *A General Theory of Authority*, 117.
[555] Aristotle, *Physics* 2.8.198b34.
[556] Simon, *A General Theory of Authority*, 116.
[557] Ibid., 117.
[558] Simon, *Philosophy of Democratic Government*, 5-6.

In Aristotle's analysis, which deals with an individual occurrence, factual order comes into existence casually, that is, by an accidental concourse of related causes. This factual order is not traceable to any essential cause, no matter how far we carry the regression. . . . Order alone can be the essential cause of order. If an effect is statistically regular, the disorder out of which it emerges cannot be initial. For instance, the ability of truth "to get itself accepted in the competition of the market" must have a cause antecedent to the set of random events made up of men's opinions, inclinations, traditions and prejudices, objections and replies, occasional pieces of valid information and occasional errors.[559]

Thus while truth may take care of itself in one or two chance cases, this could never be posited as a general principle. When truth does emerge in a human community, it will have been caused by certain intellectual forces and activities that are responsible for it and that can be identified.

vi) The Role of Authority in Teaching Transcendent Truth

Transcendent truth, therefore, needs to be given support. But how should this be done and by whom? Should it be done by the spiritual power alone, or by the state, or both? A good number of people argue that spiritual and transcendent matters should be the concern of the spiritual power alone such as the Church. According to this thinking, the role of the state is to protect human life against evil people, enforce respect for property, make laws about family life and generally be concerned with the smooth running of society. Simon argues that this is inadequate, pointing out that the massacre of millions in our times in various countries shows that the police can be persuaded to collaborate in the perpetration of evil. That is why, "if society wants to protect human life effectively, it must be concerned not only with external behavior, but also with the thoughts of men . . . the deepest ones not excluded."[560] Temporal society cannot renounce all concern with the beliefs in people's hearts. This

---

[559] Simon, *A General Theory of Authority*, 118-119.
[560] Ibid., 124.

explains why a radical preacher inciting violence is usually called to order. That is also the reason why society intervenes directly in the ethics of marriage. "Thus we are led to understand that the principal act of the social life is immanent in the souls of men. It (society) is a communion in some belief, love, or aversion."[561] If human beings are not joined together in their souls, there is no community or society. Society cannot limit its common life to the positive system without concern as to what gives its actions meaning and cohesion, in other words, their justification.[562]

But beyond this general statement of principle, Simon admits that the role of the temporal power in promoting transcendent truths is an extremely difficult question to handle when it comes down to specifics. This is so because of the abuses to which history is witness when the secular power has tried to regulate transcendent matters. These abuses include censorship, persecution, propaganda in scholarly work, syllabi that avoid questions deemed to be embarrassing, and similar issues. In a long and telling footnote on the question, it becomes clear that one of the problems Simon seeks to avoid is that of a state religion which might pervert freedom of thought. He accuses rulers of using religion in the 19th century to reinforce and support the status quo. He says:

> In several parts of the Christian world, it has been taken for granted—most of the time, silently—that the purpose of religion is to give men the additional energy needed to achieve moral decency. Accordingly, whenever temporal society gave religious belief and practice any kind of support, it was principally in view of preserving discipline in civilian and military life, honesty in economic and other transactions, the resignation of the poor and the benevolence of the rich, and some stability in family relations. All these are worthy achievements, indeed, but they belong to the moral order, which is by essence inferior and subordinated to the theological order. In many cases, peoples would rather tolerate dire privations than conspicuous absurdities. The irritating experience of reversed finality, the all-

---

[561] Ibid., 125.
[562] Ibid., 125-127.

pervading feeling that the things of eternal and divine life were valued, principally or exclusively, for the sake of things temporal, did much to shape the contemporary notion of the secular state and to develop in various peoples an impassionate determination to keep the state secular.... Believers are constantly irked by the realization that things are moving backwards, that the loftier is there to serve the less lofty, that the theological is treated as an instrument for the perfection of the moral, that the divine is subordinated to the human, the eternal to the temporal, and that ultimately the truth of religious belief is considered an issue of secondary importance.[563]

If the state is given a key role in transcendent matters, there is the added problem of what to do with dissenters[564] or those of a religion different from that of the state. At the time when Simon wrote the above thoughts, the havoc caused by states run under Islamic or sharia law was not as glaring as it is today. This shows how good his instincts were, and how right he was that the role of the state in matters of transcendent truth be circumscribed.

He thus, gives the civil power a very limited role in transcendent matters, and one may summarize his brief suggestions in two points.

1) The virtue of prudence will come into play in deciding which questions of transcendent truth the state might gainfully be interested in and how they might be tackled. This is because, as already stated a number of times in this work, moral philosophy does not deal with contingency but prudence does.

2) Simon then makes a distinction between the state and civil or temporal society[565] (earlier in his works he often treated them as synonymous, as in his definition of civil society in *Philosophy of Democratic Government*.[566]) He proceeds to argue that issues of transcendent truth should be handled by civil society rather than by the state. The reason for this is that whereas the state tends to be

---

[563]Ibid., 130-131.
[564]Ibid., 130.
[565]Ibid., 129.
[566] Simon, *Philosophy of Democratic Government*, 67.

more mechanical, and bureaucratic in its management of affairs, temporal society is suppler in dealing with such issues. The spiritual needs to be handled in a supple and subtle manner because it deals with questions that are vital. He says:

> Briefly, the loftier a function, the more strongly it demands to be exercised according to the ways of life, and the less it admits of bureaucratic management. As already said . . . promoting the order of truth in the social life of the transcendent intellect is the highest function of the civil community. It is not a function which admits of bureaucratic methods. It calls for the actualization of what is most vital in society. From this consideration it may follow that problems of truth often call for a sharp distinction between the state and the civil, or temporal, society—a distinction which we have not been using so far. When a function is directly exercised by the state, according to the ways which are those of any governing apparatus, it is inevitably exposed to what is damaging in bureaucracy.[567]

The state is too blunt an instrument to take care of transcendent matters, but since it cannot leave them out of its purview completely, its role is indirect. Simon sees this role as supporting, with the help of practical wisdom, the best among those organs which deal directly with such questions.[568]

II: The Virtue of the Ruler and the Ruled

i) Rule by the Virtuous

In the second part of this chapter, we will examine a special role that Simon accords to authority, a role that is related to the acquisition and practice of virtue. This function of authority must be distinguished from two other functions that he attributes to authority in his political philosophy.

These are his distinction between substitutive and essential authority, which constitute one of Simon's most important and well

---

[567] Simon, *A General Theory of Authority*, 129
[568] Ibid., 130-131.

known contribution to philosophy. Substitutive authority is based on a deficiency in the person or persons subject to it; such persons are, for example, immature, weak, incompetent, or vicious; they need someone to guide them in their actions. Here, the authority of someone else substitutes or makes up for their inability. Essential authority, in contrast, is based not on deficiency but on plenitude: the "subjects" are talented and proficient, but they need to be coordinated in their common effort, and so an authority must be established over them to decide how they are to work together and how their effort is to be embodied.[569] We mention these two functions of authority here in summary fashion as they have not been our main concern in this work.

In *A General Theory of Authority*, however, Simon introduces a third task for authority, which he calls its perfective character.[570] It deals with the way authority communicates excellence or virtue. In this regard, Simon places the communication of virtue from the ruler to the ruled at two levels, both of which demand that the ruler be virtuous.

The first is at the "strictly equalitarian"[571] level where the ruler passes on virtue by way of his individual "example, love and friendship."[572] As to how in general, "example, love, and friendship" communicate excellence, Simon says:

> In the case of example, action is traceable to the sheer power of attractive patterns. In the case of love, the pattern of better action receives additional potency from the desire of the lover that the beloved should be moving at all times toward higher achievements and more complete happiness. When there is reciprocity in love as friendship requires, the person who gives also expects, though disinterestedly, to receive.[573]

---

[569] Simon, *The Philosophy Of Democratic Government*, 9-10; 19-30; 59-62; 70, 129; 140-41. *A General Theory of Authority*, 20-22; 47-50; 133-42.
[570] Ibid., 136.
[571] Ibid., 134.
[572] Ibid., 135.
[573] Ibid., 135.

The second method of communication of virtue concerns the ruler who as ruler has to decide the matter and form of the common good. In this regard Simon writes:

> Here, over and above whatever is done by example, love, and friendship, the communication of excellence follows a way proper to authority, for the greater excellence of the able leader consists in his adequate relation to the common good, and it is precisely this relation which is communicated in the act of taking orders.[574]

Let us now examine each of these two in greater detail.

Regarding the first point, Simon explains that even if it may not seem to be so, people have, from the earliest of times, always wanted the running of their affairs to be taken care of by the most able. As Simon observes, most people obviously dislike the idea of being ruled by criminals and evil people, and keeping criminals from power is seen as a huge blessing.[575] Simon points to the fact that even when rulers were chosen through hereditary mechanisms, such as kings, nations fabricated "myths needed to represent the men designated by birth as excellently qualified for leadership."[576] Whereas these myths might belong to the past, Simon points out that their popularity in our times "demonstrates that the ideal of having society ruled by the best persons is not easily given up."[577]

It would be irrelevant, he says, to argue that no state actually achieves this standard since that does not take away from the ideal. People generally expect that those who lead them should surpass them in virtue and wisdom and to have such a leader is a fulfilling and gratifying experience.[578] This is what grounds love and friendship in a state. It is also the ground for the obedience of the governed, as we will show later in this chapter.

---

[574]Ibid., 145.
[575]Ibid., 137; See *Philosophy of Democratic Government*, 83-84.
[576]Ibid., 136-137.
[577]Ibid., 137.
[578]Ibid., 143.

This brings us to the second method by which virtue is communicated. Simon says that nowadays democracy is generally exercised in one of two ways: either by direct democracy or by representative government. Rule by direct democracy is a rare occurrence which happens, for instance, in a referendum, or when a small group meets regularly to take decisions about their county "as in New England towns and some Swiss cantons."[579] Simon argues that those who opt for direct democracy do so for one of two reasons. They might hold that "no selected person or group of persons can be so wise as the majority," or they might do so because it affords "clarity, stability, the avoidance of intrigues, the balance of social forces, general satisfaction and peace."[580] Both explanations, according to Simon, go beyond the substitutional and essential functions of authority and evoke its perfective function.[581] Thus even here the perfective function of authority is at work.

But people generally prefer representative government or a rule through a distinct governing personnel. Simon gives the reason for this preference. He says:

> The most obvious reason for this preference is the belief that politics is no exception to the law of proficiency through division of labor and specialization. All other things being equal, public affairs will be better run by people who have a particular inclination and a particular preparation for political leadership and who, after a while, are possessed of an experience in public affairs that other citizens cannot claim.[582]

The question that provokes disagreements, however, regards the kind of person who should run the affairs of the community. What is the kind of excellence that these persons should possess: virtue or purely technical expertise? Simon writes that "divergences are great, both among laymen and among philosophers, with regard to the kind

---

[579] Simon, *Philosophy of Democratic Government*, 149.
[580] Simon, *A General Theory of Authority*, 136.
[581] Ibid.
[582] Ibid., 139.

of excellence expected of statesmen."[583] According to Simon, the question arises because of the attitude of modern and contemporary philosophy to politics. He writes:

> Politics is often treated as if it were an art, and, accordingly, a thing foreign to morality; the political job could be done well by a morally bad man, just as a great painter may be a person of debased character. Many would even go as far as to hold that statesmen have got to do things that virtuous persons hate to do, so that power should better be in the hands of men not too particular about the morality of their means.[584]

Whereas Simon does not actually name any philosophers who defend this position, we would point to Niccolo Machiavelli (1469-1527) as one of its foremost advocates. Machiavelli reveals the origin of his quarrel with the classical view of virtue in politics in these words:

> And many have imagined republics and principalities that have never been seen or known to exist in truth; for it is so far from how one lives to how one should live that he who lets go of what is done for what should be done learns his ruin rather than his preservation. For a man who wants to make a profession of good in all regards must come to ruin among so many who are not good.[585]

For him virtues and vices, as well as whether a ruler should be concerned about praise and blame are irrelevant. The one yardstick for judging an act or its omission is whether or not it promotes the security of the state and the prince who rules. After enumerating a number of qualities which are generally held to be good, such as liberality, trustworthiness, and showing mercy to others, Machiavelli

---

[583] Ibid.
[584] Ibid.
[585] Niccolo Machiavelli, *The Prince*, trans. Harvey C. Mansfield (Chicago: University of Chicago Press, 1980), 61.

brings it all under the perspective of what is useful for the state when he says:

> And I know that everyone will confess that it would be a very praiseworthy thing to find in a prince all the above-mentioned qualities that are held to be good. But because he cannot have them, nor honestly observe them, since human conditions do not permit it, it is necessary for him to be so prudent as to know how to avoid the infamy of those vices that would take his state away from him. . . . And furthermore one should not care about incurring the infamy of those vices without which it is difficult to save one's state; for if one considers everything well, one will find something appears to be virtue, which if pursued would be one's ruin, and something else appears to be vice which if pursued results in one's security and well-being.[586]

Simon mentions another, more contemporary variant of the Machiavellian thesis, which, following Locke and the liberals, holds that morality or ethics is a private affair and should not be introduced into the running of the state. This, Simon says, is "the myth of the irreducible conflict between the ethics of man and the ethics of the state."[587] We might express the two inter-related questions thus: Are virtue and morality foreign to politics? And, Are virtue and morality a private affair?

Simon disposes of the claim that there is a dichotomy between ethics and politics by remarking, as a first argument in favor of the need for virtue in those who govern, that it "goes directly against the doctrine of the Greek philosophers who founded political science and philosophy."[588] He points to the fact that "Aristotle's ethics is political and his politics is ethical."[589] Simon does not go into any detail in support of the above assertion, but we might point to the fact that in the *Politics*, the greater part of Book III is taken up with a classification of states by the number of the rulers of each—one, few,

---

[586]Ibid., 62.
[587] Simon, *A General Theory of Authority*, 141.
[588]Ibid., 139.
[589] Ibid.

or several (III.7), and an enquiry into which of these is the best. Aristotle distinguishes six forms of government, namely monarchy, aristocracy, republic, tyranny, oligarchy, and democracy. His conclusion is that the last three are bad because they represent rule for the interest of one, a few or the mob, rather than rule for the common good. The first three are good. A republic is rule by laws, but the best state is an aristocracy or a monarchy, the choice between the two depending on the virtue or character of the citizens. If there is only one person of outstanding virtue he should be king and rule (13.1284b25-34), but if there are many, aristocracy is preferable (15.1286b3-7). Ruler-ship is an honor which should be exercised by those who merit it.

We can add another example from Book VI of the *Nicomachean Ethics* where, in discussing practical wisdom (*phronēsis*), Aristotle ascribes it to those like Pericles who look after households and are statesmen, for they understand what is good for themselves and for mankind (6.5.1140b7-11). Even if common opinion distinguishes four kinds of practical wisdom—that which enables one to decide what is best for oneself, that which helps one govern his household, that which is beneficial for a litigant in a court case, and that which one needs to rule the *polis*—Aristotle says that the last is the best.[590]

Simon's second argument for the need for virtue in the governing personnel makes use of the philosophical distinction he articulates in *The Definition of Moral Virtue*[591] between the good state of a thing such as a piano (nature) and the particular and human use into which it is put.[592] In *A General Theory of Authority*, he takes the example of a good painter who, for a variety of reasons, might decide to paint a good work of art, or a poor one, or none at all. He is a good painter, but it is the use to which he puts his talent that makes the difference. Simon points out that "any quality concerned with the good use of man's abilities is ethical by essence."[593] He refers to the saying from Aristotle's *Nicomachean Ethics* that "while there is such a thing as

---

[590] Aristotle, *Nicomachean Ethics*, 8.1142a9-10.
[591] Simon, *The Definition of Moral Virtue*, 20-29.
[592] Ibid., 33-37.
[593] Simon, *A General Theory of Authority*, 140.

excellence (virtue) of art, there is no such thing as excellence (virtue) of practical wisdom (prudence)"[594] and then proceeds to offer the following commentary on the phrase:

> From the context, this concise sentence means: one who is possessed of an art still needs a virtue—in order to make a good use of his art—but one who is possessed of prudence does not need a distinct virtue to make a good use of it, for prudence is a virtue and procures the good use of itself.[595]

Simon transfers this reasoning from the painter to the statesman and shows what happens when a statesman is seen as a mere artist or technician. He writes:

> If the statesman is, by hypothesis, an artist or a technician, there must be above him, a wise person in charge of all questions relative to use. But the *statesman* for Aristotle *is precisely this wise person*. Any description of the political leader as a technician merely serves to postpone the analysis of the main issue; a time comes when we have to consider the qualifications required for the *right use* of all the technical instruments which happen to be of relevance in political life. Then and only then we begin to study statesmanship. Thus the excellence required for political government is not of the particular, but of the *human* description. It is the highest degree of excellence in the order of things merely human.[596]

But ultimately, and this is the decisive argument, the metaphysics that demands that leaders be upright and wise has to do with a consideration of the responsibility for the matter and form of the common good with which leaders are charged by virtue of assuming rule. This brings us back to a subject mentioned briefly in our consideration of the common good in chapter 2.

---

[594] Aristotle, *Nicomachean Ethics* trans. W.D. Ross in *The Basic Works of Aristotle* ed. Richard McKeon, 1027. (6.5.1140b21).
[595] Simon, *A General Theory of Authority*, 140.
[596] Ibid., 140-141 (his emphasis).

As we saw in the last chapter, Simon claims that it is philosophically inadequate to define the common good in terms of private interests.[597] He also claims that virtue makes people capable of understanding and also willing the common good. "That virtuous people, as a proper effect of their very virtue, love the common good and subordinate their choices to its requirements is an entirely unquestionable proposition."[598] Thus the good citizen must adhere to the common good understood as what is done in common and for the good of all. The problem is to ascertain whether the virtue of the private individual concerns the whole of the common good or some aspect of it. Simon answers that the private person adheres to the *form* and not to the *matter* of the common good and this is a demand of the common good itself since "he should not be asked to take one more step and, all by himself, to will *what the common good demands. This he could not do without impairing all the perfections connected with the preservation of the particular capacity.*"[599] Simon puts the above quote in italics for emphasis and it should be noted that it is a restatement of the same idea which he again puts in italics in the *Philosophy of Democratic Government* to which we have already referred.[600] Simon considers this principle so important that he calls it "the keystone of the whole theory"[601] of the common good.

---

[597] See 205-215; 233-238.

[598] Simon, *Philosophy of Democratic Government*, 39.

[599] Ibid., 143.

[600] This quote is found above on page 123 of this book and on page 41 of the *Philosophy of Democratic Government*. James V. Schall S.J. points out that in articulating this principle, Simon draws on the Aristotelian axiom which says that for the whole to be the whole the parts have to be the parts. Schall continues: "The only way the parts could be what they are, something that was itself necessary for the common good, would be for these parts to be defended and promoted by their own authority. Both the parts and the whole will the common good, but the parts are too busy taking care of their own goods to worry about the specifics of the common good. Authority's most essential function is to allow the parts to be the parts all the while seeking to decide the particular compromises or limits that must be made in order that other parts continue and flourish in themselves and within the whole." (James V. Schall S.J., "On the Most Mysterious of the Virtues: The Political and Philosophical Meaning of Obedience in St. Thomas, Rousseau, and Yves Simon," *Gregorianum* 79 (1998): 751-752.

[601] Simon, *Philosophy of Democratic Government*, 51.

It is for the competent authority, not for the individual, to determine the matter of the common good. In the *Philosophy of Democratic Government*, Simon takes as an example going to war in the defense of the state. He writes:

> A commanding officer is ordered to hold a certain position at all costs. . . . We suppose that his will is entirely good. As a good soldier and a good citizen, he wants and intends the common good of the whole nation at war, viz., victory. It is in relation to the common good of the nation that he aims at this particular good, viz., the holding of this position. Without such subordination of purposes he would not be a good citizen. A mercenary or an adventurer might pledge himself to hold a place without caring who wins the war, but not a soldier. Thus the particular good—holding the place—is willed because of the common good, on the ground of the common good, under a determination supplied by the common good. In other words, there is, as a proper effect of civic virtue, volition and intention of the common good formally understood.[602]

Holding a particular military position belongs to the matter of the common good and winning the war belongs to the form of the common good. Thus the individual wills the common good formally and accepts a material and concrete expression of it dictated by the competent authority because he wills the common good formally. It is this reasoning that grounds the following conclusion regarding the role of authority in the volition and intention of the matter and form of the common good:

> As long as the intended achievement is personal, all takes place within the person. Only one capacity is involved. But two capacities are at work in the bringing about of the common good: individual good will procures the right form, authority determines the right matter. And thus it is only by the operation of authority that the person enjoys the

---

[602]Ibid., 42-43.

benefit of an orderly relation to the common good understood both with regard to form and with regard to matter.[603]

Simon then connects this conclusion to the need for virtue among those who rule, since rulers have to choose both the form of the common good (to which individual citizens adhere) and the matter of the common good.[604] Without virtue, the ruler would not be able to choose wisely whether a particular war should be fought (form) and where to deploy a given unit (matter). Elsewhere, he gives an example of a society which is in the process of morphological and technological change, a change which has rendered obsolete the old ways of wealth distribution. In other to enact wise laws which will ensure a just distribution of the goods of society, and thus protect the common good, the leader needs the virtue of prudence. If he is not well versed in some of the social sciences, the virtue of prudence

---

[603] Simon *A General Theory of Authority*, 144-145. Using the example of a school faculty, and on the basis of Simon's summary in *Philosophy of Democratic Government* (48), Vukan Kuic gives a beautiful rendition of Simon's meaning in a number of propositions. Here they are:

1. Mature citizenship (Simon says "virtue") includes willingness to subordinate one's own interests to the good of society (e.g., ideal faculty are loyal to their school).

2. The good of society may be intended formally without being intended materially (e.g., loyalty is not the same as commitment to a specific curriculum).

3. Mature citizenship guarantees the intention of the common good formally considered, not the intention of the common good materially considered (e.g., there is nothing wrong with the Latin teacher's loyalty [to the school] despite his strong advocacy of his subject).

4. Society would be harmed if everyone intended the common good not only formally but also materially; in a material sense, particular persons ought to intend particular goods (e.g., society cannot afford too many members like the teacher of Mathematics, minding the public business rather than his own).

5. The intention of the good of society materially considered, is the business of a public reason and a public will (e.g., the whole faculty acting as the governing board of the school).

6. The intention of the good of society by the public reason and will necessarily develops into a *direction* of society, by the public reason and will, toward that good considered not only formally but also materially; which is the same as to say that the intention of the good of society, materially considered, demands the operation of authority. (Vukan Kuic, "Simon's Contribution to Political Science," 77).

[604] Simon, *A General Theory of Authority*, 145.

might require that he take into account the consultation of specialists in economics, history, and sociology. But after finding and consulting the right experts, it remains his prerogative to take the prudential decisions required, since arriving at the right decisions regarding the matter of the common good demands not just technical expertise but righteous inclination. The individual citizen who already wills the form of the common good allows authority to choose its content (matter)—just as it chooses the particular military post to be defended during war in the quest for victory—and this demands wisdom and prudence on the part of the ruler.[605]

When this division of labor between the ruler and the ruled is not followed the results can be tragic. Simon points to the anxiety that fills the lives of the common man who finds himself burdened with the demand of taking care of the common good materially considered. If the military commander in the example given above has to choose where he will deploy his troops and for how long, rather than having to be told by the over-all command, which has a view of all that is needed for the victory of the campaign, then a tragic confusion of roles ensures. "When the private person has to emerge above his capacity and substitute for nonexistent public persons, an awe-inspiring solitude makes him realize that the structure of society has broken down."[606]

The inevitable and powerful conclusion of Simon is that when people are governed by moral giants, the power of example is infectious and "the role of love and friendship may be important."[607] People become better by seeking to be like their leaders. But leaders must be good and wise also because their public office could not be properly carried out without virtue.

Let us close this section by referring to something Simon says in *Practical Knowledge* which is very pertinent for our times. Even when a leader is upright, intelligent, well intentioned and virtuous, there are other internal factors that can ruin his stewardship. Simon especially mentions involuntary ignorance which "does not result only from

---

[605]Ibid., 145-147.
[606] Simon, *Philosophy of Democratic Government*, 44.
[607]Ibid., 143.

failure to get information that can be procured by consulting the proper memorandum or the proper man (expert)."[608] He gives us the other sources of this ignorance:

> On a deeper level, it may result from such deficiencies as lack of memory for names, faces, or traits of individual character; slow associations and slow processes of thought; inadequacy in the complex of abilities that we confusedly but meaningfully call instinct, knack, intuitive craft, practical sense; cold temperament, entailing privation of the warnings and suggestions that emotional intuition alone can procure; exposure to disturbance by irrational inclinations and aversions.[609]

A leader who becomes aware of any of the above short comings in his character will, if he is possessed of virtue, seek the help of better informed advisers. "But it often happens that no advice can substitute for personal acquaintance with the data of a problem and with the possible answers. In the case of a leader, honest awareness of harmful ignorance sometimes demands that he resign his duties."[610] Vukan Kuic is right when he concludes that, for Simon, "the requirements for political leadership seem indeed superhuman."[611] They are certainly frightfully high and daunting. For Simon, the courage to stand down when the situation clearly demands it is also an act of virtue on the part of the wise leader.

ii) Rule by the Experts or by an Elite

In the 18th century, the physical sciences developed by leaps and bounds. Generally, following on the discoveries of Galileo and others, it was widely held that advancement in science and improved conditions of living were inevitable. "The enlightened man of the eighteenth century indulged in the belief that technical progress infallibly entailed the betterment of man's condition. Coupled with

---

[608] Simon, *Practical Knowledge*, 15.
[609] Ibid.
[610] Ibid.
[611] Vukan Kuic, "Yves Simon's Contribution to Political Science," 94.

the postulate that nothing could ever stop technique in its march forward, such beliefs made up a great part of the so-called 'theory of necessary progress.'"612

One of the offshoots of this progress was the birth of technical expertise. Given the geographical expanse of modern states, their mixed cultural make up, and the complex economic factors at work in running them, there should be little surprise that Simon, in dealing with the wise ruler, mentions the need for and the role of the expert. He says:

> Occasionally, however, a leader may have to decide issues in which the human and the technical are so closely connected that wise judgment is impossible without some amount of expertness. Such occasions are increasingly frequent in technologically advanced societies.613

But the problem is the place that the expert now occupies in public decision making. This is how Simon describes the problem:

> The expert is often placed in a position of authority. Even when he retains the instrumental rank which is his, he is likely to act upon society in more than instrumental fashion. An instrument must be light; as a result of technology, the expert has become an instrument so heavy as often to get out of control.614

What Simon decries by saying that "the expert has become an instrument so heavy as often to get out of control," is the fact that the expert can frequently usurp the role of the ruler, which is an error since "leadership belongs to prudence and not to expertness."615 As we have seen, the ruler is supposed to be a man of virtue, a good man all round, who also has the complete picture of the state of the commonweal in view. Good order would decree that experts be kept

---

[612] Simon, *Philosophy of Democratic Government*, 280.
[613] Ibid., 279.
[614] Ibid.
[615] Ibid.

in subordinate positions under leaders[616] since experts have only a partial or particular view tied to their area of specialization. That is why, in Simon's view, "violence is done to the nature of public life whenever government is in the hands of an expert rather than a prudent man."[617]

In this regard, we would allude to a crucial distinction which Plato makes between being good in a particular skill, and being good absolutely speaking as a human being, which has been mentioned before in chapter one of this work,[618] and to which Simon refers in *The Definition of Moral Virtue*.[619] One of the references in support of this distinction that Simon cites is from the *Apology* 22d which reads:

> Last of all I turned to the skilled craftsmen. I knew quite well that I had practically no technical qualifications myself, and I was sure that I should find them full of impressive knowledge. In this I was not disappointed. They understood things which I did not, and to that extent they were wiser than I was. But, gentlemen, these professional experts seemed to share the same failing which I had noticed in the poets. I mean that on the strength of their technical proficiency they claimed a perfect understanding of every other subject, however important, and I felt that this error more than outweighed their positive wisdom.[620]

Someone with a particular expertise or a particular function is charged with a particular aspect of the common good. Simon thinks that "shifting from the particular function to an overall concern is possible, but generally difficult (since) the mental habits of the specialists are hard to overcome."[621] That is why someone with a

---

[616] Ibid.
[617] Ibid., 307.
[618] See p. 27.
[619] Simon, *The Definition of Moral Virtue*, 21. He mentions two other references viz., *Euthydemus* 288d and *Gorgias* 448b.
[620] Plato, *Apology*, trans. Hugh Tredennick in *Plato: The Collected Dialogues including the Letters*, ed. Edith Hamilton and Huntington Cairns (Princeton: Princeton University Press, 1996), 8-9.
[621] Simon, *Philosophy of Democratic Government*, 47.

particular leaning needs a person, or a group of persons, above him who are possessed of wisdom and are concerned with the common good in its form and in its matter. For this reason, Simon goes so far as to point out that "if the statesman is, by hypothesis, an artist or a technician, there must be above him, a wise person in charge of all questions relative to use."[622]

But Simon's intention is not to underestimate, in any way, the importance of experts, or the instrumental role played by several arts, skills, and techniques in the operation of political virtue. He says of this instrumental role of experts:

> "Instrumental" does not mean "unimportant." A man having the ethical dispositions necessary for political leadership may still fall short of qualification if he lacks the skills that are necessary instruments of political judgment and action.[623]

It is for this reason that finding and using the right experts is a part of the aptitude for wise leadership, as Simon shows in this example already alluded to:

> Consider this example: a society has recently undergone changes—say, morphological and technological—which render inadequate the traditional ways of distributing wealth. . . . We do not expect all its members to be equally aware of the situation and of its requirements. In addition to the inequality of the native gifts, it is normal, indeed, that people should be unequally versed in economics, history and sociology, and unequally informed about technological and morphological changes. Since awareness of such changes is of relevance for determining several aspects of the common good, it must be had in the highest degree by those in authority. From this it does not follow that they should be specialists in economics, sociology and economic history; but they should have the kind of good judgment it takes to find the dependable experts, (and) make them work.[624]

---

[622] Simon, *A General Theory of Authority*, 140.
[623] Simon, *Philosophy of Democratic Government*, 215.
[624] Simon, *A General Theory of Authority*, 145-146.

Being able to do so will demand, besides the virtue of prudence, the fact of living in affective communion with those one is ruling. It will demand a certain historical insertion into their reality. In *Practical Knowledge*, Simon, considering this question from the point of view of the ultimate practical judgment, says:

> We would not trust a leader who would appear to us as a fine individual disconnected from the social factors of inclination and aversion, judgment and action. Always supposing that his will is good, we would feel less confident if we realized that neither family traditions, nor historical trends, nor collective representations and drives are of much weight in his deliberations and decisions. We consider that the springs of a personality are inevitably weak unless they derive power from what is most vital in a community. Accordingly, we want a statesman to be a man of traditions, a man rooted in the history of a variety of groups, a man inspired by the needs, the ambitions, the regrets, the defeats, the great memories, and even the myths of the groups to which he belongs. We know that without all this social and historical substance his personality would be shallow and his leadership petty.[625]

In other words, rather than belong to an elite, aloof and concerned with status, the ruler must be a part of the community he leads. He must live in communion with those he rules, because judgment about political matters cannot be sound without knowledge of the past, present, and aspirations of the people one is leading.[626] Simon takes examples from history in order to prove the importance of this point. He indicates that there are examples, in various epochs, of governments run by people of great virtue who, in principle, should have taken care of the welfare of the people especially the poor and the needy but did not. They were rightly motivated by a determination to see justice done to the exploited of their societies, but they had no real idea of what was actually going on among the

---

[625] Simon, *Practical Knowledge*, 16.
[626] Simon, *Philosophy of Democratic Government*, 215.

lower classes of the people. Simon says that they "knew" but did not "realize."[627]

This kind of behavior is akin to rule by an elite, rather than by those possessed of virtue. Simon says:

> If society is ruled by an upper class—by an elite socially recognized, socially organized, having its own schools, its own books, its own leaders, its own manners—inevitably and in spite of all the wisdom used in the training of such an elite, rulers will not realize, except occasionally and in short-lived flashes, the suffering and aspirations of the common man. This elite will think merely of slow and inadequate reforms; its policy will be conservative. So far as the common man is concerned, government by this elite is government by outsiders. . . . A leader from outside is considered a blind leader. Only a leader in communion with us can realize what we are, what we need, what we are able to accomplish. . . . Blind leadership is the worst, no matter how well intentioned the blind leader may be.[628]

Prudential judgment regarding action in a given situation demands, of the leader, a certain affective connaturality with the community he serves. This permits Simon to conclude that "clearly, it is not only to the good of the political virtue that the statesman ought to be connaturalized but also to the good of this particular community, a creation of history that is unique and without any precedent."[629]

Walking in the "tattered shoes"[630] of others gives the leader an intuitive knowledge which saves leadership from blindness because it makes the leader exist, live, suffer and think inside the given community.[631] This element is a plus to moral goodness and is part and parcel of the wisdom of ruler-ship. Simon describes it as "intentional communion."[632]

---

[627]Ibid., 217.
[628]Ibid., 217-219.
[629]Ibid., 220.
[630]Ibid., 221.
[631]Ibid., 220-222.
[632]Ibid., 222.

iii) Freedom from Self: Obedience as Perfective

We are now in a position to look at the particular virtue of the ruled which answers to that of the wise ruler, namely the virtue of obedience. In our times, the virtue of obedience is not well regarded. James V. Schall S.J., whose essay we have mentioned already, in connection with the roles of the individual and authority in assuring the matter and the form of the common good,[633] calls it a counter-cultural topic.[634] Simon agrees pointing out that like authority, it has a bad name. As proof of this fact, Simon quotes W. K. Clifford (1845-1879) who says that, "there is one thing in the world more wicked than the desire to command and that is the will to obey."[635] This saying, Simon adds, is not without numerous adepts among intellectuals.

In his examination of the question of obedience to sovereign authority in chapter III of the *Philosophy of Democratic Government*, Simon points an accusing finger at Rousseau as having "probably done more than anyone else to spread the ideal of (the state as an) organization capable of doing away with the ethical substance of . . . obedience."[636] He quotes the following passage from Book 1, chapter VI, of Rousseau's *The Social Contract*:

> The problem is to find a form of association which will defend and protect with the whole common force the person and the goods of each associate, and in which each, while uniting himself with all, may still obey himself alone.[637]

Simon cites Augustin Cochin who, in *La Crise de l'histoire révolutionnaire*, interprets Rousseau as follows:

---

[633] See p. 301.
[634] Schall, "On the Most Mysterious of the Virtues," 744.
[635] Simon, *A General Theory of Authority*, 148. See William K. Clifford, *Lectures and Essays* (London: Macmillan, 1901).
[636] Ibid., 148.
[637] Jean Jacques Rousseau, *The Social Contract and the Discourses*, trans. G.D.H. Cole ("Everyman's Library" [New York: Alfred A. Knopf, 1993]), 190-91; See Simon, *Philosophy of Democratic Government*, 148.

Such is the precise and new meaning of the 'war against the tyrants' declared by the Revolution. It does not promise freedom in the ordinary sense of the word, i.e., independence, but in the sense in which Rousseau understands this word, viz., anarchy, deliverance from all personal authority, whether that of the lord to whom respect is due or that of the demagogue who exercises fascination. *If one is obedient, it will never be to man but always to an impersonal being, the general will.*[638]

This "political voluntarism"[639] of Rousseau, which "flatters the instinct of disobedience,"[640] and which distorts both the meaning of authority and obedience, was hugely influential in the French Revolution and other movements which sought to apply it.

And yet, because "the necessity of government and obedience follows from the nature of community life,"[641] obedience is not only necessary but can be communicative of virtue. This is how Simon poses the problem:

> On what grounds do some men claim a right to be obeyed? What are the reasons why they are not always disobeyed? Many would answer that they do not want to go to jail or to be shot down, and some theorists would maintain that fear and self-interest account sufficiently for the fact of obedience in civil society. Any human experience, any knowledge of history, evidences the shallowness of this explanation. . . . Things take place in civil relations, not exceptionally but regularly, as if some men had the power of binding the consciences of other men. . . . Now the proposition that a man can bind the conscience of another man raises a very great difficulty: far from being obvious, it is altogether devoid of verisimilitude. This is the very essence of the problem we propose to examine.[642]

---

[638]Augustin Cochin, *La Crise de l'histoirerévolutionnaire* (Paris: Champion, 1909), 49. See Simon, *Philosophy of Democratic Government*, 148-149 (Simon's emphasis.)
[639] Simon, *Philosophy of Democratic Government*, 191.
[640]Ibid., 149.
[641]Ibid., 154.
[642]Ibid., 145.

What is clear is that obedience is considered and justified in *Philosophy of Democratic Government* within the context of the demands of good citizenship in civil society. It is perfective but more as a civic virtue.[643]

In *A General Theory of Authority*, Simon briefly recalls the different kinds of authority, a topic he tackles in great detail in the *Philosophy of Democratic Government*.[644] The kinds of authority correspond to paternal authority and to authority that fulfils essential functions in a community.[645] We have already briefly explained the substitutional and essential roles of authority in Simon's political philosophy.[646] One might say that the stress is not on the role of obedience except in the sense indicated above. In *A General Theory of Authority*, Simon recalls that obedience as demanded by the common good can only be to the benefit of the one who obeys since he too reaps the rewards in terms of peace, development etc. When the goods of community life are assured because all obey and do their share of the work, everyone benefits. But this is only an initial answer regarding the value of obedience.

He goes on to give authority a third role not found in his *Philosophy of Democratic Government*. He says:

> But the role played by authority in the communication of excellence, is neither essential nor substitutional. It ranks above the substitutional and the essential. Since it takes place within a system of already attained perfection and aims at further development and greater perfection, it might be termed the "perfective" function of authority.[647]

---

[643] In this regard, we are aware of Arthur E. Murphy's essay, "An Ambiguity in Professor Simon's Philosophy of Democratic Government," (*The Philosophical Review* 61 [1952]: 198-211) and Simon's reply in an Appendix to *A General Theory of Authority* entitled "On the Meaning of Civil Obedience." (163-167). The debate touches on the origin of the obligation to obey political government and the various theories of the transmission of power from God to man in such fashion that governments can "bind consciences." It is thus a question of grounding obedience in society rather the different ways in which obedience ennobles as a moral virtue.

[644] Simon, *Philosophy of Democratic Government*, 7-35.
[645] Simon, *A General Theory of Authority*, 153-154.
[646] See pp. 297-298.
[647] Ibid., 136.

Obedience might, therefore, be good for the one who obeys in the context of parental authority, where it caters to a deficiency; secondly, it may also be good as a response to a call for common action, where it fulfils an essential function. Or, and here Simon gives it a third function, it can benefit the person himself who obeys and it can be perfective as a moral virtue. For him in this light, the question to be answered is whether, "beyond the goods of community life, obedience, by reason of its nature, does something for the law abiding citizen."[648] Simon pursues and answers this question in two steps:

i) By pointing to the possible results of obedience to those who are virtuous;
ii) By discussing it more philosophically.

We have already seen what Simon has to say about the equalitarian[649] way through which excellence is communicated by way of example, love, and friendship. Following on this treatment, Simon makes a first allusion to the beneficial role of obedience as a logical consequence of being ruled by the virtuous. He writes:

> To work under a leader whose qualifications are equal to his task is a happy experience, always remembered with gratitude. *In such reasonable subordination, the whole character of a man attains to higher levels*, silently, vitally, as a result of his fulfilling, every day and with all possible intelligence, the orders of the able superior.[650]

Here, Simon writes that "reasonable subordination" lifts the character of the one who obeys to new heights. In this case, what inspires is the example, love and friendship of the leader.

A little later, and more philosophically, Simon argues the case in detail as to how excellence is attained through specific obedience to

---

[648]Ibid., 154.
[649] Simon uses the word equalitarian instead of egalitarian. See *A General Theory of Authority*, 134.
[650]Ibid., 143 (our emphasis).

authority. Simon says that the question is best answered by looking at his theory of freedom, which he goes on to briefly explain.[651] We should indicate here that he gives a detailed philosophical explanation of this theory of freedom as superdetermination in *The Community of the Free*[652] and in *Freedom and Community*.[653] He also mentions it in *Philosophy of Democratic Government*.[654] Let us look at a few points from his analysis with regard to the question at hand.

Obedience would certainly be a problem, if as the moderns portray it, freedom is seen as license, or defined as Rousseau did, in terms of primitiveness and spontaneous fancy or as lack of determination. In *Freedom and Community*, Simon describes this idea of freedom:

> The identification of liberty with a lack of determination is found in a number of literary works where happy life is conceived as a continual refusal to make decisive choices. . . . Refusing to be determinately anything, trying everything without letting ourselves be steadily determined in any way, we should achieve an ability to become everything and this ability . . . is understood to be supreme liberty. It is easy to recognize in that description what philosophers technically call the potential indifference of the will, the passive indifference of the will, an indifference which is a state of non-achievement, a state of potency, *indifferentia potentialitatis*; an indifference which results from an ontological poverty: anything is good to one who has nothing.[655]

He then states the problem with this view of freedom:

---

[651]Ibid., 148.

[652] Yves R. Simon, *The Community of the Free*, trans. Willard R. Trask (Lanham, MD: University Press of America, 1984).

[653] Yves R. Simon, *Freedom and Community*, ed. Charles P. O'Donnell (New York: Fordham University Press, 2001).

[654] Simon, *Philosophy of Democratic Government*, 34-35.

[655] Simon, *Freedom and Community*, 35-36.

Far from being identical with liberty, this indifference is an obstacle that liberty has to overcome in order to assert itself. The psychological name of passive indifference is irresolution.[656]

Thus, freedom can and should be understood differently. The perspective changes as soon as we begin to see it in terms of an "active and dominating indifference" or "mastery over a plurality of possible ways of action."[657] What this means is that the biggest obstacles to freedom might be internal rather than external. Simon names these internal obstacles and grades them according to whether they are "lower" or "lofty." He says:

> Considering the lower first and then the more lofty, let us mention the power of habit, sensuous desires, lust for wealth, attachment to beloved things and persons, and in my relation to truth, excessive concern with the contributions of my own self.[658]

By way of an example of a habit to which we can become slaves, Simon takes smoking and drinking. Such a "habit or a native disposition are obstacles to our freedom if, when we see that it would be *good* to act at variance with this habit or disposition, we must confess that the power of these internal forces is all but insuperable."[659] Simon points out that our common language is accurate when it describes addiction to cigarettes or drink as slavery as when someone is said to be a slave to drink or cigarettes.

But slavery does not affect only our sensual selves but also the "operations of scientific and philosophical intelligence which stand at the peak of intellectual life."[660] Thus regarding truth, Simon indicates a particular kind of hindrance which results from being overly concerned with one's self and contribution. A researcher might develop a novel theory that explains some hitherto un-

---

[656] Ibid., 36.
[657] Simon, *A General Theory of Authority*, 148.
[658] Ibid.
[659] Ibid., 150.
[660] Ibid.

understood aspect of science such as Newton's theory of universal attraction.[661] Or it might be an attachment to a false hypothesis on the part of a scientist, historian or philosopher. Simon shows that, just like with the sensual self, such false intellectual desires can become no less addictive. He writes:

> To be sure, it is hard for a narcotic addict to break his old habit; but the history of human thought testifies that abandoning a theory for the sake of truth also takes a great degree of fortitude. . . . Whatever the case may be—i.e., whether the obstacle to the success of truth is physical and invincible or merely moral—freedom to welcome truth, without hindrance on the part of our mind, certainly is a rare privilege. That human freedom should be restricted in this high order of the mind's relation to the truth is a moral and metaphysical disaster of the first magnitude. Knowing is the creatures best chance to overcome the law of nonbeing. . . . Here, the defeat of knowledge by subjectivity originates in the intellect itself.[662]

Because human beings are deprived of many perfections, they are creatures that tend towards "becoming." Knowledge takes away the privation of what we lack by giving us other forms which complete our being. This explains the difficulty of giving up what we consider to be our discoveries, a problem which originates in the intellect, and is a special kind of selfishness peculiar to the rational being.

In the light of this situation, the question that Simon seeks to resolve is how to overcome subjectivity and achieve objectivity in that lofty part of our being. For Simon, the answer lies in obedience as remedy and method. When, in relation to authority—as far as the good is concerned, since no one is bound to obey an immoral law—I give up my judgment in favor of that of authority, the virtue of obedience comes into play. Here, it plays a perfective role.

But can one man command the interior acts of another and form their interior acts and not just what they do externally? Simon poses the question because as he observes, Thomas Aquinas declares that

---

[661]Ibid., 151.
[662]Ibid., 151-153.

regarding *purely* internal acts, no man, but God alone, can claim the obedience of another person. This means that obedience to man is concerned only with external acts. This is how Aquinas puts it:

> Consequently in matters touching the internal movement of the will man is not bound to obey his fellow man, but God alone. Nevertheless man is bound to obey his fellow-man in things that have to be done externally by means of the body.[663]

Simon, however, makes a subtle distinction: he shows that whereas human obedience does not reach *purely* internal acts, it does concern practical judgments that are the form for exterior actions and, in this way, touches our soul. He writes:

> Let it be remarked, however, that when an exterior act is voluntary, its form is something interior to the mind and heart of man, namely, a judgment. The role of obedience, which covers exterior acts also covers, by strict necessity, the judgment which is one with the exterior act in as much as it constitutes its form.[664]

He makes use of two different examples to clarify this point. The first concerns obedience to pirates. "All that is exacted by the pirates is money and merchandise,"[665] and my action in handing the money over does not touch on my internal convictions or acts. My action does not concern or shape my internal beliefs, since I do not think I should give them the money. Simon contrasts this, with my paying of taxes,[666] which involve a practical judgment that this is the right thing to do. I may think that the taxes charged me are too heavy, or reasonable, or have no opinion at all, but the inner conviction that I should obey this law and accept the judgment of those I obey, is not shaken. This internal obedience curbs my subjectivity, and aids the process of maturation.

---

[663] Aquinas, *Summa Theologiae*, II, II, q. 104, a.5.
[664] Simon, *A General Theory of Authority*, 155.
[665] Ibid., 156.
[666] Ibid., 155.

Willingness to act to whatever degree, falls under the virtue of obedience and ennobles the one who obeys to the extent of the nobility of the act. When I bring my will and volition into line with that of legitimate authority regarding the common good, the excellence of the virtue of obedience becomes mine. When I curb the rebellious acts of my subjectivity, voluntarily and freely, "for the sake of the law, for the sake of the good, and for the sake of God,"[667] I become a virtuous person.

I would like to conclude this chapter by asking whether Simon's account of obedience as perfective is convincing. James V. Schall S.J., who compares Simon's philosophical contribution on the question with that of Aquinas and Rousseau, does not think Simon is completely successful in doing away with the bad name of obedience. He says:

> Yves Simon, in the "Introduction" to his *A General Theory of Authority*, had discussed the "bad name" that the correlative of obedience, that is, "authority", had in the modern world. Though authority's "bad name" was, I think, largely alleviated by the work of Simon, the bad name of "obedience," to which he also addressed himself, is not so well redeemed.[668]

After an analysis of the quote from St Thomas on obedience which we saw above, for the most part along the same lines as Simon, Schall comes to the following view of the heart of Simon's contribution on the virtue of obedience:

> In his analysis, Simon has located obedience as an aspect of authority's presentation of good laws. He had recognized that to do a good act, we must have our interior thoughts properly ordered, to will what is good in the particular as that appears in a legitimate law. However, even assuming that God has commanded us to rule our thoughts, commanded us not to covet, we are still much subject to pride and opposing desires that will deflect us from the acts of the law.

---

[667]Ibid., 156.
[668]Schall, "On the Most Mysterious of the Virtues," 744-745.

Obedience relies on the nature of the superior reasonableness of the good law over against those disturbing temptations and movements in our own soul that might at any time seem more suasive than the precept of the law itself. The law ultimately intends that we be good, though it does this through our performing good acts, the goodness of which are found in the law. Obedience to the law or authority, thus, takes the process one step backwards into our souls to touch the very freedom we have to see the good in a particular case, the case before the law, in this case.[669]

By way of an assessment, Schall brings in John Finnis and compares his view with that of Simon.[670] Finnis, he points out, never uses the word obedience but rather obligation since, in his reasoning, one follows the law not because it is willed by the superior or God, but because it is good and reasonable. Obedience, therefore, is not directly to the superior or God. Finnis, he continues, would find problems with Simon because the will as such has no contents but the good as presented in reason. Rather than obedience to an authority, we are obliged to the good as it appears in reason.

Are Simon and Finnis at odds? Is Simon a volutarist? Schall says:

> Simon in his view of obedience is not so much concerned with the good or reason in the formulation of the law. The law is itself attractive to the reason because the law is itself also reasonable. The reason of the legislator speaks to the reason of the law observer. Simon is aware, however, of the tremendous pulls within the law observer that would deflect him from seeing or following the good in reason found in the law. For Simon, obedience is a protection from our own subjective moods and desires. These passions and tendencies are formidable especially if we see them, after the manner of St. Augustine, in terms of pride and self-will, rebellion against any rule not our own. In this

---

[669] Ibid., 754-755.
[670] John Finnis, *Natural Law and Natural Right* (London: Oxford, 1980), 297-342. See Schall, "On the Most Mysterious of the Virtues," 755-756.

sense, obedience is directed to that one intellectual form in the practical intellect that is needed that we might observe the law.[671]

Schall thus implies that, for Simon, obedience engages the will. He continues:

> Simon conceives obedience as that virtue that overcomes our subjectivity so that we can act well in each particular case. He is aware of the strength of the subjective forces within us and seeks to overcome them through obedience. Finnis, on the other hand, is concerned with the attractiveness of the good that is itself choiceworthy because it is true. That which draws us will be a particular good.[672]

For Schall, the emphases of Simon and Finnis are different. They are looking at the same thing from different angles, as obedience or as obligation. On the one hand Simon stresses the law and obedience to it as an antidote to the evil that lies in our hearts always pushing us to do what is wrong; and on the other hand Finnis lays emphasis on the good in the law as what to aim at in action.

In order to avoid any ambiguity or suspicion of voluntarism on Simon's part, we would point out that if for the reasons adduced by Schall Simon is concerned about the virtue of obedience to the law, it is necessary to keep the rest of his philosophy in view and stress that he is no voluntarist. In fact, he argues forcefully against it in his *The Tradition of Natural Law*.[673] Even for Simon, one follows authority because what is commanded is good, and not just because it is commanded. For instance, he says that "the virtue of obedience implies that my own judgment is irrelevant in any *normal* relation of myself to authority."[674] This is how he explains the presence of the word *normal* in the above quote:

---

[671] Schall, "On the Most Mysterious of the Virtues," 756

[672] Ibid.

[673] Yves R. Simon, *The Tradition of Natural: A Philosopher's Reflections*, ed. Vukan Kuic (New York: Fordham University Press, 1992), 72-78.

[674] Simon, *A General Theory of Authority*, 154-155. (our emphasis).

The word normal is inserted here in order to exclude those extreme cases in which it is lawful and perhaps obligatory to act at variance with orders that are plainly absurd or criminal. . . . Things bearing all the externals of law and therefore called "laws" may really be no laws at all for lack of justice, and an agency bearing the externals of authority, and therefore called authority, government or administration, may be ungenuine and have no real power to command obedience.[675]

Granted the above, it often takes authority to command what is good.[676] That is why in *Philosophy of Democratic Government*, Simon argues forcefully for a recognition of the essential functions of authority even in a community of virtuous people. Simon's metaphysics of obedience does show how it can be an important virtue in public action. But he also shows, in this chapter, the relevance of the virtue of those who rule in an age in which technical expertise is highly prized, and the pursuit of 'what works' or is useful is taken as the norm.

---

[675] Ibid., 154.
[676] Simon, *Philosophy of Democratic Government*, 19-35.

Chapter 4

Virtue in Public Life: Virtue and Law

Introduction

Clarke E. Cochrane and Thomas Rourke observe that the relationship between virtue and natural law is "not obvious"[677] in the work of Simon. This means that one has to be attentive to find it. That is what we try to do in this concluding chapter, namely, to find the sometimes subtle, sometimes overt manifestations of virtue in what Simon has to say about law.

In this effort, Simon's work *The Tradition of Natural Law* is the main source of our exposition of what he thinks about virtue and law. This book, edited by Vukan Kuic, has been put together from the lectures of a course Simon taught at the University of Chicago in 1958. It is not a systematic treatment of the subject of natural law but was meant by Simon to clarify certain contemporary problems of natural law. We have also found certain sections of his works, *Practical Knowledge* and *The Definition of Moral Virtue*, useful.

This chapter is divided into two parts. Part I, which tackles mainly issues of definition, opens with Simon's general idea of nature. For Simon, natural law applies to things in general, to the animal world, and to rational beings. This means that it applies to the physical and moral worlds, or shows its double character as "natural law and natural right,"[678] to borrow the terminology of St Thomas. Things act for an end and nature recommends a naturally right way of acting. The virtue of a thing is its ability to act in an excellent way and according to its nature. In the case of man, Simon says that it is

---

[677] Clarke E. Cochrane and Thomas Rourke, "Moving Beyond Ideology in Christian Economic Thought: Yves R. Simon and the Recent Debates," in *Freedom, Virtue and the Common Good*, ed. Curtis L. Hancock & Anthony O. Simon (Notre Dame: University of Notre Dame Press, 1995), 311.

[678] Simon, *The Tradition of Natural Law*, 42.

necessary to take cognizance of the fact of freedom that is characteristic of rational beings. This is where moral virtue comes in to complete natural virtue. While virtue is immanent in things generally, in the case of man it needs to be chosen. There is thus a certain unity and difference, in the concept, as it applies to the physical and moral worlds.

In order to make this idea stand out even more clearly, we look at some of the storms that the idea of a naturally just has undergone in the history of philosophical thought. In *The Tradition of Natural Law* Simon discusses three of these philosophical challenges: these are Epicurean indeterminism and existentialism, the mechanism of Descartes and the problem of ideology. In addition, therefore, to looking at Simon's idea of nature, Part I will examine his treatment of Epicureanism, Cartesianism, and Existentialism, as well as his discussion of ideology; it will present his explanation of how these ways of thinking vitiate the truth that exists in nature and thus undermines the role of virtue and its place in natural law.

With Part I acting as an introductory backdrop, Part II is intended to provide outstanding instances of the interplay between virtue and law. We must distinguish between positive law, natural physical law, and natural moral law. We will examine four important facets of the interaction between virtue and these kinds of law. The first problem we address will be the difficult and basic question about the very existence of the just by nature or natural moral law. We then, secondly, proceed from the question of the existence of natural law to that of how it is known. Simon's answer that it is known by inclination and cognition takes us back to Aristotle and Thomas Aquinas. Of great importance here is the fact that the knowledge of natural law is progressive, which, for Simon, provides an answer to those who deny the existence of the naturally just by pointing to the multiplicity of sometimes contradictory customs and beliefs in different parts of the world. In addition, Simon makes the point that the virtue of a people plays no small part as to whether knowledge of natural law advances or suffers reversals. The third point in this part will show how each kind of law—positive, natural physical, natural moral—can function as premise and as conclusion in moral reasoning, and how virtue plays a role in the way they carry out these functions.[679] We close this chapter with an exposition of the argument of Simon showing that God is the author of the naturally just. This argument, which relies on the philosophical principles of the five ways of Aquinas, is regarded by some scholars as no small contribution to the question of virtue and law.

I: Virtue and the Idea of Natural Law and Philosophical Challenges to the Idea

The Idea of Natural Law

In his book *The Tradition of Natural Law* Simon mentions Sophocles' *Antigone* as being at the very origins of the idea of a law written into the fabric of nature. He refers to Aristotle who, in one of only two references[680] to natural law, relates the contribution of Sophocles. Aristotle writes:

> For there really is as everyone to some extent divines, a natural justice and injustice that is binding on all men, even on those who have no association or covenant with each other. It is this that Sophocles' Antigone clearly means when she says that the burial of Polyneices was a just act in spite of the prohibition: she means that it was just by nature.
>
> Not of to-day or yesterday it is,
> But lives eternal: none can date its birth.[681]

Simon gives the following clarifying commentary to this passage of Aristotle's:

---

[679] As will be explained later in this chapter, law as premise refers to natural law as providing justification and grounding for the norms of positive law, which norms in turn are the conclusions from natural law. See pp. 374-379 and 393- 400.

[680] The two references are found in *Nicomachean Ethics* 5.7. 1134b and in *Rhetoric* 1.13.1373b.

[681] Aristotle, *Rhetoric*, trans. W. Rhys Robert, in *The Basic Works of Aristotle*, ed. Richard McKeon, 1370. (1.13.1373b6-13). See Simon, *The Tradition of Natural Law*, 131.

The reference is to the famous page of *Antigone*. Antigone is blamed for having buried her brother against an order of the ruler of the city. Her brother was a rebel and was therefore to be denied the honor of a decent burial. But Antigone gave him this honor, and when challenged by the ruler, who was her own uncle, she explains to him that over and above the written laws there are some that are unwritten, that are eternal—no one knows when they had been enacted. *Antigone* is justly recognized as one of the greatest documents in the history of natural law.[682]

But if *Antigone* is one of the first works to allude to the existence of a law of nature, Simon says that Aristotle's is among the earliest of attempts to give an explanation of how we are to understand it. Aristotle provides the philosophical clarification for what the poet describes. In the passage of the *Nicomachean Ethics* alluded to above, Aristotle distinguishes the naturally just (*to dikaion phusikon*) from the legally just (*to dikaion nomikon*).[683] What brings the two sides of the coin together Simon says, is the idea of "the adjusted, the adequate, that which fits exactly in relation to something else."[684] The idea of the exact and the true is implied. The adjusted is that which is right for the thing and is measured by the thing. Simon says:

> The natural just of Aristotle—and the same remark holds, by all means, for the natural right and the natural law of Thomas Aquinas—ignores the . . . contrast between the physical and the moral worlds. Between the two communication is insured not only by the notion of nature but also by that of justice, which fundamentally signifies adjustment.[685]

What this means is that, for Aristotle, everything has a way of acting proper to it or adjusted to its being. If a tree acted like a horse

---

[682] Simon, *The Tradition of Natural Law*, 131-132.
[683] Aristotle, *Nicomachean Ethics*, 5.7.1134b18; See Simon, *The Tradition of Natural Law*, 41.
[684] Simon, *The Tradition of Natural Law*, 41.
[685] Ibid., 42.

this would not be naturally just because it would not be adjusted to the nature of the tree. The notion of adjustment is true of the physical and moral worlds.

Elsewhere in *The Tradition of Natural Law*, Simon pursues the question and further explains the meaning of an adjusted way of acting. He points out that the naturally just is "that which is right by reason of what the things are."[686] This, he says, applies equally to the physical and the moral worlds, namely, to physical nature and to man. Simon gives the example of sulphuric acid, which refers to both worlds—the physical and the human—and connects them. He writes:

> For instance, we all assume that sulphuric acid has a steady way of behaving which is definitely at variance with that of some things which outwardly look very much like it, say, sherry wine. But mistaking the former for the latter would be frightful in its consequences. And it is agreed that *no drinks are served in laboratories*. Do you recognize here not only a discreet example of the general consensus on laws embodied in things but also an important aspect of the unity between the physical and the moral worlds?[687]

There is therefore a law inherent in things according to which they act in a way proper to their nature. He says that "plainly it is *because* natural law is first embodied in things that we declare such and such an action to be right, and such and such an action to be wrong."[688]

Even if this fact is true of the physical and moral worlds, Simon does make a distinction between virtue as it exists in the physical world and as it exist in the moral world, that is, in man. He says that there is a "unity and then a contrast in the expressions "natural law" or "law of nature" as applied to the physical and as applied to the moral worlds."[689] It exists as a rule inherent in the nature of things"

---

[686]Ibid., 120.
[687] Ibid., 121
[688]Ibid., 137.
[689]Ibid., 120.

because "there is an interior, an immanent law of operation which connects the universe of mankind with the universe of physical nature"[690] but in addition, for man, it has to be freely chosen. Simon says:

> What is particular about the natural law of man, of the moral world, is that essentially it operates through free choice. It exists as a rule inherent indeed in the nature of things but which does not direct operation in determinate fashion. It governs behavior through judgment and through free choice.[691]

What this means is that since man, unlike physical things which act by rote, is a thinking being, natural virtue besides existing in things has, for him, to be freely chosen.

In order to make his meaning as clear as possible, he uses a threefold division of natural law that he adopts from Aquinas.[692]

1) The first division of natural law concerns those tendencies which man shares with all things. They are not particular to man, or to animals, or to living things, but are common to all things. The biggest of these, is the tendency to keep existing, to hold on tenaciously to one's life, or to persevere in being. Man shares this virtue with all being.

2) The second division of natural law concerns those inclinations that man shares in common with animals. Simon says that these touch on issues of generation, sex and procreation, the association of male and female, and the care for offspring, which normally should be the business of the mother.[693]

3) The third division of natural law has to do with the natural inclinations proper to rational beings. Simon puts in this division of natural law issues which are right or wrong by reason of what the

---

[690]Ibid., 121-122.
[691]Ibid., 122.
[692]Ibid., 122-125. See Aquinas, *Summa Theol.* I-II q. 94, a. 2.
[693]Ibid., 123.

rational being is such as "the desire to know the truth, problems of obedience, (and) problems of government."[694]

Simon's conclusion which speaks to what differentiates and unites the three groups is instructive. He writes:

> Thus everything that is right by nature is right either because the universal nature of a being is such, or because the universal nature of animal is such, or because the rational nature is such. This threefold classification insures the community between the natural law of the moral world and the natural law of the physical world, no matter how sharply these laws may be contrasted in some respects. After all, man is part of this universe.[695]

The difference between the natural law of the moral world and that of the physical world is that, whereas the things of the physical world act simply by nature, man acts by nature, by animal nature and by rational nature.[696] Thus the concept of the 'adjusted' or of virtue exists independently of my being. It is immanent in a thing, an animal or a human being. The addition for the human being is that, as a rational agent, I have to judge and choose for or against "the inclinations of being, the inclinations of the animal nature, and the inclinations of the rational nature."[697] For man, virtue has the double meaning of immanence and of being freely chosen.

Philosophical Challenges to the Idea of Natural Law

We would now like to mention some philosophies which Simon indicates as disruptive of this idea of virtue working in nature. These deviations, and the philosophical arguments advanced to support them, help us to understand even better how virtue works in the law of nature.

---

[694] Ibid., 124.
[695] Ibid., 124.
[696] Ibid., 125.
[697] Ibid.

i) The Indeterminacy of the Epicureans and the Existentialists

Epicurus (341-270 B.C.) and the Epicureans provide, for Simon, a good example of the denial of nature as the stable source of being and appropriate action. We might give a little background information to what Simon says, by pointing out that Epicurus borrows elements for his philosophy from the atomism of Democritus and Leucippus. Aristotle tells us in *On Generation and Corruption*, that the work of the atomists was motivated by a desire to reconcile the observable facts of motion and change with Parmenides' denial of these facts.[698] The single treatise with which Parmenides is credited, largely preserved for us by Sextus Empiricus and Simplicius, lays claim to knowledge of a unique truth namely, that there is no change. A thing either is or it is not. A third way is metaphysically impossible. In a fragment of his he says, "what is there to be said and thought must needs be: for it is there for being, but nothing is not."[699]

Parmenides' "astonishing deductive *tour de force* that if something exists, it cannot come to be or perish, change or move, nor be subject to any imperfection"[700] had to be dealt with. According to Aristotle, whereas Anaxagoras sought to resolve the question by postulating primary things, observable stuffs, and properties, and Empedocles posited earth, air, fire, and water, the atomists, Democritus and Leucippus, proposed physical individuals or atoms as the basic elements constitutive of things.[701] But the atomists think that the movement of atoms is governed by mechanical necessity. Regarding this aspect of their doctrine, C.C.W. Taylor writes:

> The atomists' universe is purposeless, mechanistic, and deterministic; every event has a cause, and causes necessitate their effects. Broadly speaking the process is mechanical; ultimately,

---

[698] Aristotle, *On Generation and Corruption*, trans. Harold H. Joachim, in *The Basic Works of Aristotle*, ed. Richard McKeon, 1.7-8.324a35-325a31.

[699] Quoted in G.S. Kirk, J.E. Raven, M. Schofield, *The Presocratic Philosophers*, 247.

[700] G.S. Kirk, J.E. Raven, M. Schofield, *The Presocratic Philosophers*, 241.

[701] Aristotle, *On Generation and Corruption*, 1.7-8.324a35-325a31.

everything in the world happens as a result of atomic interaction. The purpose of atomic interaction has neither beginning nor end, and any particular stage of that process is causally necessitated by a preceding stage .... The fundamental text is the single fragment of Leucippus (DK 67 B1) "Nothing happens at random, but everything by necessity."[702]

Epicurus prefers to go with the solution proposed by the atomists, but their doctrine of mechanical necessity in the movement of these atoms riles him.

Let us return to Simon, who says that mechanical necessity is a problem for Epicurus because it implies the acceptance of fate.[703] While adopting aspects of atomism, he works out a system of philosophy designed primarily to address the question of how to attain human happiness. His is above all an ethical system or moral philosophy, whose aim is "to liberate man from the fear of death, from the fear of the gods, and from the fear of fate."[704] Because the atoms of Democritus "move in a vortex ruled by mechanical necessity,"[705] a thing he finds more uncongenial than the whims of gods and goddesses,[706] Epicurus decides to do away with this necessity by introducing the atomic swerve (*clinamen*), a device through which falling atoms deviate from the vertical. Simon says:

---

[702] C.C.W. Taylor, "The Atomists," in *The Cambridge Companion to Early Greek Philosophy*, ed. A.A. Long (Cambridge: Cambridge University Press, 2006), 185.

[703] Within his system which describes nature as based on atomistic materialism, it is easy to find an answer to his ethical concerns and explain why man should not fear death or the gods. With regard to the former, fear of death, he explains that when we die, the soul made up of finer atoms does not survive, and together with the atoms of the body simply disintegrates and that is the end of us. From this it follows that there can be no punishment after death, nor regrets for the life that is gone. As regards the latter, namely, fear of the gods, Epicurus explains that they are too busy enjoying their happiness to be concerned about human affairs. See Philodemus, *On Piety*, ed. Dirk Obbink (Oxford: Clarendon Press, 1996), 321-323.

[704] Simon, *The Tradition of Natural Law*, 59.
[705] Ibid.
[706] Ibid., 29.

According to Epicurus, atoms fall like rain but also have the property of deviating from the vertical. This property helps to explain the constitution of aggregates, but most of all it is designed to rule out the inescapable necessity asserted by Democritus' philosophy. The swerve of the atom is the principle of free choice in Epicureanism.[707]

In other to buttress this view, Simon quotes the following passage of Lucretius who (together with Cicero) is largely responsible for explaining the idea of the swerve:

> This point too herein we wish you to apprehend: when bodies are borne downwards sheer through void by their own weights, at quite uncertain times and uncertain spots they push themselves a little from their course: you just and only just can call it a change of inclination. If they were not used to swerve, they would all fall down, like drops of rain, through the deep void, and no clashing would have been begotten nor blow produced among the first-beginnings: thus nature never would have produced aught.[708]

Simon notes that unlike Aristotle's idea of chance, which as we saw does not have an essential cause but several accidental causes (*Physics* 2.5.196b; *Metaphysics* 6.3.1027b), Epicurus's swerve is even worse as an explanatory cause. The swerve is simply not a cause. It is random and irrational. This philosophizing, of course, eliminates the idea of teleology or a law immanent in natures by which they act and develop.[709]

Simon also briefly alludes to the existentialists, who generally deny the idea of a given human nature and hold that it is made up progressively on the bases of our choices. While describing the threat they pose in dire terms, Simon mentions their challenge only in a few brief and cryptic phrases. For instance, he says that "existentialism (is) a philosophy dedicated to the proposition that man has no nature

---

[707] Ibid., 59.

[708] Lucretius, *De ReumNatura* II, trans. H.A.J. Munro (London: George Bell & Sons, 1908), 216-225. See Simon, *The Tradition of Natural Law*, 180-181.

[709] Simon, *The Tradition of Natural Law*, 59-60.

but only history."[710] From this premise, he draws the following conclusion for belief in natural law:

> No natural law would be conceivable in a world of all-embracing indeterminacy, in a world from which all determinate natures would be excluded; this seems to be the way things are represented by at least the most extreme forms of existentialism.[711]

ii) The Mechanism of Descartes and Others

Simon traces the origins of mechanism to Parmenides (b. 515 B.C.). We have already mentioned the essence of his theory above while dealing with the indeterminacy of the Epicureans and the Existentialists. For Simon, Parmenides ignores the three key qualities of the concept of nature viz., plurality, teleology, and growth, and sees "the world of reality (as) made of one single, large, definitely corporal, motionless thing, without qualities, and without any other diversity than that resulting from the fact that its parts are external to each other."[712] If change and multiplicity are illusory, then there is no idea of natures in the world of Parmenides. Simon points to the following passage from Aristotle's *Physics*, in which he shows the paradoxical and absurd consequences of the teaching of Parmenides:

> But if all things are one in the sense of having the same definition, like 'raiment' and 'dress,' then it turns out that they are maintaining the Heraclitean doctrine, for it will be the same thing 'to be good' and 'to be bad,' and 'to be good' and 'to be not good,' and so the same thing will be 'good' and 'not good' and man and horse; in fact, their view will be, not that all things are one, but that they are nothing.[713]

Parmenides' mechanism is a fitting introduction to René Descartes, who conceives of reality in terms of extension and thought

---

[710] Ibid., 3.
[711] Ibid., 57.
[712] Simon, *The Tradition of Natural Law*, 45.
[713] Aristotle, *Physics*, trans. R.P. Hardie and R.K. Gaye in *The Basic Works of Aristotle*, ed. Richard McKeon, 221 (1.2.185b19). See Simon, *The Tradition of Natural Law*, 46.

and, therefore, does not admit of natures in his philosophy either. Simon names him as the most thorough going of all the mechanists,[714] "at least as far as corporal reality is concerned."[715] Descartes posits only two substances (if they can be called substances), viz., the thinking thing and the extended thing, that is, consciousness and space, neither of which is a nature as such, nor is there any interaction between the two. How, it may be asked, does Descartes explain the regularity in the action of bodies which we experience all around us? Simon explains Descartes' answer:

> The truth is that there are no natures in the universe of Descartes. Stability in natural processes, not being guaranteed by any nature, has to be guaranteed by an extrinsic power, and this is how the theory of divine immutability comes to play an essential part in Cartesian physics: the laws of motion are such as we know them not by reason of any necessity immanent in things, but because God once decided that they would be such. Do not worry: God is not subject to whims, and He will not change his mind; the science of physics is possible.[716]

Just as he has problems explaining the relationship between thought and extension, it is equally difficult for him to explain how the physical and the mental parts within man relate. Descartes adopts a spiritualistic explanation according to which consciousness moves the body and the body influences consciousness. The details as to how this takes place between two substances that differ *toto genere* are beyond Descartes. He has recourse to the pineal gland. Simon quotes Maritain in support of this understanding of Descartes:

> Cartesian dualism breaks man up into two complete substances, joined to one another no one knows how: on the one hand, the body which is only geometric extension; on the other hand, the soul which

---

[714]Ibid., 49.

[715]Ibid., 45.

[716] Simon, *The Tradition of Natural Law*, 45-46. Simon refers to Descartes' *Meditations on First Philosophy*: Fourth Meditation; and the second part of the *Principles of Philosophy*.

is only thought—an angel inhabiting a machine and directing it by means of the pineal gland.[717]

Given the unsatisfactory nature of Descartes' explanation, other philosophers picked up the question and tried to find a solution to it. Thus Leibniz developed his doctrine of a pre-established harmony which sees the world of consciousness and that of extension as two clocks that have both been set and synchronized by a wise horologer, in such fashion that when one of the clocks strikes twelve, the other does the same.[718] In this way, when the mind wants something of the body, it responds.

Simon contrasts Descartes' view to that of Aristotle for whom the multiplicity of physical nature is an obvious fact and concludes that "wherever there is nature there is direction toward a state of accomplishment, and in order to get rid of teleological considerations, mechanism has first to replace nature by something else, e.g., extension."[719] But extension is not a nature and experience clearly shows that a nature tends to act in a certain way in order to fulfill its being. An acorn will grow into an oak tree and not into an orange tree. In fact, when we talk of an acorn, progression to an oak tree is postulated. This is teleology.

Simon asks why something so obvious would be disputed so doggedly by biologists who call teleology "primitive, archaic, pre-scientific, foreign to science, (and) anti-scientific?"[720] He tells us why in these words:

> The reasons why teleological notions are held suspicious by the scientific mind are numerous. One of the most profound is already familiar to us: there are no natures and no final causes in mathematics.

---

[717] Jacques Maritain, *The Dream of Descartes*, trans. Mabelle L. Andison (New York: F. Hubner& Co., Inc., 1944), 179. See Simon, *The Tradition of Natural Law*, 177.

[718] Gottfried Leibniz, *The Monadology and Other Philosophical Writings*, trans. Robert Latta (London: Oxford University Press, 1898), 331-334. See Simon, *The Tradition of Natural Law*, 50; 178.

[719] Simon, *The Tradition of Natural Law*, 47.

[720] Ibid., 47.

When we watch a geometrical figure or an equation develop its properties, we are aware that it is not in order to achieve a better state of affairs that this equation or this figure is effecting this development .... It is easy to see what the consequences are for a problem like that of natural law. When the Cartesian universe displaces the universe of Aristotle, when a universe made of natures is displaced by a single huge thing, extension, whose parts and their arrangements and rearrangements lend themselves beautifully to mathematical treatment, we have to deal with a world picture in which teleological considerations are as irrelevant as considerations of color and taste would be in geometry.[721]

The reason for the persistent refusal to accept nature and its ways is based on the scientific mindset. Dealing with beings that grow—a boy will mature into a man—and develop their actualization over time calls for a mentality different from the mentality at work in the sciences that deal with elements and quantities.

This description of modern science, Simon observes, helps us to understand another tendency that is favored by the modern world, a tendency to exalt the power and freedom of the human being. In a universe in which natures are replaced by extension, and "whose parts and their arrangements and rearrangements lend themselves beautifully to mathematical treatment," man is the main actor and he is consequently also the one who gives values to things. When things are thus conceived as not having natures and, therefore, as not having any innate finalities of their own, the tendency is for man to attribute to them values of his own making. This is how Simon puts it:

When we hear today of moral values, esthetic values, social values, political values, etc., we should know where these come from. They come from the mind, they come from outside the things, they are not embodied in entities, in nature. Thus, "this has value" does not mean that by reason of what the thing is .... Its value is something assigned

---

[721]Ibid., 47-48.

to it by the mind while, in itself, it remains without value, without nature.[722]

Since these modern values do not exist in nature, they are subjective, and Simon holds Kant as having a huge responsibility for this subjectivist trend which has resulted in a multiplication of values in modern times.

iii) The Misuse of Natural Law as Ideology

For Simon, the biggest danger threatening efforts aimed at discovering and explaining the workings of natural justice resides in the problem of ideology. Simon is of the view that philosophy has been more or less tainted by ideology in every age[723] and unfortunately, contemporary times have not been spared. He gives one of the reasons why ideology has infiltrated the philosophy of natural law in our times:

> Our times have witnessed a new birth of belief in natural law concomitantly with the success of existentialism, which represents the most thorough criticism of natural law ever voiced by philosophers. Against such powers of destruction we feel the need for an ideology of natural law.[724]

Since ideology is often mistaken for philosophy and truth, a proper understanding of its characteristics is essential. Simon thus defines what he means by ideology in these terms:

> According to the familiar use of the word, an ideology is a system of propositions which, though indistinguishable so far as expression goes from statements about facts and essences, actually refer not so much to any real state of affairs as to the *aspirations* of a *society* at a certain *time* in its evolution. These are the three components which, taken together distinguish ideology from philosophy. The notion of truth

---

[722] Ibid., 51.
[723] Ibid., 29-30.
[724] Ibid., 23.

which an ideology embodies is utilitarian, sociological, and evolutionistic. When what is actually an expression of aspirations assumes the form of statements about things, when these aspirations are those of a definite group, and when that group expresses its timely aspirations in a language of everlasting truth—then, without doubt, it is an ideology that we are dealing with.[725]

Cochrane and Rourke capture Simon's meaning beautifully when they say that an "ideology is a body of claims, expressed in universal moral terms, which are useful for a particular group of people in their efforts to attain their social, political or economic goals, at a particular point in time."[726]

Simon takes as an example of the workings of an ideology masquerading as a philosophical explanation, John C. Calhoun's justification of slavery in the south of the United States early in the nineteenth century. The mule-jenny, which caused a rapid increase in the production of cotton, had just been invented and Calhoun, Vice President of the United States from 1824 to 1832, realized the utility of this machine to the south, as far as the abundant and cheap production of cotton by slaves was concerned. He then argued that it was a universal law of society for one part of the community to exercise control over a section on which it depended for cheap labor. It had always been this way in the history of mankind, therefore, it must be a universal law, he said.[727]

While the sources of Calhoun's theory are traced by some scholars to Aristotle's *Politics*,[728] what is crucial here is that Simon

---

[725]Ibid., 16-17.

[726]Cockrane and Rourke, "Moving Beyond Ideology in Christian Economic Thought: Yves R. Simon and the Recent Debates," in *Freedom, Virtue, and the Common Good*, 309.

[727] Simon, *The Tradition of Natural Law*, 17-18.

[728] The reference here is to *Politics*, Book 1, chapter 5 on the question of slavery where Aristotle says: "For he who can be, and therefore is, another's, and he who participates in rational principle enough to apprehend, but not to have, such a principle, is a slave by nature." Aristotle, *Politics*, trans. B. Jowett, in *The Basic Works of Aristotle*, ed. Richard McKeon, 1133.(1.5.1254b20). Simon examines the various theories in this regard in a long footnote and takes the different positions for what they are, namely, as the views of the given authors on Calhoun's sources for his

shows how Calhoun's theory exhibits all three characteristics of an ideology: it defends the aspirations of a social group at a given time under the pretence that it is a philosophical application of timeless universal principles.[729] However, the workings of philosophy are completely different, as Simon indicates:

> In contrast with ideology, the law of philosophy is altogether one of objectivity. The object of an aspiration is not a pure object, it is an object and it is something else, viz., an end, just as the object of transitive action is an effect. The object of cognition alone is a pure object.... The object of an ideology is, in spite of appearances without which the ideology would not work, an object of desire. The object of philosophy is a pure object.[730]

Simon is equally clear in *An Introduction to Metaphysics of Knowledge*:

> We are looking at the relation of the object of knowledge to the faculty of knowing. What kind of relation is it? Well, it is a relation of pure qualitative determination, innocent of everything involved in the order of movement, effectuation, or desire.... Knowing is not making, creating, or transforming: we could say that in knowing we touch an object, but we never interfere with it .... Indeed, to conceive knowledge either as some sort of making or as the result of some sort of desire is to misconstrue its nature.[731]

More importantly for our purposes, Simon points out that if keeping philosophy pure of ideological influences is difficult, it is even more so with regard to moral philosophy, including questions of natural law. He asserts that "a treatise on natural law which would be purely philosophic and in no way influenced by the ideological

---

ideology of slavery (171-172). Elsewhere and independently of Calhoun, Simon accepts that Aristotle's treatment of slavery amounts to an ideological rather than a philosophical consideration. (*The Tradition of Natural Law*, 29-30).

[729] Simon, *The Tradition of Natural Law*, 17-18.
[730] Ibid., 21.
[731] Yves R. Simon, *An Introduction to Metaphysics of Knowledge* (New York: Fordham University Press, 1990), 8.

needs of the time is, in fact, almost impossible. Ideological currents will at least influence the choice of the questions treated; we shall be fortunate if they do not exert any perverse influence on the actual treatment of these questions."[732]

However, while no philosopher can fully escape the ideological influences of his community,[733] using ideology, masquerading as natural law, to combat all the relativisms of our time does a disservice to natural law. It is thus essential to specify the role of the philosopher:

> A philosopher is not equipped to handle contingent matters[734] . . . . But a philosopher knows what prudence is; he knows what conditions must be satisfied for the handling of contingent matters to be prudential . . . . By providing standards by which it may be possible to distinguish between prudential action and sheer expediency, or between a good law and a bad one, a philosopher makes not an insignificant contribution.[735]

And this is where mistakes have been made. Some thinkers have failed to distinguish natural law from its prudential application to concrete situations, and this failure results in natural law being turned into an ideology, a rational system that resolves practical problems. Simon shows that given the challenge of existentialism, "with its powers of destruction," some have unwittingly and unnecessarily had recourse to ideology as a tool with which to fight back in defense of natural law, but in fact they replace the natural law by an ideology. They want to use natural law deductions to prove things that can only be settled by prudential judgments; they do so because they want a purely rational argument, with the authority of pure reason, to resolve the more ambiguous problems of practical life. Simon gives the

---

[732] Simon, *The Tradition of Natural Law*, 23.

[733] Ibid., 25

[734] Simon distinguishes clearly the role of the philosopher from that of the wise and prudent ruler. The one deals with essences and objective realities, and the other with political contingencies which require experience and the wily ways of virtue. See *The Tradition of Natural Law*, 24-26.

[735] Simon, *The Tradition of Natiural Law*, 25-26.

example of moral agents trying to prove too much from natural law. He says:

> For a number of years we have been witnessing a tendency, in teachers and preachers, to assume that natural law decides, with the universality proper to the necessity of essences, incomparably more issues than it is actually able to decide. There is a tendency to treat in terms of natural law questions which call for treatment in terms of prudence. It should be clear that any concession to this tendency is bound promptly to cause disappointment and skepticism. People are quick to realize what is weak, or dishonest, in pretending to decide by axioms of natural law, or by airtight deduction from these axioms, questions that really cannot be solved except by the obscure methods of prudence.[736]

The role of virtue is thus denied when a purely rational version of natural law turns into an ideology that attempts to solve prudential problems. The role of well-formed inclinations is removed and replaced by a purely logical argument that makes no appeal to virtue. If the other theories inimical to natural law, such as existentialism and mechanism, err by defect, the replacement of natural law by an ideology errs by excess, in the sense of moralists "taking advantage of the will to believe on the part of their followers"[737] in order to pretend, through the use of sophistry, that natural law can do more than it can actually do.

In *Practical Knowledge*, Simon points to the "breakdown in tradition"[738] as the reason for the failure to distinguish natural law from its prudential application. When firm traditions that guide action are lost the tendency is to multiply precepts of natural law in compensation. In order to show how this happens Simon argues that in spite of the sufficiency of the answers provided by righteous inclination in prudential decisions, a trait of the culture of our times is continually to demand explanation for the truth of such actions.

---

[736] Ibid., 23.
[737] Ibid., 31.
[738] Simon, *Practical Knowledge*, 97.

"The people of our times are less willing than those of other times to fulfill without understanding." [739] Simon attributes this need and demand to the "breakdown of tradition." Russell Hittinger writes that what "Simon has in mind is the breakdown of the pre-theoretical bases for moral consensus—bases that owe more to affective sources of order and common striving than to philosophy."[740] Hittinger is surely right since Simon says the following in *Practical Knowledge*:

> This particularly strong demand for explanation, this particular reluctance to fulfill rules that are not explained, can be traced to . . . the breakdown of tradition. . . . Now, it is tradition that proposes rules that have to be fulfilled whether they are understood or not. It is tradition that is supposed to conserve and to utter the rules that are established by the inclinations of just hearts without being, as yet, provided with the character of rational clarity.[741]

It may well be this breakdown of the pre-theoretical bases for the functioning of society and frantic efforts to replace it that is responsible for the excessive claims of some teachers and preachers and the proliferation of theories of natural law in our times. These overdone efforts that neglect the role of the virtue of prudence constitute a disservice to natural law and breed skepticism.

II: Virtue and Facets of Positive Law and Natural Law

On the Existence of the Just by Nature

Having examined Simon's definition of the naturally just and some philosophies that radically negate this idea, we will now look at what he says about some of the substantive questions touching on law and virtue. It is a question of looking at the interaction between virtue and aspects of law. We will begin with the arguments Simon gives for the existence of the just by nature.

---

[739] Ibid.
[740] Russell Hittinger's Introduction to *The Tradition of Natural Law*, xxiv.
[741] Simon, *Practical Knowledge*, 97.

The existence of the just by nature is an extremely difficult question, Simon says, because people point to different mores and practices around the world today and all through human history in order to deny its existence. Simon gives the example of euthanasia to illustrate the point:

> Take, for instance, a subject like euthanasia. In our society one finds people having tea, playing bridge, and doing more important things together, being good friends. And yet some of them think that killing a patient who has incurable cancer is murder, while others say that it is a charitable thing to do. He is in this world for a few more weeks or months, with no prospect but to stand terrible suffering; give him a pill of morphine and let that be the end of it for him and everybody around him . . . . What is the right thing to do by nature?[742]

If natural law exists, why is there so much disagreement regarding its contents? A discussion of the question of the existence of natural law has the aspect of virtue written all over it.

Simon's approach is to use positive law as foil to get to the existence of natural law. He asks "whether the understanding of the positive law leads rationally to an antecedent, to a more profound or universal law, which we might call the 'law of nature.'"[743] After answering the question affirmatively, he informs us that it is best tackled by way of "three lesser questions."[744]

The first question is whether "it makes sense to ask whether a positive law is just or unjust?"[745] Noting that only a few legal positivists and some skeptical lawyers might answer negatively, Simon says that there is unanimity that such a question makes sense. In fact, people ask such questions of positive law all the time, the implication being that there is another yardstick, a natural moral law, against which positive law is measured.

---

[742] Simon, *The Tradition of Natural Law*, 126.
[743] Ibid., 111.
[744] Ibid., 112.
[745] Ibid.

Simon observes that in our times, pragmatists, seeking to avoid the use of the terms good and bad, and thus the idea of virtue with regard to the law, prefer to say that we enact laws because they "work." In like manner they say that we prefer democracy because it "works."[746] Simon argues that this is a cover that seeks to avoid the issue. To say that something works implies a set goal and an agreed end. And an end is agreed because people think it is good. He gives the example of the vaccine against paralytic poliomyelitis.[747] When we say that the vaccine works, it is because we judge that it is better not to have any people suffering from paralytic poliomyelitis. It is relative to this goal that the vaccine is judged to work. Without this prior setting of ends, judged to be good and worthy of pursuit and given as something good by nature, it would make no sense to say that the vaccine works. The same is true of positive law. If it said to work it is because prior goals, judged to be good, have been set.

Simon formulates the second question, which takes us from positive law to natural law, by asking the reasons for which we are sometimes moved to effect changes in positive law.[748] In framing and giving a response to this question, Simon is inspired by Aquinas who treats of the topic in "Of change in Laws" in the *Summa Theologiae*.[749] Simon notes that the issue of the reasons for changing a law is implied in the preceding question since a law might be changed because it is judged to be unjust. He adds that a law might also be changed because of changed circumstances which make the particular law obsolete. He gives the example of credit organizations which might crop up in society pretending to offer higher dividends than the banks but involving greater risks of clients losing all of their money. A change in the law designed to address the new situation would be in order, the underlying principle being that "it is better that people should not be robbed of their savings."[750] The presumption is that people who have worked hard and honestly for their money

---

[746]Ibid., 113-114.

[747]Ibid., 114.

[748] Ibid., 115; See Jacques Maritain, *Philosophy of Nature*, trans. Imelda C. Byrne (New York: Philosophical Library, 1951), 102-114.

[749]Aquinas, *Summa Theologiae*, I-II q. 97 a. 1 & 2.

[750] Simon, *The Tradition of Natural Law*, 116.

should not be duped by unscrupulous money dealers. Positive law is changed, therefore, because the virtue of justice has been violated and also to achieve a better application of what is perceived to be naturally just in different or changed circumstances.

The third question has to do with the reasons for obedience to positive laws. The question here is why law should be obeyed. Is it just for extrinsic reasons especially fear of the consequences of disobedience such as being thrown into jail or worse? Simon asks if "the ground for obeying the law (can) be reduced, completely and in all cases, to a desire to avoid the trouble which would follow if the law was disobeyed?"[751] He admits that it is possible that in some cases such considerations play a role. But this could not be the case in "all legal propositions in all respects" since it "would void positive law of all obligation and ground it in sheer power."[752]

Citing the work of Iredell Jenkins,[753] Simon points to the fact that there is quasi unanimity that the obligations of positive law should not be interpreted in such a way that freedom, choice and morality are shoved to the background and pride of place given to external constraints. The reasons for obedience to positive law are evident in the definition of law as "an ordinance of reason for the common good made by him, who has the care of the community, and promulgated."[754] Law, therefore, is obeyed because it is reasonable, and because it is ordered to the common good, and not just out of fear of punishment. Simon reasons that "when a society is in such a condition that its laws are obeyed only insofar as there is fear of being caught and punished, it has already disintegrated and even the fear of punishment cannot do much to hold it together."[755] Rather law is obeyed because of an intrinsic justice at its heart. "*Nothing would be right by enactment if some things were not right by nature.*"[756] We bow before natural moral law because our virtue is measured by it.

---

[751] Ibid.

[752] Ibid.

[753] Iredell Jenkins, "The Matrix of Positive Law," *Natural Law Forum* 6 (1961): 1-50 especially 3-16. See Simon, *The Tradition of Natural Law*, 184.

[754] Aquinas, *Summa Theologiae*, I-II q. 90 a.4.

[755] Simon, *The Tradition of Natural Law*, 118.

[756] Ibid., 117-118 (his emphasis).

On Knowledge of Natural Moral Law

We have already touched on this topic at the end of chapter one within the context of the definition of moral virtue. Our treatment there was within the context of the definition of virtue as requiring consistency in choosing the good in contingent circumstances. We noted that if virtue has to do with choice of the good there must be moral axioms that basically point out the good as distinct from what is evil. These axioms, we said, are known primarily by instinct.

The question to be examined here is whether virtue is operative in our ability to know natural moral law or what Aquinas refers to as the natural right. We know positive laws by being told about them or by the intellectual study of jurisprudence; do we know natural law in the same way?[757] Clearly, how we know natural moral law, like everything touching on natural law, is a difficult question to answer, but following a tradition going back to Aristotle and Aquinas,[758] Simon answers that there are two ways to such knowledge: by inclination and by cognition.

We have already indicated Simon's reference to Sophocles' contribution, in the *Antigone*, to the idea of natural law. Simon adds that Aristotle, who quotes from the *Antigone*, goes on to make an important contribution on this question, pointing out that this law is first known by inclination. In the passage from *Rhetoric* already referred to, he writes that "there really is, as everyone to some extent *divines*, a natural justice and injustice that is binding on all men."[759] In order to show this particular contribution of Aristotle's Simon analyses the word "divines" found in the above quotation (the Greek word is *manteuomai* which is related to the English "mantic"). Going into its Greek roots he shows that it comes from a verb which means "to perceive through sympathy or intuition; to detect; to foretell; to

---

[757] Robert Sokolowski, "Knowing Natural Law," in *Pictures, Quotations and Distinctions: Fourteen Essays in Phenomenology* (Notre Dame: Notre Dame University Press, 1992), 278-279.

[758] Aquinas, *SummanTheologiae*, I-II q. 51 a.1.; See Simon, *The Tradition of Natural Law*, xxix.

[759] Aristotle, *Rhetoric*, trans. W. Rhys Robert in *The Basic Works of Aristotle*, ed. Richard McKeon, 1370 (1.13.1373b6-8). (our emphasis).

have or feel a presage."⁷⁶⁰ He concludes by saying that "no doubt Aristotle in this passage maintains that natural law is known by inclination,"⁷⁶¹ the inclination of a good and honest will, one shaped by virtue, before it is known by way of cognition.⁷⁶²

Sokolowski points us in the same direction:

> How then does the sense of what is good or bad by nature arise? It occurs primarily in an *immediate*, particular criticism of customary behavior within which one lives. Someone gradually *appreciates* that something we all do really ought not to be done . . . (or) that something we do not do should really be done.⁷⁶³

Sokolowski further uses such phrases as "moral perception"⁷⁶⁴ or "there may be a rather clear conviction," or "there may arise suspicions that," in order to indicate this inclination⁷⁶⁵

Where knowledge by cognition exists, it is to be preferred but when inclinations are sound, that is, when they are the inclinations of a virtuous person, judgments by them are certain. Simon argues that quite often, inclination "is the only way to ascertain practical judgments when they are considered concretely."⁷⁶⁶ To buttress this position, he gives an example in *The Tradition of Natural Law*⁷⁶⁷ which we find in *Practical Knowledge*⁷⁶⁸ and in *The Definition of Moral Virtue*.⁷⁶⁹ Let us narrate it as Simon gives it in *The Definition of Moral Virtue*:

> Let us imagine a smart businessman, who is also a good, prudent man, being approached by a smart crook. The project he is offered to

---

⁷⁶⁰ Simon, *The Tradition of Natural Law*, 132.

⁷⁶¹ Ibid.

⁷⁶²Ibid. See also Aristotle, *Ethics*, 10.5.1176a17; Aquinas, *Summa Theologiae* I-I q. 6 ad. 3; I-II q. 65 a. 1&2; q.95 a.2 ad.4; II-II q. 45. a.2.

⁷⁶³Sokolowski, "Knowing Natural Law," in *Pictures, Quotations and Distinctions: Fourteen Essays in Phenomenology*, 279 (our emphasis).

⁷⁶⁴ Ibid., 284

⁷⁶⁵Ibid., 280.

⁷⁶⁶ Simon, *The Tradition of Natural Law*, 128.

⁷⁶⁷ Ibid.,

⁷⁶⁸Simon *Practical Knowledge*, 19.

⁷⁶⁹ Simon *The Definition of Moral Virtue*, 109.

join looks perfect in every way: no risk to speak of, very little work, and great expectations. Because the plan is so attractive, our businessman goes over it again very carefully and still cannot find anything wrong with it. Nevertheless, he rejects the offer and tells the man not to call back. And when a friend puzzled by his decision asks what was wrong with the project he says: I did not see anything wrong, but I smelled it. The deal stinks.[770]

The decision is arrived at by inclination or instinct. In the version narrated in *The Tradition of Natural Law*, Simon adds the idea that inclination operates in *all* contingent circumstances when he says:

> When moral problems are considered concretely—in all their concreteness and individuality—the last word belongs always to sound inclination. There are no exceptions. There is always some aspect of the entirely concrete, circumstantiated issue—individual, unique, unprecedented, unrenewable—some aspect that can be decided only by inclination.[771]

Inclination is sometimes followed by knowledge through cognition. The two forms of knowledge are not mutually exclusive. Simon says that inclination and cognition often work together and gives an example that connects the two. It is of a man who negotiates a contract to execute a certain job. Some parts of the job will be difficult to carry out and will demand a lot of work, but he accepts the terms and freely signs the contract. However, in executing the job he bails out on those parts that are difficult. Given this situation we immediately conclude that what he has done is wrong. How do we know that? At first, by instinct, because the proposition "let us cheat in the execution of a contract" is naturally repugnant. But we also know that it is wrong by rational apprehension, since a contract that was negotiated with the full cooperation and acceptance of all parties and freely signed by them has been violated.[772]

---

[770] Ibid., 109.
[771] Simon, *The Tradition of Natural Law*, 129.
[772] Ibid., 132-134.

Simon repeatedly mentions Kant as the philosopher who tried to drive a wedge between the universe of nature and the universe of morality.[773] For Kant, cognizing the moral law by instinct is unthinkable. Kant appeals to reason alone regarding our knowledge of the moral law. It is instructive here to refer to Sokolowski who gives us an account of how Kant does this. He points to Kant's work *Groundwork of the Metaphysics of Morals* in which Kant's aim is to seek out and establish the supreme principle of morality. Kant finds this principle in the categorical imperative which he states as follows: "I ought never to act except in such a way that I could also will that my maxim should become a universal law."[774] Kant appeals to reason to demonstrate that one would be deterred from stealing or any other crime, through the test of generalization, if one realized that such action by everyone would make life in society impossible. As is clear, there is no question of cognizing through instinct here but by reasoning.

Sokolowski then goes on to indicate the problem with this approach:

> Kant suggests that we determine moral obligation by turning, primarily, to abstract reasoning. He finds nothing compelling or obligatory in moral sensibility as such. Only the necessitating force of reason instills a prohibition or a command into behavior. This move into abstract argument implies that the person who reasons about morals loses his engagement in situations.[775]

Kant's account fails to take into consideration at least two important factors: the "loss of engagement in situations" indicated in the above quote and the significance of the character of the person in moral activity.[776]

---

[773]Ibid., 42; 121; 124.

[774] Immanuel Kant, *Groundwork of the Metaphysics of Morals*, ed. & trans. Mary Gregor (Cambridge: Cambridge University Press, 2010), 15.

[775]Sokolowski, "Knowing Natural Law," in *Pictures, Quotations, and Distinctions: Fourteen Essays in Phenomenology*, 285.

[776]Ibid., 286.

It remains true that fulfillment without understanding is often all we can manage and this raises the question as to whether we can trust our inclinations and why. How can we be sure that our inclinations shorn of understanding can lead us to virtuous action? Simon addresses this question in *Practical Knowledge*. And what he says there—which is good for all practical judgments seen as the form of human actions—is also good for the judgments we make regarding natural law. This is how Simon poses the question:

> Is it possible for our heart, i.e., our will and our sense appetite, to be in such steady agreement with the object of virtue that our inclinations and aversions no longer be exposed to the arbitrariness of subjectivity but assume the reliable power of an object?[777]

He answers as follows:

> If a person is known for unflinching dedication to justice, we think that his example can be safely followed, in difficult problems of justice, provided all the relevant circumstances are the same in his case and ours. We trust that the instincts of people whom we know to be really virtuous cannot be at variance with what virtue demands. Clearly, there exists a harmony, a sympathy, a dynamic unity, a community of nature, in short, a connaturality, between the virtuous heart and the requirements of virtue.[778]

That our inclination has to be righteous rather than warped to get us there is a basic position of Simon. Whereas someone with a debased morality is not ruled out by any objective necessity from metaphysical excellence, the psychological relation between some metaphysical truths and dispositions of the human appetite, make his grasp of such truths improbable.[779] This is the reason for Simon's strong language regarding the writings of Bertrand Russell on questions of ethics, marriage and religion in general. He says:

---

[777] Simon, *Practical Knowledge*, 20.
[778] Ibid.
[779] Ibid., 40.

An excellent negative example here is Bertrand Russell. In his writings on these subjects there is a total absence of inclinations and repugnances, rational or emotional . . . . When he writes on marriage, sex, and morals, he reveals not only his ignorance but also a considerable perversion of judgment. His writings illustrate convincingly what is left when judgment by inclination is completely gone, when there are no prepossessions left, when freedom from tradition is recklessly asserted. Then, what is left, in fact, is nothing, and the attempt to substitute something strictly rational for that nothing is a vain illusion.[780]

What we have seen about knowledge of natural law by inclination and rational knowledge, and the reliable nature of the one or the other, should not, however, be construed to mean that such knowledge is given all at once. It is not—and here Simon answers one of the main arguments against the existence of natural law. He leans on Aquinas for support for his argument specifically Aquinas' treatment of the question as to whether natural law is the same for all men. We might point to the following passage, in which after making a distinction between the speculative and the practical reason, Aquinas says:

> The speculative reason is differently situated in this matter, from the practical reason. For, since the speculative reason is busied chiefly with necessary things, which cannot be otherwise than they are, its proper conclusions, like the universal principles, contain the truth without fail. The practical reason, on the other hand, is busied with contingent matters, about which human actions are concerned . . . . As to the proper conclusions of the speculative reason, the truth is the same for all: thus it is true for all that the three angles of a triangle are together equal to two right angles, *although it is not known to all*. But as to the proper conclusions of the practical reason, neither is the truth or

---

[780] Simon, *The Tradition of Natural Law*, 136.

rectitude the same for all, *nor, where it is the same, is it equally known by all*.[781]

In the above passage Aquinas distinguishes, among others,—in the context of the *per se nota* status of the first premises of natural law—that which is *per se notum secumdum se* (evident in itself) from that which is *per se notum quo ad nos* (evident to us).[782]

On the basis of passages such as the above, Simon draws two conclusions regarding our knowledge of the content of natural law:

1) Firstly he points out that knowledge of natural law is progressive.[783] He argues, quite rightly, that if we do not acquire knowledge of biology or chemistry all at once but gradually and over time, neither should we expect to know everything about natural law in a moment of inspiration. He writes:

> The moral world is no less mysterious than the physical world. And if mankind advances rather slowly in the knowledge of the physical world, there is absolutely no reason to postulate that it should do better in the understanding of the moral universe, which is incomparably more mysterious because it includes the mystery of freedom.[784]

Thus there is nothing conclusive about the argument against natural law, which is based on differences of perception from one epoch to another, and from one society to another.[785] To indicate this progress in moral knowledge, Simon gives the example of how people have progressively moved from polygamy to monogamy, and how polyandry which jeopardizes knowledge of the paternity of the child, is virtually non-existent today.[786]

---

[781]Aquinas, *Summa Theologiae*, I-II q. 94 a. 4 (p. 1011); See also article 6 of the same question. See Simon, *The Tradition of Natural Law*, 158. (our emphasis).
[782]Simon, *The Tradition of Natural Law*, xxxii.
[783]Ibid., 158, 161-162.
[784]Ibid., 162.
[785]Ibid., 158.
[786]Ibid., 157; 164.

2) Secondly, Simon points to the possibility of an "abnormal blinding" in the understanding, not just of individuals, but of societies. He writes:

> We must be aware of the possibility of an abnormal blinding of our understanding of what is naturally right. We observe that in individuals all the time. . . . Now what happens to individuals can also happen to societies. . . . The possibility of corrupt judgment in a social group cannot simply be excluded. In fact, it is to be suspected that the judgment of every social group is blind or corrupt in some respect and to some extent.[787]

This lack of the virtue of discernment, this corruption of judgment, means that entire social groups can get it wrong when it comes to natural moral law. This might result from human vice or from the influence of an ideology.

On Law as Premise and Conclusion: The Role of Virtue

Even though Simon often writes quite simply about natural law when he means natural moral law, he distinguishes three senses in which the idea of law can be understood. He says we might talk about "the law of the land" (positive law), "the law of gravity" (natural law of the physical world), or "the law of the moral world" which he also refers to as "the natural law of morality"[788] (natural moral law). He insists, again and again, that the use of the word law in the above instances is to be understood analogically. But the analogy is not metaphorical, nor one of attribution, but one of proper proportionality since law belongs properly to each of the cases here and does not apply through attribution or through metaphor.[789] Our task here is to see what role Simon gives virtue, as premise and as conclusion, especially in the relationships that exist between natural law and positive law.

---

[787]Ibid., 158.
[788]Ibid., 110.
[789]Ibid., 110; 69-70.

The question with which we are concerned under this heading is posed by Simon in *The Tradition of Natural Law* in his examination of the rational nature of law in these terms:

> Let us now ask in what capacity law is a work of reason and more precisely, whether it is a work of reason in the capacity of conclusion or in that of premise.[790]

This question is important since, as will become clear shortly any system of laws needs to be applied to concrete situations and has the ground of its justification outside of itself. It is clear that whether as premise or as conclusion the interactions between natural moral law and positive law reveal the workings of virtue.[791]

Simon begins with positive law since he says that "sound method" demands we begin by examining those "judgments which apply to actions immediately."[792] Is positive law a premise or a conclusion and does virtue play any role in its application? Simon describes a positive law as a rule and points out that as such "there is nothing more essential to it than the intelligible features implied in the concept of rule (which) include universality and necessity."[793] The universality and necessity of the law of a society take into consideration, and without sacrificing objectivity, the diversity in the beliefs and mores of its members. Simon writes that "law is more at home in the realm of necessity" and "if any law is so grounded in a necessary state of affairs as to be unqualifiedly immutable, this is law in the most excellent sense of the term."[794]

The problem is that when it comes to putting the law into practice, that is when it comes to action, we are always confronted by features that are the opposite of law, namely, singularity and contingency. Simon writes:

---

[790] Ibid., 82.
[791] Ibid., 161.
[792] Ibid.
[793] Ibid., 83.
[794] Ibid., 84.

The individual case with which practical judgment ultimately has to deal may always be in some significant respect unique, unprecedented, and unrenewable. Thus, the last conclusion of the practical discourse is marked in essential fashion by features of strict singularity and of contingency.[795]

What the above means is that not everything can be written into law since there are a multiplicity of situations to which it must be applied some of them not even foreseen when the law is written.

This means that between the law and action there is always a space. This space Simon tells us is filled by the soundness of inclination. He says:

> A practical judgment fully adjusted to the circumstances is not so much a work of reason as that of an inclination. It cannot be connected logically with any first principle. It ought indeed to be connected with principles but owing to the contingency of its matter, the soundness of an inclination is the only thing that can effect this connection.[796]

Simon thus repeats what we have seen elsewhere in this work. Its relevance here is that positive law is treated in the capacity of premise and its application in that of conclusion with the need for virtue in sound inclination being an ever present arbiter. The last practical judgment, "which is congruent to action as form is congruent to matter,"[797] is the conclusion mediated by virtuous inclination from premises whose rational bases have much receded to the background.

It should be mentioned here that Simon uses the idea of law as a premise rather than a conclusion to debunk the idea of a universally applicable social science. He says:

> If law is a premise rather than a conclusion, if, universally, law admits of no immediate contact with the world of action, the ideal of a social science which would, in each particular case, procure a rational

---

[795]Ibid., 82.
[796] Ibid.
[797]Ibid., 83.

solution and render governmental prudence unnecessary is thoroughly deceptive.[798]

Simon is very good on this point. Social science could be universally applicable only if human beings were only subject to *physical* natural law. In such a case there would be no room for deliberation, prudence, and virtue, all of which would really be illusory. Clearly, no human being can live under such an assumption, no matter how much a mechanistic reductionist might profess it in theory.

But—and this brings us to the second case in which law can be premise or conclusion—while positive law is a premise needing virtue with regard to its application in contingent circumstances, it is also a conclusion from a set of premises, namely natural moral law. It should be added that in this case as well there is a role for virtue, viz, a need for virtue in the formulation of positive law itself. This is what Simon says about the existence of this particular relationship of premise and conclusion:

> Law is a premise; it is a work of the reason having the character of premise. And among laws, the natural laws have more the character of premises than positive laws; they are prior premises.[799]

Regarding the role of virtue here, the relevant question concerns the nature of this derivation of positive law from natural law. Simon explains its nature and why it requires virtue:

> Are these derived legal formulas determined by logical connection with axioms, or are some of them the work of prudential determination? The answer is plain: indefinitely many legal formulas are the work of a legislative prudence and their determination has been worked out by the sensible, the dependable inclinations of experienced and well-intentioned persons. The obscure methods of prudence, which are at work in the space between the last legal expression and

---

[798]Ibid., 85.
[799]Ibid., 129.

the ultimate form of action, are already at work, on a very large scale, within the system of legislation itself.[800]

Thus the virtue needed in the application of positive law in concrete situations is already necessary in its formulation from the premises of natural law. We have already seen how Simon shows this in three questions he proposes to show the existence of natural law.[801] Each of these questions leads from positive law to natural law by the obscure ways of prudence.

On God as the Author of Natural Law and Natural Moral Law

We will conclude this last point of the last chapter by looking at how Simon ties natural law and natural moral law and thus virtue to God as its origin. Simon indicates that whereas this question would be a non issue for atheistic existentialist philosophers, who propose a comprehensive indeterminacy, and deny both nature as we know it, and God,[802] it is not for that reason not worth exploring. He takes as his starting point the question of obligation under natural law, that is, the issue of why we obey positive law, a topic we have examined in another context.[803] As we have already seen, Simon's analysis leads him to the conclusion that "natural law exists in nature before it exists in our judgment." He says:

> Natural law, in the very meaning of that expression, exists ontologically before it exists rationally in our minds; it is embodied in things before it is thought out, thought through, understood, intelligently grasped.[804]

But the key question is whether we should stop here; it is whether the "last word belongs to things."[805] That is, is it possible to talk about

---

[800] Ibid., 86.
[801] See pp.202-205.
[802] Simon, *The Tradition of Natural Law*, 63.
[803] See pp. 205.
[804] Simon, *The Tradition of Natural Law*, 137.
[805] Ibid.

natural law as existing in things without raising the question of its ultimate grounding? If we do, then we are confronted with the unpleasant fact of the rational being controlled by the non-rational. That is, if we stop here, it would seem that things control reason. We, therefore, need to go further in our analysis.[806]

Reverting to the witness of philosophical history, Simon mentions Aristotle and the reasons for his failure to arrive at a proper idea of God by reflecting on nature. This, he says, is because Aristotle saw God more as final cause rather than as an efficient cause, and, given this fact, as moving the universe as an object of desire or love. Simon says that the "gaps in his metaphysics" prevented him, as one of the founders of natural law theory, from making a clear philosophical connection between the world and God. Simon quotes Eduard Zeller who writes of Aristotle:

> The absolutely perfect being, the highest good, is also the end to which all things move and strive. On him the uniform order, the cohesion and life of the world depend. Aristotle did not assume the action of the divine will on the world or any creative activity or influence of the deity in the course of the world.[807]

Simon thinks that Zeller is a bit too categorical in his assertions and prefers a more nuanced approach when he says that, "Aristotle never worked out the metaphysical instruments necessary to understand God as efficient cause without having him bear the counter impact of his own causation." "Aristotle was unable," he continues, "to explain how God's cognition of the world involves no influence of things upon him, no passivity on the part of his intellect."[808] It is rather that, given the tools he had, he could not say more on the question. Simon continues:

---

[806]Ibid., 136-138.
[807] Eduard Zeller, *Outlines of the History of Greek Philosophy*, trans. L.R. Palmer (London: Routledge & Kegan Paul Ltd., 1931), 177-178. See Simon, *The Tradition of Natural Law*, 175.
[808] Simon, *The Tradition of Natural Law*, 28.

When we consider the relation between natural law and intelligence, we realize that a metaphysician who lacks the instruments needed for treating the relation between natural law as a rule of behavior immanent in things and natural law as the judgment of an ultimate governing intelligence—we realize that such a metaphysician is reasonably inclined to economy of words on the subject.[809]

In various parts of *The Tradition of Natural Law* Simon gives other examples of philosophers who forge various kinds of links between God and natural law. He mentions Hugo Grotius[810] and Descartes, who, as we have seen, works out a relationship between God and the world that serves his purposes. Within the context of his mechanism, we have already mentioned how he resolves the question of the relations between the thinking thing and the extended thing by positing a certain kind of god in order to guarantee stability in nature. Simon further mentions eighteenth century deism whose thinking was along similar lines. For it also, it is God who guarantees stability in nature such that bodies will fall downwards and not upwards.[811]

Simon is of the view that there is today a greater readiness to accept a link between nature and God. But there is in dispute a prior methodological question to be resolved. He says:

> The connection of the problem of natural law with the problem of God is perhaps more commonly acknowledged in our time than in any other period. . . . But it is not easy to show precisely what this connection is. One may wonder whether the study of moral nature and of natural law is a way to the knowledge of God or whether the knowledge of God must be had before the proposition that there exists a natural law of the moral world is established. We may be able to show that the truth is better expressed by the first part of this alternative.[812]

---

[809] Ibid.

[810] Hugo Grotius, *The Rights of War and Peace*, trans. A.C. Campbell (Washington: M. Walter Dunne, 1901), 22. Simon, *The Tradition of Natural Law*, 62.

[811] Simon, *The Tradition of Natural Law*, 138-139.

[812] Ibid., 62.

As the last sentence above says, Simon proposes to anchor his proof in the experience of nature. In this recourse to experience we can see the influence of the five ways of Aquinas. He writes:

> Just as the consideration of beauty in things perishable leads to unparticipated Beauty—remember the speech of Socrates in the *Symposium*—so the consideration of law in human affairs leads to the unparticipated Law, the eternal law which is identical with the divine intellect and the divine substance.[813]

In an assessment of Simon's contribution to natural law theory, Steven A. Long highlights this recourse to the premises of the five ways of Aquinas as a *"tour de force."*[814] He regards the "assimilation of the proof for the existence of God proceeding from moral obligation to the pattern of the proofs from contingency, motion, causality" as one of the high points of Simon work in this domain.[815]

Regarding the proof itself as developed by Simon, let us return to the deists. Purified of extraneous elements, Simon indicates that the following syllogism, derived from the deists, and which regards the order of discovery, would be metaphysically acceptable:

1. Natural law exists in our minds as a proposition.
2. Before it is apprehended, it exists embodied in things.
3. In the third stage, we are led to the recognition of the "author of nature."[816]

Simon asks why it is that we cannot go back *ad infinitum* in our search for the "author of nature" and thus drive it into inexistence. That is, why is it that the regulating intellect does not need to be regulated and so on *ad infinitum*? In answer, he argues that the

---

[813] Ibid.

[814] Steven A. Long, "Yves Simon's Approach to Natural Law," *The Thomist* 59 (1995): 133.

[815] Ibid.

[816] Simon, *The Tradition of Natural Law*, 139.

problem of an infinite series is resolved at the point where being and knowing are one.[817] This is the substance of Simon's rebuttal of the possibility of an infinite series:

> The proof of God from the fact of obligation is of the same logical type as the other aposterioristic proofs, i.e., from the facts of motion, efficient causality, contingency and necessity, degrees of being, and the order in the universe. The argument from the fact of obligation shares with these other philosophical proofs the formal principle of demonstration, viz., the necessity of a first cause which is pure act or being, itself subsistent in its own right. Applied to our case, what ends the allegedly infinite series is an attribute, a characteristic of that pure act: the identity of "to be" and "to think". . . . For Aristotle, God is an act of intellectual consciousness. God's "to be" is an act of thinking whose object is itself *Met.* 12.9.1075a)."[818]

As can be seen above, Simon refers to Aristotle for support of his basic argument that since in God there is identity of "to be" and "to know,"[819] the existence of things with a certain nature leads directly to God. Simon clinches the point as follows:

> Between the "to be" of God and the "to think" of God there is no distinction whatsoever; it is like two names designating exactly the same thing. And it is this identity of being and knowing that stops the regression into infinity in our search for the ground of obligation under natural law. . . . The facts of order in the universe and the facts of obligation under natural law, i.e., that our reason bows before things, both require rationally a transcendent First Being in whom 'to be" and "to act" and "to think" are one and the same."[820]

Things are what they are because God knows them in the very act of knowing himself.

---

[817]Ibid., 141-142.
[818] Ibid.
[819]Ibid., 143.
[820]Ibid., 144-145.

We might summarize the relationship between virtue and law in Simon's thinking as follows. For Simon, that natural law exists and can be defined is not difficult to discern. That is why the attacks of the Epicureans, the Existentialists and the Mechanists must be set aside. That natural law can be known by instinct and cognition is clear in Aristotle, Aquinas and others. As to the interplay between virtue and natural law, two approaches are possible. The first would emphasize the role of natural law in determining the moral content of our actions. This, for Simon, is a false path, the by-product of ideology. The second, and the right one for Simon, is that whereas natural law contributes broad principles, the modalities of their application belongs to the realm of virtue in such fashion that the ultimate choice is made by inclination of the will rather than intellectual cognition. In everyday life, the example of the virtuous person is indispensable and this is what rescues inclination from the throes of subjectivity. For Simon, the law of nature is ultimately anchored in God as its author.

Conclusion

Vukan Kuic, who was one of Simon's students and later edited some of his works after his death, pays glowing tribute to his teacher when he tells us that, "Yves Simon may have shed enough light on some of the most difficult problems of political theory to help us out of our present confusions."[821] It would be safe to say that Kuic, for the most part, has in mind Simon's philosophical work on the question of authority and its relation to liberty understood as superdetermination, the theory of decision making and the role of the virtue of prudence in it, and his masterly exposition of the philosophy of work, among others themes.

Even if his work on virtue, its definition and how it applies to politics have not yet received as much attention, his contribution on this issue is no less remarkable as this work would have shown. Regarding the definition of virtue, Simon explains three modern theories whose aim is to replace virtue, namely, the recourse to natural or spontaneous goodness, the attempt to make people better through social engineering, and the thinking that people can be made good through psychological manipulation. Simon tells us that what these ideas have in common is the desire to find alternatives to the need to acquire the virtues. In a beautiful passage he says:

> The theory of the interconnection of virtues entails the conclusion that the cost of prudence is frightfully high. No wonder that much ingenuity is spent in finding ways out of such a predicament, albeit with the complicity of the most improbable illusions. Socratic theories identifying science and virtue, casuistic extensions of moral science into the domain of contingency, the calculus of probabilities replacing good judgment in magistrates and rulers, a social science which would say what we need to know in order to make our societies rational—these

---

[821]Kuic, "Yves Simon's Contribution to Political Science," 56.

products of rationalistic optimism, no matter how fantastic, are easier to accept than the prospect of having to acquire all virtues.[822]

The key to understanding Simon's idea of virtue is to examine how he contrasts it with habit in three areas. Whereas habit is characterized by subjective necessity, a lack of vitality and excludes voluntariness, virtue possesses the opposite traits of objective necessity, vitality, and freedom. In order to explain the first, we might take the example of a chain smoker. In habit, his urge to smoke is not on account of health reasons, or for any other personal good, but is the result of a purely internal compulsion. This is what we refer to as a subjective necessity, whereas in objective necessity the reasons for repeated actions are objectively good. The second trait, that of vitality means that by habit we mechanically repeat certain actions formed over time. Virtue on the other hand is creative, taking account of contingent circumstances. The virtuous person, grounded in the right, gives fresh and original answers to the different situations in which he finds himself. Thirdly and finally, in contrast to habit which excludes voluntariness being a mechanical repetition through internal compulsion, Simon defines virtue in terms of freedom understood as superdetermination, or the mastery one possesses over his rational and emotional powers. It is the highest form of freedom because the person who is truly free is not the one swayed by every wind, but the one who through right choices has fixed his character in the good.[823]

Quite apart from the theoretical contribution Simon makes in helping us define and understand the meaning of freedom and other concepts, Simon's clarification of the true definition of virtue is of major importance. His explanation of what a true understanding of virtue means is designed to save modern man from illusory alternatives that do not deliver. While accepting that psychotic cases exist and can be helped by modern medicine, Simon's work

---

[822] Simon, *Practical Knowledge*, 22.
[823] Simon, *Freedom of Choice* (New York: Fordham University Press, 1992), 152-153

encourages us to get down to the difficult work of acquiring and living the virtues.

Simon's definition of virtue leads to the political realm because his aim was always to clarify the ideas by which men live whether in their individual lives or in the public space that they share in common. He tells us that "political society is not brought about by instincts and infra-rational forces but by rational judgment and free will."[824] If virtue is understood as that which directs us to choose the objective good in contingent circumstances, there is little doubt it would play a central role in politics, which is about choice in an important area of human activity. The question to be answered in this domain is usually, "what is to be done."

Given the central character of the common good in politics, Simon applies his ideas on virtue to the important question of defining it. Not the least of his contributions on the common good is how it should not be conceived, namely, as a work of art (something external to man) or as the concourse of individual interests. Simon is adamant that "beyond the satisfaction of individual needs the association of men serves a good unique in plenitude and duration."[825] He works out with adroitness how legitimate individual interests may be reconciled with the common good, and articulates, in terms of the preeminence of the supernatural, the one reason for which the individual good and the personal good might sometimes override the common good. Whereas Virginia Held proposes the elaboration of an ethical system with minimum criteria on which all can agree, a quasi impossibility in contemporary society which is culturally diverse, Simon gets to the principles that can guide people in their choice when individual goods, or personal goods clash with the common good.

We mentioned briefly Simon's division of authority into the substitutional or paternal and the essential. Before Simon's work on this question a good many scholars saw authority as mainly a coercive force (the deficiency theory of government). Simon tells us that "according to Tom Paine and a few others, 'society is produced by

---

[824] Simon, *Philosophy of Democratic Government*, 191.
[825] Simon, *A General Theory Of Authority*, 29.

our wants and government by our wickedness.'"[826] Simon argues persuasively for its essential function, showing how governing is necessary even among angels. This is an original contribution to political philosophy.[827] We recall the above because Simon goes on to make an important distinction in the essential function of authority, arguing that taking care of the common good of society materially considered is the "most essential function"[828] of authority. As we have seen society would disintegrate if the citizens besides assuming the common good formally considered have to take charge of this aspect as well. David Easton says society would cease to exist without this "authoritative allocation of values."[829] Simon's metaphysics of the responsibilities of various parties in society regarding the common good considered materially and formally, is unrivalled in our times.

It is logical to assume that a ruler could not perform properly this function of "allocating values" if he were not virtuous. Thus Simon goes further and gives authority another role, its perfective function. The entire question of virtue in politics must be jarring to some in our society steeped, as it is, in Machiavelli's philosophy of the useful, and in which the expert is now an omnipresent reality. But any feelings of surprise dissipate when one becomes acquainted with the different facets of Simon's arguments and their roots in classical philosophy. In sum, Simon's argument is a straightforward one: in general since all practical knowledge always joins facts or theories to human desires, the person making the decision makes the difference. In unique situations, decision making must forever be left to prudence and love. If this is true of every citizen, it is even more so of the ruler who has the care of the community. His character is decisive. Besides right reason and a good will, Simon adds a deep insertion in the social and historical reality of the people one is

---

[826] Simon, *Philosophy of Democratic Government*, 61.

[827] Kuic, "Yves Simon's Contribution to Political Science," 61, 70.

[828] Simon, *Philosophy of Democratic Government*, 71

[829] David Easton, *The Political System: An Inquiry into the State of Political Science*, (New York: Alfred A. Knopf, 1953), 129-141. See, Kuic, "Yves Simon's Contribution to Political Science," 78.

leading. This discourse should be required reading for all who aspire to rule.

For the ruled, the particular virtue that answers to that of the ruler is obedience. As we have seen, ever since Rousseau explained genuine obedience as obedience to oneself, albeit within the context of the general will through which one person unites himself to all, obedience to another has had a bad name. Modern ideas of freedom as indetermination have not helped. It is against this backdrop that Simon's achievement must be measured. Simon's work is the first of its kind that explains how given our capacity to become all things through knowledge, the virtue of obedience saves us from that failure which might result from our subjectivity, and thus perfects us.

Just as it is difficult to see the need for virtue in the ruler in a world that values technical competence above all else, it is also difficult to imagine the multiplicity of connections between virtue and law till one reads Simon. Simon attributes a denial of teleology to the mentality engendered by transferring the elements found in the study of mathematics to the rest of life. Since there are no natures and no final causes in mathematics, it is presumed that that is how the whole of life is.[830] Once the mentality of the mathematician is seen not to apply to nature, one recognizes more clearly the workings of teleology in nature and the role of virtue in recognizing it. Knowledge of natural moral law which is first had by instinct demands virtue, as does the drafting of positive law which has its justification in natural law.

In conclusion, we would make two points:

i) Clearly, one of the keys to understanding Simon is that he sees the good of society as predominantly a moral good.[831]

ii) The scholar Willis D. Nutting, who has studied Simon's work closely, makes a remark that is very fitting as an evaluation of Simon's work, when he writes as follows in his review of *Work, Society, and Culture*:

---

[830] Simon, *The Tradition of Natural Law*, 47-48.
[831] Kuic, "Yves Simon's Contribution to Political Science," 64.

And so I would repeat, you will find that you will understand any problem better if you can read something that Yves Simon has written about it. 'He touched nothing that he did not adorn.'[832]

One could not agree more.

---

[832] Willis D. Nutting, "Work and Culture," *The Review of Politics*, 34 (1972): 239.

Bibliography

Primary Sources

Simon, Yves R. "Common Good and Common Action." *Review of Metaphysics* 22 (1960): 202-44.

———. *The Community of the Free*. Translated by Willard R. Trask. Lanham, MD: University Press of America, 1984.

———. *A Critique of Moral Knowledge*. Translated and introduced by Ralph McInerny. New York: Fordham University Press, 2002.

———. *The Definition of Moral Virtue*. Edited by Vukan Kuic. New York: Fordham University Press, 1986.

———. *The Ethiopian Campaign and French Political Thought*. Translated by Robert Royal. Edited by Anthony O. Simon. Notre Dame: University of Notre Dame Press, 2009.

———. *Foresight and Knowledge*. Edited by Ralph Nelson and Anthony O. Simon. New York: Fordham University Press, 1996.

———. *Freedom and Community*. Edited by Charles P. O'Donnell. New York: Fordham University Press, 2001.

———. *Freedom of Choice*. Edited by Peter Wolff. New York: Fordham University Press, 1969.

———. *A General Theory of Authority*. Introduction by Vukan Kuic. Notre Dame: University of Notre Dame Press, 1980.

———. *An Introduction to the Metaphysics of Knowledge*. Translated by Vukan Kuic and Richard J. Thompson. New York: Fordham University Press, 1990.

———. *The March to Liberation*. Translated by V.M. Hamm. Milwaukee: The Tower Press, 1942.

———. *Nature and Functions of Authority*. Milwaukee: Marquette University Press, 1948.

———. *Philosophy of Democratic Government*. Notre Dame: University of Notre Dame Press, 1993.

———. *Practical Knowledge*. Edited by Robert J. Mulvaney. New York: Fordham University Press, 1991.

———. "Progress in Metaphysics." *Commonweal* 42 (1945): 5-6.

―――――. *The Road to Vichy: 1918-1938*. Translated by James A. Corbett and George J. McMorrow. Lanham, MD: University Press of America, 1988.

―――――. *The Tradition of Natural Law: A Philosopher's Reflections*. Edited by Vukan Kuic. New York: Fordham University Press, 2001.

―――――. *Work, Society, and Culture*. Edited by Vukan Kuic. New York: Fordham University Press, 1971.

Maritain, Jacques, and Yves Simon. *Correspondance 1927-1940*. Tome 1.Établieetannotée par Florian Michel. Tours: Éditions CLD, 2008.

Secondary Sources

Aquinas, Thomas. *Summa Theologiae*. Complete English Edition in Five Volumes. Translated by the Fathers of the Dominican Province. New York: Benziger Brothers Inc., 1981.

―――――. *The Basic Writings of Thomas Aquinas*. Edited by Anton C. Pegis. New York: Random House, 1945.

Aristotle. *Nicomachean Ethics*. Translated by David Ross. Oxford: Oxford University Press, 1998.

―――――. *On Generation and Corruption*. Translated by Harold H. Joachim. In *The Basic Works of Aristotle*. Edited by Richard McKeon. New York: Random House, 2001.

―――――. *Physics*. Translated by R. P. Hardie and R. K. Gaye. In *The Basic Works of Aristotle*. Edited by Richard McKeon. New York: Random House, 2001.

―――――. *Politics*. Translated by H. Rackham. Cambridge: Harvard University Press, 1932.

―――――. *Rhetoric*. Translated by W. Rhys Roberts. In *The Basic Works of Aristotle*. Edited by Richard McKeon. New York: Random House, 2001.

―――――. *The Politics of Aristotle*. Edited and translated by Ernest Baker. New York: Oxford University Press, 1962.

Arrow, Kenneth. *Social Choice and Individual Values*. 2d ed. New York: Wiley, 1964.

Augustine. *The City of God against the Pagans*. Edited and translated by R.W. Dyson. Cambridge: Cambridge University Press, 2006.

Bacon, Francis. *The New Organon*. Edited by Lisa Jardine and Michael Silverthorne. Cambridge: Cambridge University Press, 2000.

_____. *The New Atlantis*. In *The Major Works including New Atlantis and the Essays*. Edited by Brian Vickers. Oxford: Oxford University Press, 2008.

Barry, Brian. *Political Argument*. New York: Humanities Press, 1965.

Baumol, William J. *Economic Theory and Operations Analysis*. 2d ed. Englewood Cliffs, N. J.: Prentice-Hall, 1961.

Bay, Christian. *The Structure of Freedom*. Stanford, California: Stanford University Press, 1958.

Benestad, Brian J. *Church, State, and Society: An Introduction to Catholic Social Doctrine*. Washington D.C.: The Catholic University of America Press, 2011.

Benn, S. I. "'Interests' in Politics." *Proceedings of the Aristotelian Society* 60 (1960): 123-40.

Bentham, Jeremy. *An Introduction to the Principles of Morals and Legislation*. New York: Hafner, 1948.

Bergson, Henry. *Matter and Memory*. Translated by Margaret Paul and W. Scott Palmer. London: Allen, 1912.

Bobonich, Christopher. *Plato's Utopia Recast: His Later Ethics and Politics*. Oxford: Clarendon Press, 2002.

Bruell, Christopher. "On Plato's Political Philosophy." *The Review of Politics* 56 (1994): 261-82.

Buchanan, James M., and Gordon Tullock. *The Calculus of Consent: Logical Foundations of Constitutional Democracy*. Ann Arbor: University of Michigan Press, 1965.

Cicero. *Republic*. Translated by C. W. Keyes. Cambridge: Harvard University Press, 1928.

Cochin, Augustin. *La Crise de l'histoire révolutionnaire*. Paris: Champion, 1909.

Cochran, Clarke E. "Political Science and 'The Public Interest.'" *The Journal of Politics* 36 (1974): 327-55.

_____."The Politics of Interest: Philosophy and the Limitations of the Science of Politics. *American Journal of Political Science*. 17 (1973): 745-66.

_____. "Yves R. Simon and 'The Common Good': A Note on the Concept." *Ethics* 88 (1978): 229-39.

Cochran, Clarke E. and Thomas Rourke. "Moving Beyond Ideology in Christian Economic Thought: Yves R. Simon and the Recent Debates." In *Freedom, Virtue, and the Common Good*, edited by Curtis L. Hancock and Anthony O. Simon, 307-31. Notre Dame: University of Notre Dame Press, 1995.

Cohen, Julius. "A Lawman's View of the Public Interest." In *The Public Interest*. Nomos V, edited by Carl J. Friedrich, 155-61. New York: Atherton Press, 1962.

Coleman, James S. "Foundations for a Theory of Collective Decisions." *The American Journal of Sociology* 81 (1966): 615-27.

Colm, Gerhard. "In Defence of the Public Interest." *Social Research* 27 (1960): 295-307.

Deane, Herbert A. *The Political and Social Ideas of St. Augustine*. New York: Columbia University Press, 1963.

de Montaigne, Michel. *Montaigne's Essays and Selected Writings*. Edited and translated by Donald M. Frame. New York: St. Martin's Press, 1963.

Descartes, René. *The Philosophical Writings of Descartes*, Vols. 1 & II. Translated by John Cottingham, Robert Stoothoff, and Dugald Murdoch. Cambridge: Cambridge University Press, 2005.

Downs, Anthony. "The Public Interest: Its meaning in a Democracy." *Social Research* 29 (1962): 1-36.

Durkheim, Emile. *The Rules of Sociological Method and Selected Texts on Sociology and its Method*. Edited by Steven Lukes. Translated by W.D. Halls. New York: The Free Press, 1982.

Easton, David. *The Political System: An Inquiry into the State of Political Science*. New York: Alfred A Knopf, 1953.

Emerson, Ralph Waldo. *The Selected Writings of Ralph Waldo Emerson*. Edited by Brooks Atkinson. New York: Modern Library, 1950.

Finnis, John. *Natural Law and Natural Right*. London: Oxford, 1980.

Flathman, Richard E. *The Public Interest: An Essay Concerning the Normative Discourse of Politics*. New York: Wiley, 1966.

Foot, Philippa R. "Hume on Moral Judgment." In *David Hume: A Symposium*, edited by D. F. Pears, 67-76. London: Macmillan & Co. Ltd., 1963.

Fourier, Charles. *The Utopian Vision of Charles Fourier*. Edited and translated by Jonathan Beecher and Richard Bienvenu. Boston: Beacon Press, 1971.

Fried, Charles. "Two Concepts of Interests: Some Reflections on the Supreme Court's Balancing Test." *Harvard Law Review* 76 (1963): 755-78.

Friedrich, Carl J., ed. *The Public Interest*. Nomos V. New York: Atherton Press, 1962.

Gammon, Francis L. "The Philosophical Thought of Yves Simon: A Brief Survey." *Revue de l'Université d'Ottawa* 42 (1972): 237-44.

Grotius, Hugo. *The Rights of War and Peace*. Translated by A. C. Campbell. Washington: M. Walter Dunne, 1901.

Hancock, Curtis L., and Anthony Simon O. ed. *Freedom, Virtue, and the Common Good*. Notre Dame: University of Notre Dame Press, 1995.

Hayek, Friedrick A. *The Constitution of Liberty*. Chicago: The University of Chicago Press, 1960.

Hegel, G.W.F. *Philosophy of Right*. Translated by T. M. Knox. Oxford: Clarendon Press, 1942.

Held, Virginia. "On the Meaning of Trust." *Ethics* 78 (1968): 156-58.

_____. "Rationality and Social Value in Game-Theoretical Analyses." *Ethics* 76 (1966): 215-20.

_____. *The Public Interest and Individual Interests*. New York: Basic Books Inc., 1970.

Herring, Pendleton E. *Public Administration and the Public Interest*. New York: McGraw-Hill Book Co., 1936.

Hobbes, Thomas. *De Cive or The Citizen*. Edited and introduced by Sterling P. Lamprecht. New York: Appleton-Century-Crofts, 1949.

_____. *The Elements of Law: Natural and Politic*. Edited by Ferdinand Tonnies. London: Frank Cass & Co. Ltd., 1969.

———. *Leviathan.* Edited by Richard Tuck. New York: Cambridge University Press, 1996.

Holmes, Oliver Wendell. "Ideals and Doubts." *Illinois Law Review* 10 (1915): 1-4.

———. "Natural Law." *Harvard Law Review* 32 (1918): 40-44.

———. *The Essential Holmes: Selections from the Letters, Speeches, Judicial Opinions, and Other Writings of Oliver Wendell Holmes.* Edited by Richard A. Posner. Chicago: The University of Chicago Press, 1992.

Hume, David. *A Treatise of Human Nature.* Edited by David Fate Norton and Mary J. Norton. New York: Oxford University Press, 2001.

———. "Of the First Principles of Government." In *Hume's Moral and Political Philosophy.* Edited by Henry Aiken. New York: Hafner, 1948.

Jenkins, Iredell. "The Matrix of Positive Law." *Natural Law Forum* 6 (1961): 1-50.

John of St. Thomas. *The Material Logic of John of St. Thomas: Basic Treatises.* Translated by Yves R. Simon, John J. Glanville, and G. Donald Hollenhorst. Chicago: University of Chicago Press, 1955.

Kant, Immanuel. *Groundwork of the Metaphysics of Morals.* Translated by Mary J. Gregor. Cambridge: Cambridge University Press, 2010.

———. *Prolegomena to any Future Metaphysics.* Translated by Gary Hartfield. Cambridge: Cambridge University Press, 2004.

Keys, Mary M. "Politics Pointing Beyond the *Polis* and the *Politeia*: Aquinas on Natural Law and the Common Good." In *Natural Moral Law in Contemporary Society*, edited by Holger Zaborowski, 170-94. Washington D.C.: The Catholic University of America Press, 2010.

Killoran, John. "A Moral Realist Perspective on Yves R. Simon's Interpretation of Habitus." In *Freedom, Virtue and the Common Good*, edited by Curtis L. Hancock and Anthony O. Simon, 88-103. Notre Dame: University of Notre Dame Press, 1995.

Kirk, G. S., Raven J. E., and Schofield, M. *The Presocratic Philosophers.* Cambridge: Cambridge University Press, 2003.

Klosko, George. *The Development of Plato's Political Theory*. New York: Methuen & Co. Ltd., 1986.

Kuic, Vukan. "Yves Simon's Contribution to Political Science." *The Political Science Reviewer* 4 (1974): 55-104.

──────. "Yves R. Simon on Liberty and Authority." In *Acquaintance with the Absolute: The Philosophy of Yves R. Simon*, edited by Anthony O. Simon, 128-46. New York: Fordham University Press, 1998.

──────. *Yves Simon: Real Democracy*. Lanham, MD: Rowman & Littlefield Publishers Inc. 1999.

Laski, Harold. *Liberty in the Modern State*. New York: The Viking Press, 1949.

Leibniz, Gottfried. *Philosophical Essays*. Translated by Roger Ariew and Daniel Garber. Indianapolis: Hackett Publishing Company, 1989.

Leys, Wayne. A. R. and Chamer Marquis, Perry. *Philosophy and the Public Interest*. Chicago, Ill.: Committee to Advance Original Work in Philosophy, 1959.

Lloyd, Dennis. *Introduction to Jurisprudence*. Rev. ed. New York: Praeger, 1965.

Long, Steven A. "Yves R. Simon's Approach to Natural Law." *Thomist* 59 (1995): 125-35.

Lucretius. *De Rerum Natura*. Translated by H. A. J. Munro. London: George Bell & Sons, 1908.

Machiavelli, Niccolo. *The Prince*. Translated by Harvey C. Mansfield. Chicago: University of Chicago Press, 1980.

Maritain, Jacques. *Man and the State*. Chicago: Chicago University Press, 1951.

──────. *Philosophy of Nature*. Translated by Imelda C. Byrne. New York: Philosophical Library, 1951.

──────. *The Dream of Descartes*. Translated by Mabelle L. Andison. New York: F. Hubner & Co., Inc., 1944.

──────. *The Person and the Common Good*. Translated by John J. Fitzgerald. Notre Dame, Indiana: University of Notre Dame Press, 1966.

──────. *The Range of Reason*. New York: Scribner, 1952.

_____. *The Rights of Man and Natural Law*. Translated by Doris C. Anson. New York: Gordian Press, 1971.

Marx, Karl and Engels Friedrich. *The Communist Manifesto*. Edited by Joseph Katz. Translated by Samuel Moore. New York: Washington Square Press Inc., 1965.

McInerny, Ralph. "On Yves R. Simon as a Moral Philosopher." In *Freedom, Virtue and the Common Good*, edited by Curtis L. Hancock and Anthony O. Simon, 76-87. Notre Dame: University of Notre Dame Press, 1995.

Mulvaney, Robert J. "Practical Wisdom in the Thought of Yves R. Simon." In *Acquaintance with the Absolute: The Philosophy of Yves R. Simon*, edited by Anthony O. Simon, 147-81. New York: Fordham University Press, 1998.

Murphy, Arthur E. "An Ambiguity in Professor Simon's Philosophy of Democratic Government." *The Philosophical Review* 61 (1952): 198-211.

Murphy, Mark C. *Natural Law in Jurisprudence and Politics*. Cambridge: Cambridge University Press, 2006.

Nemetz, A. and Massaro, T. "Common Good." In *New Catholic Encyclopedia*.16-22.

Nicgorski, Walter. "Yves R. Simon: A Philosopher's Quest for Science and Prudence." *The Review of Politics* 71 (2009): 68-84.

Nutting, Willis D. "Work and Culture." *The Review of Politics* 34 (1972): 237-39.

Paine, Thomas. *Common Sense in the Writings of Thomas Paine*. New York: G. P. Putnam's Sons, 1894.

Pareto, Vilfredo. *Manual of Political Economy*. London: Macmillan, 1972.

Pascal, Blaise. *Pensées*. New York: E. P. Dutton, 1958.

Peirce, Charles Sanders. *Collected Papers of Charles Sanders Peirce*. Edited by Charles Hartshorne and Paul Weiss 6 vols. Cambridge: Cambridge University Press, 1931- 1935.

Phelan, Gerald B. "Justice and Friendship." *Thomist* 5 (1943): 153-70.

Plamenatz, John. "Interests." *Political Studies*. Vol. II. Oxford: Clarendon Press, 1954.

Plato. *Laws*. Edited by Jeffrey Henderson. Translated by R. G. Bury. Cambridge: Harvard University Press, 2004.

_____. *The Collected Dialogues including the Letters*. Edited by Edith Hamilton and Huntington Cairns. Princeton: Princeton University Press, 1996.

Poggi, Gianfranco. *Durkheim*. Oxford: Oxford University Press, 2000.

Pollard, Christopher J. *The Concept of Virtue as Habitus in the Moral Philosophy of Yves Simon*. M.A. thesis. The Catholic University of America, 1994.

Popper, Karl. *The Open Society and Its Enemies* 2 vols. New York: Harper Torchbooks, 1962.

Pound, Roscoe. "A Survey of Social Interests." *Harvard Law Review* 57 (1943-1944): 1- 39.

Randall Jr., John Herman. *Aristotle*. New York: Columbia University Press, 1962.

Rapoport, Anatol and Albert A. Chammah. *Prisoner's Dilemma*. Ann Arbor: University of Michigan Press, 1965.

Rist, J. M. *Stoic Philosophy*. Cambridge: Cambridge University Press, 1969.

Rousseau, Jean Jacques. *Discourse on the Origin and Foundations of Inequality Among Men or Second Discourse*. In *The Discourses and other early political writings*. Edited and translated by Victor Gourevitch. Cambridge: Cambridge University Press, 2002.

_____. *On the Social Contract*. Edited by Roger D. Masters. Translated by Judith R. Masters. New York: St. Martin's Press, 1978.

_____. *The Social Contract and the Discourses*. Translated by G. D. H. Cole. Everyman's Library. New York: Alfred A. Knopf, 1993.

Schall, James V. "On the Most Mysterious of the Virtues: The Political and Philosophical Meaning of Obedience in St. Thomas, Rousseau, and Yves Simon." *Gregorianum* 79 (1998): 743-58.

Schubert, Glendon. *The Public Interest*. Glencoe, Ill.: The Free Press, 1960.

Skinner, B. F. *About Behaviorism*. New York: Vintage Books, 1976.

_____. *Beyond Freedom and Dignity*. New York: Knopf. 1971.

Smith, Howard R. *Democracy and the Public Interest.* Athens: University of Georgia Press, 1960.

Smith, Michael A. *Human Dignity and the Common Good in the Aristotelian-Thomistic Tradition.* Queenston, Ontario: The Edwin Mellen Press, 1995.

Speath, Robert L. "Simon's Moderate Pessimism." *The Review of Politics* 48 (1986): 121-22.

Sokolowski, Robert. "Knowing Natural Law." In *Pictures, Quotations, and Distinctions: Fourteen Essays in Phenomenology*, 277-91. Notre Dame: University of Notre Dame Press, 1992.

Sorauf, Frank. "The Conceptual Muddle." In *The Public Interest*, Nomos V, edited by Carl J. Friedrich, 183-90. New York: Atherton Press, 1962.

Stone, Julius. *Human Law and Human Justice.* Stanford: Stanford University Press, 1964.

Strauss, Leo. *Natural Right and History.* Chicago: University of Chicago Press, 1949.

Taylor, C. C. W. "The Atomists." In *The Cambridge Companion to Early Greek Philosophy*, edited by A. A. Long, 181-204. Cambridge: Cambridge University Press, 2006.

Weber, Max. *On the Methodology of the Social Sciences.* Translated by Edward Shils and Henry A. Finch. Glencoe, Ill.: Free Press, 1949.

Weil, André. "The Future of Mathematics." *American Mathematical Monthly* 57 (1950): 295-306.

Zaborowski, Holger. *Natural Moral Law in Contemporary Society.* Washington D.C.: The Catholic University of America Press, 2010.

Zeller, Eduard. *Outlines of the History of Greek Philosophy.* Translated by L. R. Palmer. London: Routledge & Kegan Paul Ltd., 1931.

www.ingramcontent.com/pod-product-compliance
Lightning Source LLC
Chambersburg PA
CBHW021352300426
44114CB00012B/1185